MW01148867

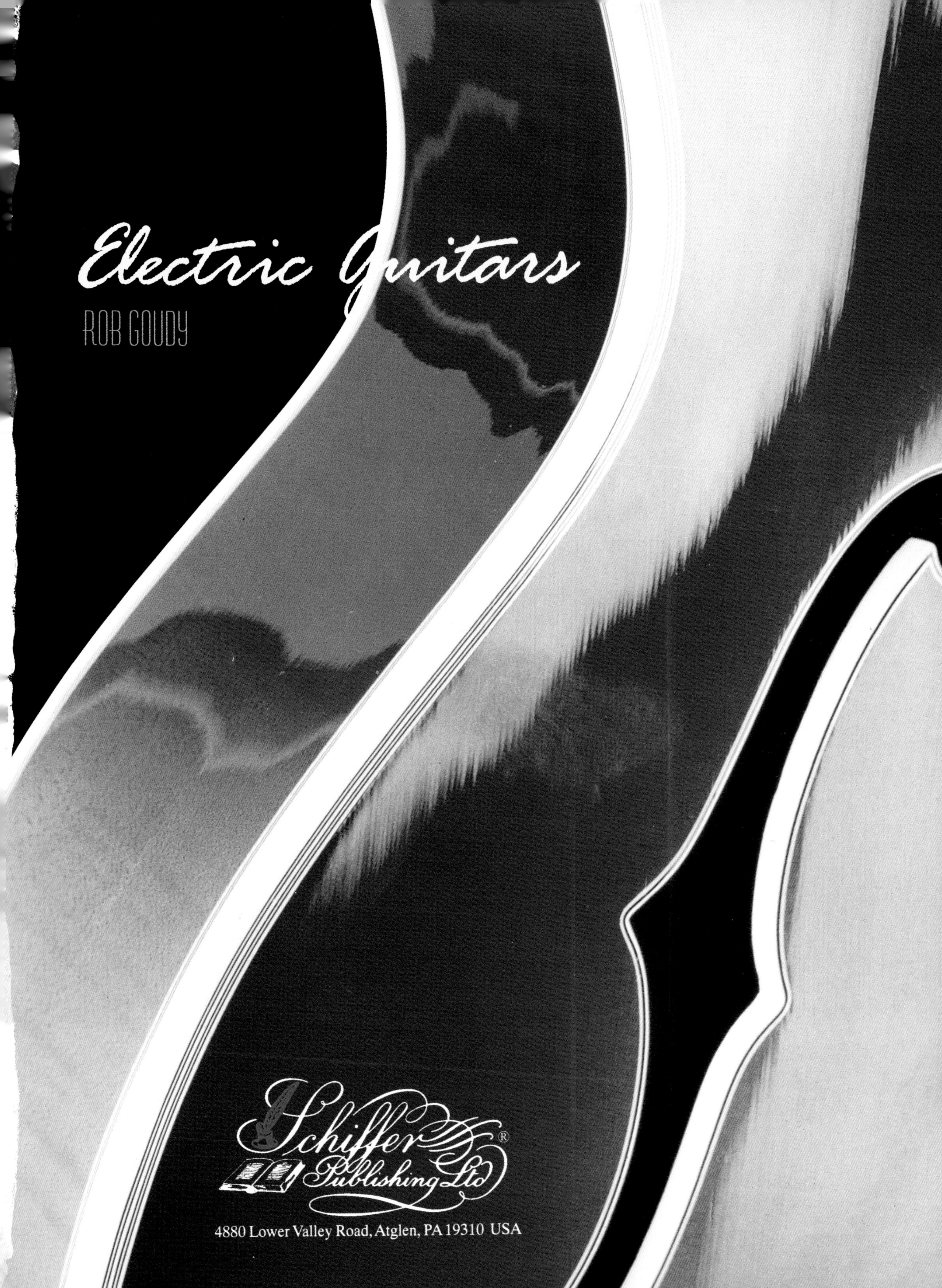

Electric Guitars
ROB GOUDY
Schiffer® Publishing Ltd
4880 Lower Valley Road, Atglen, PA 19310 USA

Library of Congress Cataloging-in-Publicatrion Data
Goudy, Rob.
Electric guitars / Rob Goudy.
p. cm.
Includes bibliographical references.
ISBN 0-7643-0964-1
1. Electric guitar. I. Title.
ML1015.G9G68 1999
787.87'19--dc21 99-32935
CIP

Design by Blair Loughrey
Type set in Rage Italic/HuxleyVertiacal/Goudy Olst Bt/ Humanist 521/ Zapf Humanist BT

ISBN: 0-7643-0964-1
Printed in China

Published by Schiffer Publishing Ltd.
4880 Lower Valley Road
Atglen, PA 19310
Phone: (610) 593-1777; Fax: (610) 593-2002
Please visit out web site catalog at
www.schifferbooks.com
or write for a free catalog.
This book may be purchased from the publisher.
Please include $3.95 for shipping.

In Europe, Schiffer books are distributed by
Bushwood Books
6 Marksbury Rd.
Kew Gardens
Surrey TW9 4JF England
Phone: 44 (0)181 392-8585; Fax: 44 (0)181 392-9876
E-mail: Bushwd@aol.com

Please try your bookstore first.

We are interested in hearing from authors
with book ideas on related subjects.

CONTENTS

Acknowledgments **4**
Introduction **5**
In the Beginning **6**
Electric Guitars **10**

Acoustic 11
Airline 12
Alembic 12
Ampeg 13
Aria Pro II 14
Baldwin 14
B.C. Rich 15
Bigsby 17
Carvin 18
Charvel/Jackson 18
Coral 19
Custom Kraft 20
Danelectro 20
D'Angelico/D'Aquisto 22
Dean 23
Eko 25
Epiphone 26
Fender 33
Framus 58
G & L 58
Gibson 59
Greco 104
Gretsch 104
Guild 116
Hagstrom 125
Hamer 126
Hang Don 127
Harmony 128
Höfner 130
Ibanez 132
Kay 136
Kramer 137
Kustom 138
Martin 138
Micro/Fret 140
Mosrite 141
Music Man 145
National 147
Ovation 148
Paul Reed Smith 150
Peavey 154
Premier 155
Rickenbacker 155
Robin 161
Schon 161
S.D. Curlee 162
Silvertone 162
Steiberger 164
Supro 165
Teisco 166
Tokai 166
Universal 167
Veillette-Citron 167
Vox 168
Wandré 170
Washburn 171
Yamaha 171
Zeidler 173
Zemaitis 174
Zorko 174

Glossary **175**
Bibliography **176**

ACKNOWLEDGMENTS

I have many of people to thank who have made this book possible. First has to be the people at Schiffer Publishing for having an interest in making a book on guitars. Most notably Doug Congdon-Martin and Jeff Snyder and their team took my hand written chicken scratch and put it into print. I would like to thank the photographers at Schiffer, Jeff Snyder, Blair Loughrey, Molly Higgins, and Bruce Waters, for coming out to several guitar shows to photograph most of the guitars illustrated in this book.

To the dealers, collectors, and enthusiasts who let me handle and photograph their instruments, the pictures of your guitars are what make this book special. Thank you.

Special mention for guitar phots must go to Stan Jay of Mandolin Brothers Ltd., who sent me pictures of Paul McCartney's priceless Hofner bass. Craig Brody of the Guitar Broker sent me many photos of some really cool guitars, including several metalflake Fenders. Larry Hendrikson of Axe In Hand, made many rare guitar photos available. Scott Chinery allowed me to photograph some of his priceless, one-of-a-kind instruments.

I would like to thank the folks at the Kaman Music Corporation for sending me information on Ovation and Hamer guitars, the folks at Carvin and Martin for serial number information,. Much of the rest of the serial number information was acquired by cross referencing the information in the fine books listed in the Bibliography. I would like to thank Jay Pilzer of New Hope Guitar Traders for his information on Guild guitars.

Lastly, but mostly, I would like to thank my family for their constant support in my many endeavors, and Jennifer for her love, patience, and understanding of my passion for vintage electric guitars. I love you all.

INTRODUCTION

The electric guitar has been the prominent instrument of popular music in the last half of the twentieth century. It should therefore be of no surprise that this instrument, in its many configurations, has become such an icon. It should also be of no surprise that, because of the electric guitar's popularity, certain vintage models of this instrument have become quite valuable in collectors' circles. Of course, as in all collectible markets with vast diversity, values can vary greatly. And in the case of vintage guitars, these figures can range from under one hundred dollars, to over one hundred thousand dollars!

Most of this book will focus on the vintage electric guitar. It is the intention of this author to familiarize the reader with the major and not-so-major manufacturers and their products. Some of these companies still exist, some are now defunct, some resurrected, and some have been juggled around so much that their trademark name is the only thing that remains from the original company. As with the manufacturers themselves, the instruments that they have produced have paralleled this theme.

The information in this book has been acquired over the twenty year love affair I have had with the guitar through personal research, by collecting and dealing with the guitars, reading most of the books published on this subject and through periodicals such as Vintage Guitar Magazine.

This book will focus mostly on U.S. made instruments since most collectors agree that these guitars make up 95% of the real collectible market. But it will also feature Spanish style electrics manufactured from around the world.

Although of paramount importance to the development of the electric "Spanish" guitar, the Hawaiian or lap steel and the later pedal steel guitar that they spawned will not be covered in this book. These instruments, in all their colorful and technical diversity deserve a book of their own.

The text covered within will be in alphabetical order of companies by trademark names, followed by brief histories, model names, descriptions, serial numbers, and photographs with captions and values. Note on instrument values: the retail price on the guitars photographed represent the instruments in those photographs specifically at the time of publication and are meant only as a general guide. A better example of the same exact guitar would be worth more, a worse example would be worth less. Condition, and originality are of paramount importance when placing values on vintage guitars. Also, this market, not being completely matured yet, can be extremely volatile. If you are in the market either to purchase or sell an instrument and are not sure of its current value, an independent appraisal could be very beneficial.

I would like to thank all of the dealers, players, and collectors who let us photograph their guitars. I am indebted to you all, for without the photos, there would be no book. Credits of ownership are listed at the end of each caption and refer to the time at which the instruments picture was taken. I also wish to thank those who chose to remain anonymous.

IN THE BEGINNING

Volume. Its the only reason for the existence of the electric guitar. Throughout the evolution of the modern acoustic guitar, builders strove to make their instruments louder. In Madrid, Spain, during the mid-to-late 1850s Antonio De Torres[1] practically developed the classical guitar to modern standards. By increasing the body size and basically perfecting the soundboard's fan bracing to a seven strut design, he effectively increased the volume and tonal response of his guitars, making all of his contemporaries' designs obsolete. Across the Atlantic, in Nazareth, Pennsylvania, during the same time period, Christian Frederick Martin[2] was developing the "X" bracing pattern, which has now become standard on all steel string flat-top guitars. This development, along with increasing the size of the body and changing from gut to steel strings was aimed at increasing volume as well as improving tone. The quest for volume didn't end there. Gibson's carved or arch-top guitars of the twenties just kept growing in size up to the Super 400 Model of the mid-to-late 1930s. These "orchestra" style guitars had to keep up with whole horn sections and so the guitarists, wanting to be heard, kept their pursuit for a louder instrument.

There were offshoots of the acoustic guitar designed to increase volume. The resonator guitars of National and Dobro of the late 1920s and early 1930s were among the more successful attempts to produce an instrument with greater volume.

Of course, during all of these advancements in acoustics, there was a totally new technology developing: the electronic amplification of sound. In 1907, the vacuum tube was invented by Lee de Forest. This device made the amplification of electrical currents possible. Four years later, in 1911, he was granted a patent for an amplifier for radio frequencies. By the end of that decade, the technology was being used for AM radio and for amplification of recorded music, which was previously accomplished with a stylus connected to a diaphragm which was attached to a huge horn.

By the mid-1930s, all of the major acoustic guitar designs had been fully developed: Epiphone's, Stromberg's[3], and D'Angelico's[4] archtop guitars; Gibson's archtop and flat-top guitars; Martin's flat-tops; and National's and Dobro's resonators had been basically perfected. Today's vintage guitar market bears testament to this era of acoustics in that certain models of acoustic guitars produced at this time fetch the highest prices in their respective market.

Only a decade before this a few visionaries had foreseen the limiting factors of a mechanically amplified (strings vibrating across a diaphragm, soundboard, or resonator) guitar. They had envisioned the future in an electronically amplified instrument.

Gibson's Lloyd Loar (1886-1943), an acoustics engineer credited for their highly esteemed Style Five instruments left the company in late 1924 after disputes over the viability of an electrically amplified guitar. He would go on to start up Vivi-Tone, a company devoted to electrically amplified instruments.

At the end of the 1920s, Vega, a prominent banjo company, and Stromberg-Voisinet, whose name would later be changed to Kay, both made unsuccessful attempts at marketing electrically amplified instruments. It would be Ro-Pat-In (a company that would see several name changes, finally becoming Rickenbacker) an upstart company in 1931, who would be the first to market a successful electric guitar with their initial instrument, a Hawaiian lap steel. With this came the first modern electromagnetic pickup. All other previous attempts were microphonic and although probably giving a truer acoustic tone, the electromagnetic pickup's greater efficiency gave it greater volume.

To this day, the operating principals of this pickup have been applied to the units built and used by all of the world's electric guitar manufacturers.

From the mid-1930s to the late 1940s, the electric guitar was in its developmental stages. The success of the lap steel guitar had ushered in many electronic advancements in pickup and amplifier design, and these developments were applied to the electric Spanish guitar. Of course, the final major development of the electric Spanish guitar was the utilization of the solid body. Rickenbacker made a Spanish necked version of the Bakelite lap steel called the Model B, in

1935, and in 1937 a thicker bodied model with a motorized vibrato was launched, called the Vibrola Spanish Model. In 1938 or 1939, Slingerland also made in very limited quantities a Spanish necked solid instrument, based on their Songster lap steel model. This all wood guitar with neck-through construction and bound curly maple top and back could be considered the first solid body electric.

Les Paul, better known for his namesake guitars built by Gibson, also pioneered the solid electric guitar. In 1940 he built a guitar that would later become known as "The Log." It was constructed of a solid 4" x 4" block of pine wood for the body's center section. The rest of the body was built by attaching the halves of an Epiphone archtop to both sides of this block of wood. The Gibson-made neck, pickups, bridge, and tailpiece all attached to the solid center section, in effect making a solid electric guitar.

Paul Bigsby, who would later become famous for his vibrato units that were used on many other companies' instruments, built some very modern solid electrics in the late 1940s. His typical instrument, which was co-designed by country musician Merle Travis, was a Les Paul-shaped neck-through body guitar made of figured maple. The maple neck had a headstock shape very reminiscent of the famous Fender Stratocaster which debuted seven years later. He also built multi-necked guitars as well as instruments with varying body shapes.

This brings us to Leo Fender (1909-1991), who, in 1946, founded the company that bears his name. As early as 1943, Fender built an electric guitar prototype resembling a lap steel with a rounded Spanish style neck. This instrument was the predecessor to the most famous line of solid body electrics in the world. By the early 1950s, all of the elements of the electric guitar had pretty much been perfected. Throughout the next decade manufacturers refined and produced instruments of exceptional quality and this shows in the values that the vintage guitar market has placed on these instruments.

In late 1945, Fender, with Californian guitarist and inventor Clayton Orr (Doc) Kauffman, formed the K & F Company. Building small amps and lap steel guitars, the company lasted less than one year. Kauffman, not having the foresight or faith in the electric instrument market that Fender did, bailed out on the company in early 1946. Later that year, Fender Electric Instrument Company was formed and within three years Fender had completed the prototype for the Telecaster.

Like the decade of the early 1930s to the early 1940s is considered the golden era of the acoustic, so it is for electric models built from the early 1950s to the early 1960s.

From its humble beginnings .when a conservative bunch of people known as guitarists rejected the idea of an electrically amplified instrument to today's worldwide acceptance, the electric guitar has proven to be a dominant force in all popular music styles. With this in mind, let's take a trip through the world of electric guitars.

Endnotes

1. Torres (1817-1892) is considered by many, if not all, to be the most influential builder of classical guitars during the 19th and 20th centuries.
2. Martin (1796-1873) founded C.F. Martin & Co. in 1833, and to this day his company is regarded as building the worlds finest production acoustics in the world.
3. Elmer Stromberg (1895-1955) worked at his family's business that was founded by his father, Charles, in about 1905. Elmer was responsible for producing some of the largest and loudest archtop guitars ever built.
4. John D'Angelico (1905-1964) of New York hand made some of the worlds most esteemed archtop guitars during his lifetime. Late in his career, he built some electric models utilizing imported bodies. James D'Aquisto, apprenticed by John in 1952, carried on D'Angelico's tradition of building instruments to extraordinary standards of quality. He also ventured into the electric field by building some Les Paul shaped solid body electrics in the late 1970s. D'Aquisto's career was cut short by his untimely death in 1995.

1953 Fender Champion Lap Steel with a 1958 Fender Princeton Amp Guitar. *Courtesy of Michael Homsher*.

Mid 1930s OAHU Lap Steel with an Era Supertone Amp. The Supertone name was used by Sears up until the end of the 1930s when it was changed to Silvertone.

Late 1930s Epiphone Electric model M. SN: 1977 with an Epiphone electric Amp. *Courtesy of Michael Homsher*.

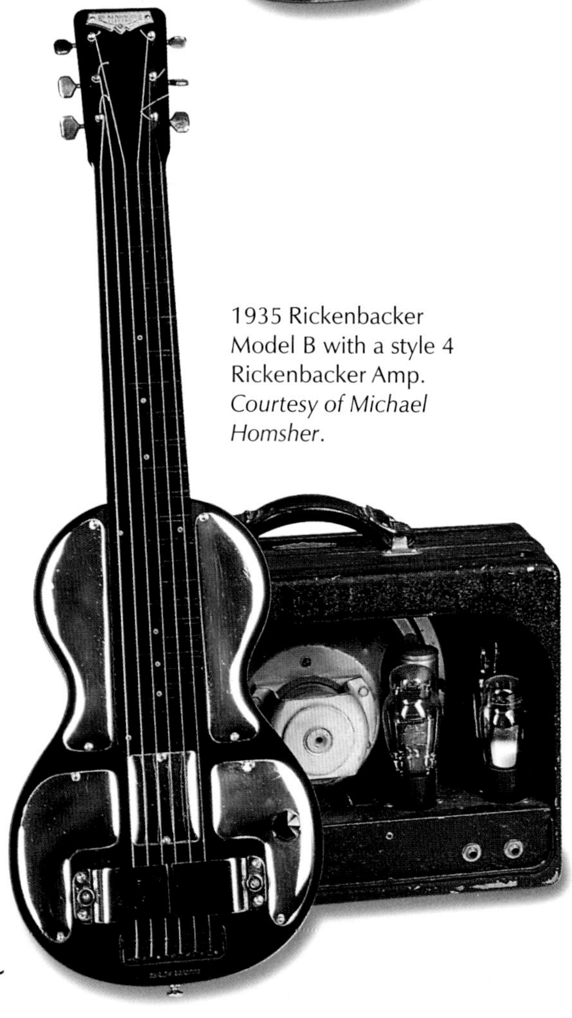

1935 Rickenbacker Model B with a style 4 Rickenbacker Amp. *Courtesy of Michael Homsher*.

1940 Gibson EH150 with its original case. SN: F 1481-4. *Courtesy of Michael Homsher.*

MOCKIN' BIRD HILL

(TRA-LA LA TWITTLE DEE DEE DEE)

Words and Music by VAUGHN HORTON

Sincerely
LES PAUL
and
MARY FORD

SOUTHERN MUSIC PUB. CO., INC.
1619 BROADWAY, NEW YORK 19, N.Y.

An early 1940s photo of Les Paul and Mary Ford playing some of Les's early electric guitars, including Les Paul's "Clunker."

Electric Guit

ELECTRIC GUITARS

Acoustic

Better known for their well made solid state amplifiers, the Southern California Company also marketed an electric guitar and bass. In 1972, the Acoustic Black Widow guitar and bass made their debut. Besides sharing names, they both sported all black paint, a red pad on the body's back, and the same general silhouette. Early instruments were imported from Japan, but most seem to have been made by Semie Moseley of Mosrite fame. Instruments made by Moseley share much of the hardware, electronics, and design features of Mosrite guitars from the same period. By the end of 1973 production of Acoustic's Black Widows ceased.

1972 Acoustic. Black Widow. BC1110.
Courtesy of Mark Hayes. $600.

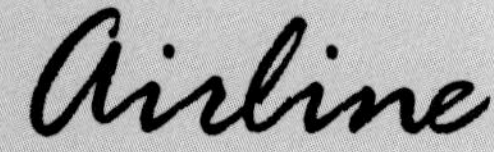

Airline

Airline is the trademark name of an entry level line of instruments marketed by Montgomery Ward. Airline guitars and basses were built by several different companies during the 1950s and 1960s, with Kay, Valco, and Harmony making the lion's share.

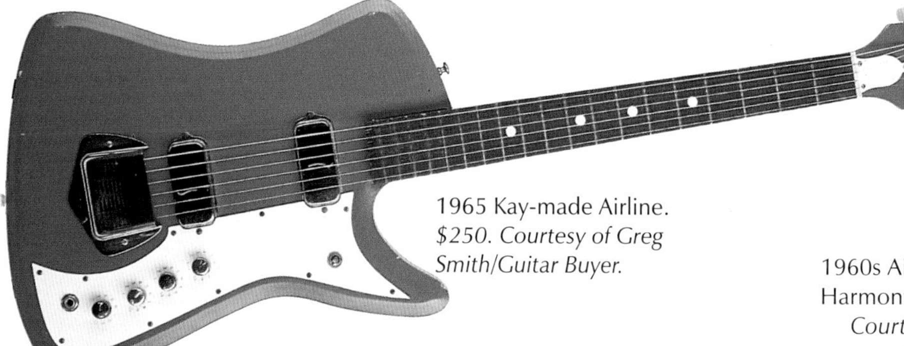

1965 Kay-made Airline. *$250. Courtesy of Greg Smith/Guitar Buyer.*

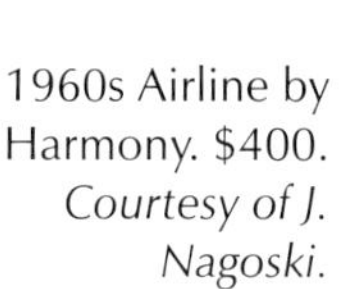

1960s Airline by Harmony. $400. *Courtesy of J. Nagoski.*

Alembic

Founded in 1969 by Ron Wickersham and his wife Susan, Alembic was originally conceived to engineer, construct, and maintain the sound system of the Grateful Dead band. During the first year, Alembic expanded their duties to include recording with sound engineer Bob Matthews, and guitar repair and development with Rick Turner, all the while sharing space in the Novato, California, warehouse that the Dead used for practice. In March 1970, Alembic relocated to San Francisco and three months later incorporated with Wickersham, Matthews, and Turner each holding equal shares.

By 1971, Alembic was building complete guitars using lessons learned from earlier repairs and experiments. One of their breakthroughs was the use of on-board active electronics which Alembic successfully incorporated into their new designs.

In 1973, L.D. Heater became Alembic's distributor and production began to take off. Also during this time Bob Matthews' shares of the business were bought out by company employees and Sam Field, Turner's successor to President, joined the company.

In 1978, Turner left Alembic to start Turner Guitars and Field became President. In 1989, Alembic relocated to its current location in Santa Rosa, California, where a staff of approximately 25 people build these neck-through high quality instruments. Alembic currently offers many production models as well as customer ordered one-offs.

1986 Alembic Spoiler Bass . SN: 86S3869. $1500. *Courtesy of The Bass Place.*

Alembic Serial Numbers

Starting with 1971, Alembic started stamping serial numbers on the back of the headstock. Generally, the first two numbers correspond with the year the instrument was produced. If the serial number includes a letter, this indicates the model of the instrument. Example: instrument number 86S3869 is a 1986 Spoiler Bass.

Ampeg

Ampeg was founded in 1949 by New York City jazz bassist Everet Hull. The company is famous for its instrument amplifiers, which included stand out models such as the B-15 Portaflex bass amp, the Jet, Reverberocket, and Gemini combo models, as well as the thunderous SVT bass amp. Its first product was an amplified support peg for the acoustic upright bass that Hull had perfected in 1947. It is from this amplified peg that Hull took the name Ampeg for his company. By 1957, the company, with the help of Jess Oliver, had designed and marketed a complete line of amps which included the B-15.

In 1962, Ampeg acquired the design rights from Zorko for a downsized upright electric bass made of fiberglass. After making some improvements to the original's design, Ampeg debuted the Baby Bass. Also during this period, the company moved from New York City to Linden, New Jersey.

From the early to mid-1960s, Ampeg imported a line of electric guitars and basses from Burns of England. These instruments are the same as Burns's own models, differing only in the pickguards that are engraved with "Ampeg by Burns of London."

In 1966, Ampeg introduced their own solid electric bass models. This line consisted of two instruments that were available with or without frets. First came the fretted AEB I and fretless AUB I models. These featured a scrolled style headstock and cosmetic "F" holes that were cut completely through the body. These were followed by the ASB I and AUSB-I fretted and fretless models with exaggerated symmetrical body horns. The shape of this instrument has earned it the nickname "The Devil Bass."

In 1967, Hull sold Ampeg and by 1968 the new owners, Unimusic, bought the Grammer acoustic guitar plant in Nashville. Ampeg was planning to produce acoustic guitars, but was persuaded by Dan Armstrong, a design consultant, that the electric guitar market would be more lucrative. Ampeg contracted Armstrong to design a guitar and bass, and the instruments were ready for production by 1969. Featuring a clear Lucite body (a very few were made in black), 24 fret fingerboard, and interchangeable pickups on the guitar model, they were revolutionary as well as shocking to the eye. By the end of 1971, Armstrong broke his contract with Ampeg and production ceased in the Linden, New Jersey, factory.

In the 1970s, Ampeg imported a line of cheaply made instruments from the far East. The Stud series as they were named featured a thick plywood-style laminated body.

Also in the 1970s, Ampeg imported Hagstrom model guitars, most notably was the Swede model that was the basis for their Patch 2000 guitar synthesizer system.

Ampeg in 1997 has re-issued some of their classic 1960s models, though updated by using contemporary electronics and construction methods. Ampeg's original guitars of the 1960s to the early 1970s are fairly collectible and command prices from $500 to $2000, depending on model and condition.

Ampeg Baby Bass. $2000. *Courtesy of New Jersey Guitar and Bass Center.*

1966 Ampeg Scroll Bass, AEB1. $1300. *Courtesy of Gary's Classic Guitars.*

1969 Ampeg Dan Armstrong Model. $1200. *Courtesy of New Jersey Guitar and Bass Center.*

1969 Ampeg Scroll Bass, with magnetic pickup. $1300. *Courtesy of Neil's Guitars.*

Aria Pro II

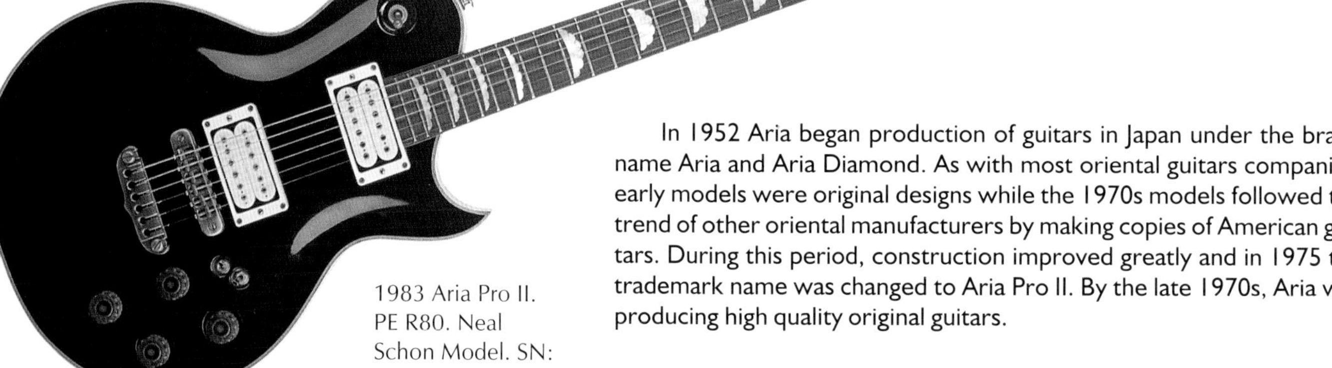

1983 Aria Pro II. PE R80. Neal Schon Model. SN: 108024. $500

In 1952 Aria began production of guitars in Japan under the brand name Aria and Aria Diamond. As with most oriental guitars companies, early models were original designs while the 1970s models followed the trend of other oriental manufacturers by making copies of American guitars. During this period, construction improved greatly and in 1975 the trademark name was changed to Aria Pro II. By the late 1970s, Aria was producing high quality original guitars.

Baldwin

1967 Baldwin Vibraslim. SN: 17648. $500. *Courtesy of Nationwide Guitars.*

1967 Baldwin Jazz Split Sound. SN: 19579. $650

Baldwin, a major piano and organ company, was looking to get a piece of the guitar boom pie in the 1960s. After being out-bid by Columbia Broadcasting Systems to purchase Fender in 1965, they turned to Burns. In September of that year, they acquired the production facilities from Jim Burns and began importing Burns guitars that were labeled with the Baldwin trademark. In 1967, Baldwin acquired Gretsch from Fred Gretsch Jr., and, by 1970, phased out the Burns style instruments so as to concentrate on the production of Gretsch guitars. Gretsch instruments of this period share some of the Burns/Baldwin traits including the key adjustment for the truss rod and the vibrato mechanisms.

1968 Baldwin Baby Bison Bass. SN: 15759. $600. *Courtesy of Lee Cunningham.*

B.C. Rich

Bernardo Chavez Rico, a Los Angeles native, built classical and flamenco style guitars at his family's business, Bernardo's Valencian Guitar Shop. In the mid-to-late 1960s, he began to build steel string guitars to capitalize on the folk rock boom, and, on the advice of his distributor, changed his professional name to B.C. Rich. In 1970, after repairing a Gretsch guitar for Bo Diddley, he developed an interest in electric guitars and by 1971 had introduced his first solid body electric, the Seagull. Like the instruments that would follow, it had a sexy, curvaceous body that was directed toward the hard rock market. These guitars featured a neck-through body construction and active electronics. In the late 1970s, Rico imported a line of electrics in very limited quantities. These shared the construction methods of their American counterparts, but without active electronics. These fairly rare guitars feature the name B.C. Rico on the headstock. Throughout the 1980s, there were American and imported B.C. Rich guitars.

In 1988, Rico went into semi-retirement, licensing the B.C. Rich name for imported instruments. In 1989 it was licensed to Class Axe for U.S.A.-made instruments.

In 1994, Rico regained control of the B.C. Rich trademark, and with partner Bill Shapiro is once again producing quality domestic and imported guitars.

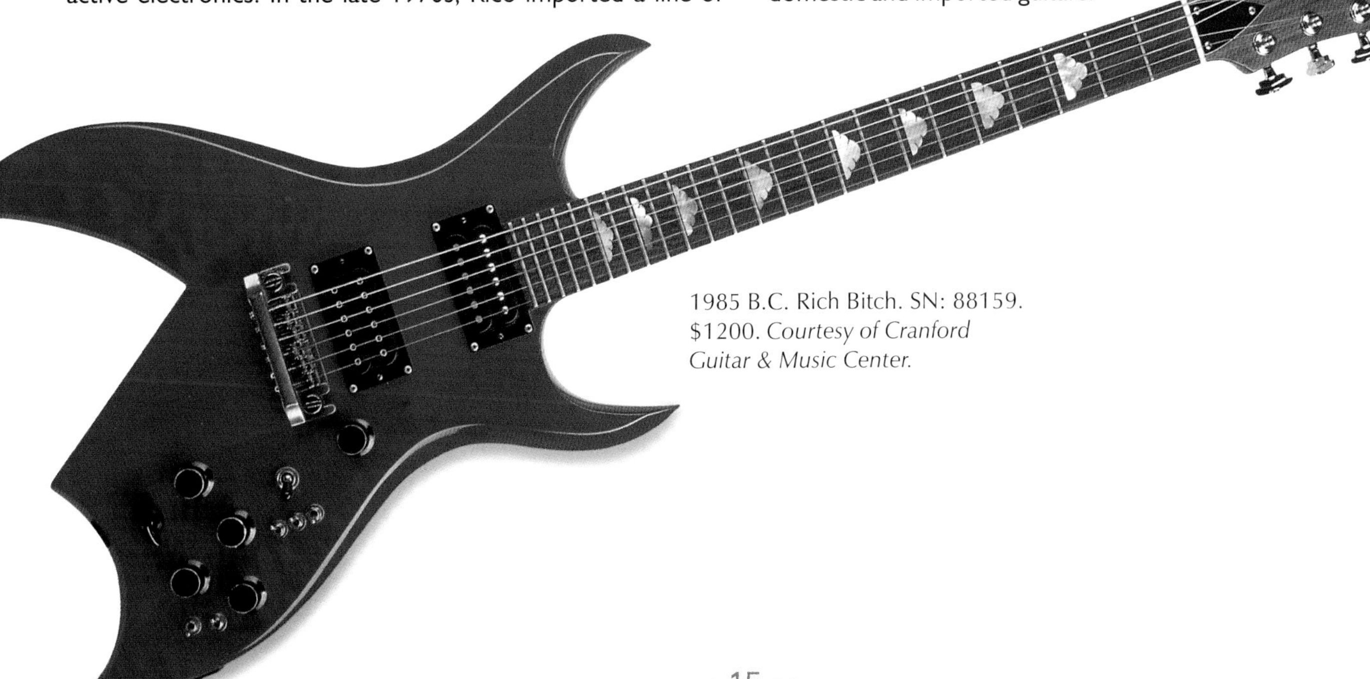

1985 B.C. Rich Bitch. SN: 88159. $1200. *Courtesy of Cranford Guitar & Music Center.*

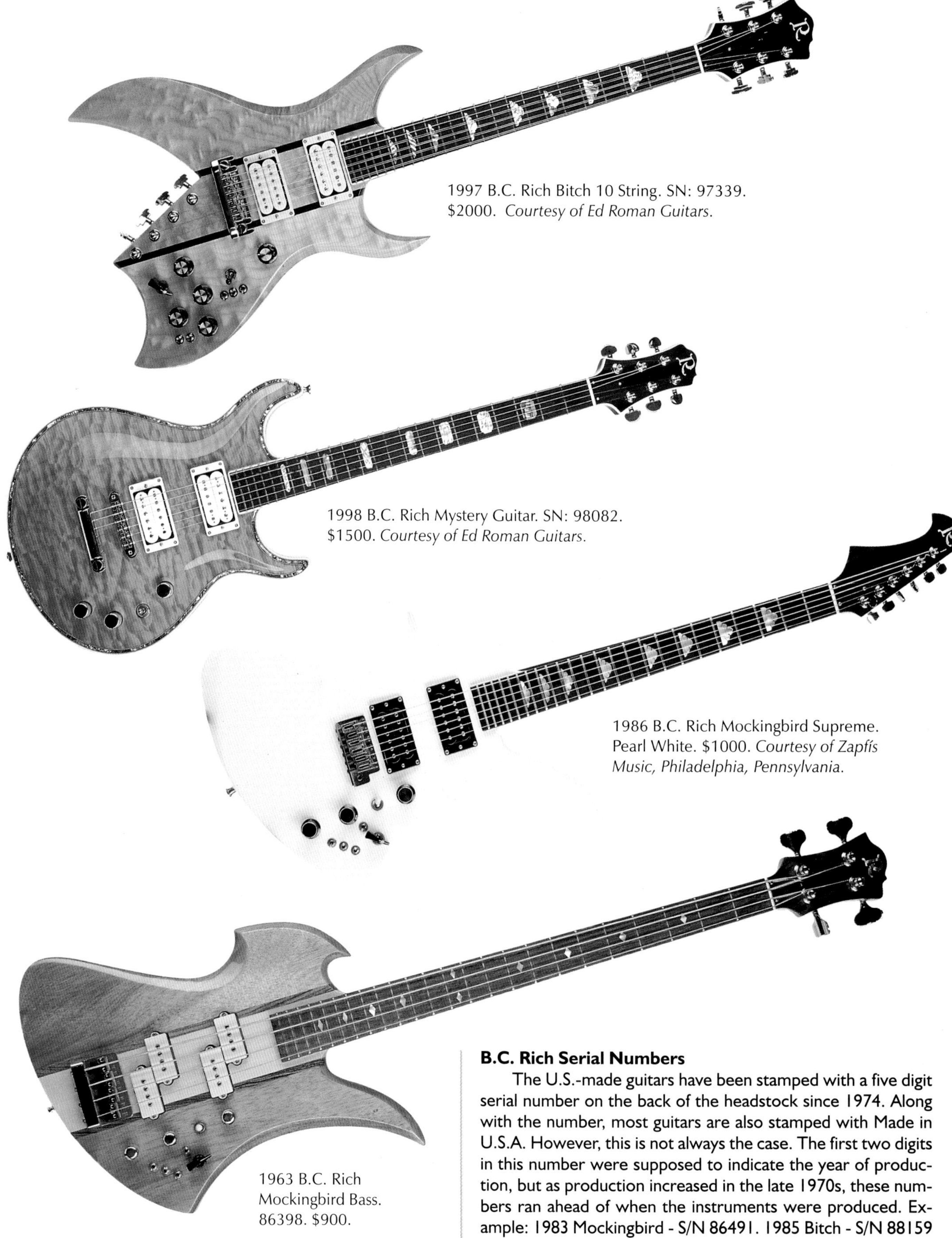

1997 B.C. Rich Bitch 10 String. SN: 97339. $2000. *Courtesy of Ed Roman Guitars.*

1998 B.C. Rich Mystery Guitar. SN: 98082. $1500. *Courtesy of Ed Roman Guitars.*

1986 B.C. Rich Mockingbird Supreme. Pearl White. $1000. *Courtesy of Zapfís Music, Philadelphia, Pennsylvania.*

1963 B.C. Rich Mockingbird Bass. 86398. $900.

B.C. Rich Serial Numbers

The U.S.-made guitars have been stamped with a five digit serial number on the back of the headstock since 1974. Along with the number, most guitars are also stamped with Made in U.S.A. However, this is not always the case. The first two digits in this number were supposed to indicate the year of production, but as production increased in the late 1970s, these numbers ran ahead of when the instruments were produced. Example: 1983 Mockingbird - S/N 86491. 1985 Bitch - S/N 88159

Current U.S. models, however, do follow this code. Example: 1997 Bitch- S/N 97339.

Bigsby

1952. Bigsby Grady Martin Double Neck. SN: 10152. "Priceless." *Courtesy of The Chinery Collection.*

1950 Bigsby Mandolin. SN: 51550. "Priceless." *Courtesy of The Chinery Collection.*

Paul Bigsby, known by his peers as P.A., was a pattern maker by trade who loved to tinker with the mechanics of motorcycles. In 1946, Merle Travis, a professional guitarist and friend of Bigsby, commissioned him to repair a vibrato on a Gibson L-10. Instead of fixing the worn out unit, Bigsby designed and built his own, replacing the old one completely. This vibrato would become the forerunner of the famous Bigsby vibrato that is still available today. About a year later, in 1947, Travis sketched out a complete guitar that he wanted Bigsby to build for him. This instrument, with its single cut-away birdseye maple body, neck-through construction, and sleek headstock design was way ahead of its time. The headstock shape would be made world famous by a man named Leo Fender, when, in 1963, he would introduce to the world the Stratocaster with a similar shaped headstock. Bigsby would continue to build guitars up until 1950 on a special order basis only, after which he referred people to Fender. Bigsby's other accomplishments include the re-necking of a few acoustic guitars and revolutionizing the pedal steel guitar. In 1956, he designed a couple of guitars for Magnatone, but had no involvement in production.

In 1965, he sold his vibrato company to Ted McCarty (a Gibson ex-president) and in 1968 Paul Bigsby passed away. Bigsby's guitars can be dated by the serial number, which corresponds to the date that the instrument was built.

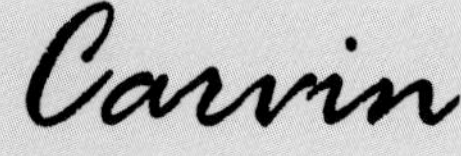

Carvin was founded in 1946 by Lowell Kiesel, building pickups, small amps, and lap steels. In 1949 Carvin, whose name derived from Kiesel's two eldest of five sons, Carson and Gavin, moved from Los Angeles to Covina, California. Throughout the 1950s, 1960s, and most of the 1970s, Carvin marketed kits and completed instruments made from necks and bodies that were either imported or domestically made by other manufacturers. Since 1978, Carvin guitars have been made in-house in Escondido, California, where Carvin has resided since 1969. Throughout their history, Carvin has marketed most of its products through mail order catalogs and today most of their business is carried out in this same fashion.

Early 1960s Carvin Hollow Body Electric. $600. *Courtesy of Johnny's Guitars.*

1989 Carvin Ultra V. SN: 23292. The bridge pickup is not original. $600. *Courtesy of Vince Perri.*

Carvin Serial Numbers

Carvin did not implement numbers until 1970. However, it is possible to assess the approximate manufacturing date of early models by the styles and methods of construction.

1954-1961: Archtop models were made by Kay or Harmony and came with or without Carvin pickups.
1954-1961: Solid bodies were Telecaster-style.
1962-1968 : Solid bodies were JazzMaster-style.
1968-1969: Solid bodies were Japanese-made Strat-style with a sunburst finish.
1970-1976: Solid bodies were German made Strat-style with a squared off lower bout.
1964-1977: Hofner bolt-on necks were used on all Carvin products.
1963-mid 70s: Bigsby vibratos were an option.
1978 : Instruments featured a glued-in neck and all American construction.
1988: Carvin changed to a neck-through the body construction method.
Serial numbers on models produced after 1970 can be located at the end of the fingerboard or on the input jack plate.
1970: First number is 5000
1980-1983: Numbers are in the 11000 range, approximately 1000 units produced a year.

Example:

1981 Koa	DC200—S/N 11815
1983-1984	13000-15000
1985-1987	17000-22000
1988-1989	22000-25000
1989-1991	26000-33000
1992	35000

Examples:

1986 DC150	21538
1988 Ultra V	23292

Serial number information was courtesy of Carvin.

Charvel/Jackson

Wayne Charvel operated a guitar repair shop in Azusa, California, during the late 1970s. In 1977, Grover Jackson was employed by the shop, which by this time had gained a reputation for making high quality replacement necks and bodies. In 1979 Jackson bought the Charvel operation and moved it to San Dimas, California. A year later Jackson debuted their first guitar at the 1979 NAMM show. With this the "Super Strat" was born. The guitars featured a Stratocaster™-shaped body, flashy paint jobs, a Humbucking pickup, and sleek bolt-on necks that sported a Fender-style headstock. By 1981, Charvel published their first catalog which featured the company's ability to custom paint graphics, and various options available to the customer. It was also during this time that Charvel introduced a headstock design that would be copied by guitar manufacturers the world over. The styling exercise featured a 6 on one side ExplorerTM-style headstock that was chopped off at the tip to end in a sharp point. Early Charvel's had Fender-style vibratos, but these soon gave way to locking style units which allowed for dive-bombing techniques while maintaining a stable tuning, which were becoming quite popular with 1980s hard rock.

By late 1981, Charvel had introduced their Jackson line of neck-through body models. These included the Rhodes "V", so named from its association with the late, great guitarist Randy Rhodes, which has a V shaped body with a radical extended upper horn that ended in a sharp point. Features included two Humbuckers, a V shaped string anchor plate, and a plain 22 fret dot-inlaid neck. These soon changed to a locking tremolo and a bound neck with "shark fin" style fingerboard inlays. The other model was the Strat-shaped Soloist, which shared these features plus a two octave neck.

Charvel would market the bolt neck series as Charvels and the neck-through series as Jacksons until 1985. Instruments built during that time were available with endless custom options. In 1985, Grover Jackson licensed the company name to IMC (International Music Corporation) and a year later he sold the company to them.

The Charvel/Jackson line of guitars would expand tremendously over the next few years. IMC-made Charvels and the Jackson Professional series are made in Japan while the Jackson U.S.A. and Jackson Custom Shop models are made in Ontario, California.

Charvel has recently introduced the U.S.A.-made Charvel San Dimas models, probably to capitalize on the growing desirability of the original Charvel guitars.

1996 Charvel Surfcaster. SN: 375381. $450. *Courtesy of Mark Hoover, Guitars Plus.*

1988 Jackson Soloist. SN: J4060 in yellow crackle finish. $900.

Coral

The Coral line of guitars was introduced in 1967 by Danelectro, after the company's acquisition by the entertainment conglomerate MCA. The Coral instruments were meant to be upscale Danelectros that were to go head to head in competition with brand name guitars, such as Fender. The Coral instruments were built in Danelectro's Neptune City, New Jersey, factory and featured upgrades such as Kluson tuners and Bigsby vibratos. The bodies that were used on the hollow archtop models were imported from Japan. Production of Coral instruments ceased in 1968 when MCA folded Danelectro.

1967 Coral Firefly. $500.

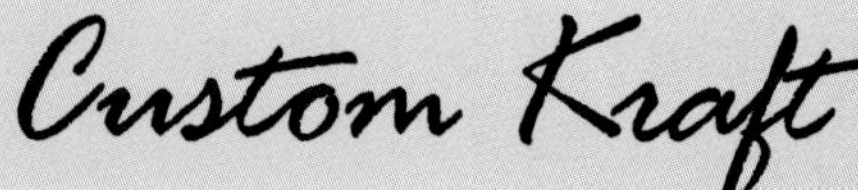

Custom Kraft. $350. *Courtesy of Bruce Barr c/o Sound Barrier Int'l*

Custom Kraft guitars were built from 1961 to the early 1970s by Kay, Harmony, and Valco as a house brand of St. Louis Music, an importer, distributor, and manufacturer of musical instruments since 1922.

Danelectro

Danelectro 4021. $1000. *Courtesy of Rod & Hank's Guitars.*

In 1934, Nathan Daniel (1912-1994), an electronics enthusiast residing in New York, started making his first home built amplifiers. Soon after, he was contracted by Epiphone to design and build their electric line of amps.

In 1948, Daniel founded the Danelectro Corporation. The factory relocated to Redbank, New Jersey, where it produced amplifiers and echo units. Danelectro designed their first guitar in 1955 and it was introduced to the public in 1956. By 1960, the factory had again moved, to its final location in Neptune City, New Jersey.

Early Danelectros featured a wider "Coke bottle" shaped headstock and a different neck and body construction compared to what was to become the "classic" Danelectro guitar. This was a narrow Coke bottle shaped headstock, twin rod reinforced neck, and body constructed of a stapled poplar wood frame core and masonite top and back. The edge of the guitar's body featured a white pebbled vinyl strip that concealed the method of construction. Some later solid wood body models do not share this feature. All Danelectros shared the cheesy, inexpensive hardware and all featured the same pickups that make these cheaply made instruments so desirable today. The pickups are single coil units mounted inside of a chrome plated tube which has earned them the name "Lipsticks." The rich single coil sound that these pickups emit has resulted in the use of these guitars by many professional players.

About 80 to 85 percent of Danelectro's guitars were sold under Sears's Silvertone name.

Danelectro produced some very original designs like the Guitarlin which featured a 31 fret fingerboard, the Long Horn bass with a 2 octave neck, and a couple of electric sitars, one of which came complete with 13 drone strings and was marketed under the Coral brand name.

Vincent Bell, an East Coast session player, became a design consultant and product demonstrator for Danelectro in the 1960s. His inspiration resulted in the designs of the sitars as well as the 12 string models. His signature can be found on the pickguards of some of the Coral model instruments.

In 1967, Danelectro was sold to the entertainment conglomerate MCA. By 1968, Danelectro was folded due to poor business operations and was sold to William C. Herring for $20,000 in late 1968.

Dan Armstrong, who designed Ampeg's Lucite guitars, met Herring at a swap meet in Englishtown in early 1969. He acquired an interest in Danelectro after visiting the factory with Herring and seeing piles of unfinished guitars. Armstrong contracted with Ampeg to build some Danelectros prior to the release of their see-through models. These instruments featured the single cut-away body style with a single Humbucker, and a pickguard sporting the phrase "Dan Armstrong modified Danelectro" on it. The neck's headstock was unlabeled. It is estimated that about 700 of these guitars were made before Herring got sued and lost the stock to Danelectro in August of 1969.

In 1995, Danelectro was resurrected by the Evett Company. They are currently producing effects pedals, small amps, and reissues of some of the classic Danelectro guitars. All of the reissues are imported from overseas sources.

Original Danelectros, despite being produced as an inexpensive student level instrument, enjoy a healthy vintage marketplace, with prices ranging from $200 to over $1500 depending on color, rarity, and desirability of the model.

Danelectro Serial Numbers

Most guitars are stamped in the neck pocket with a 4 digit code, although some instruments will be stamped elsewhere on or in the body. The first two digits denote the week of construction from 01 to 52. The third digit's meaning is unknown, and the fourth digit denotes the years of manufacture. Also, since Danelectros were produced in the 1950s and 1960s, numbers could be repeated. In this case, features of the instrument's construction can determine the decade of manufacture. Danelectros Coral line utilizes a three digit code with the first number being the year and the last two being the week.

Early 1960s Danelectro Convertible. $500.

1961 Danelectro Short Horn Bass. Copper finish. $550 *Courtesy of Bradley Guitars.*

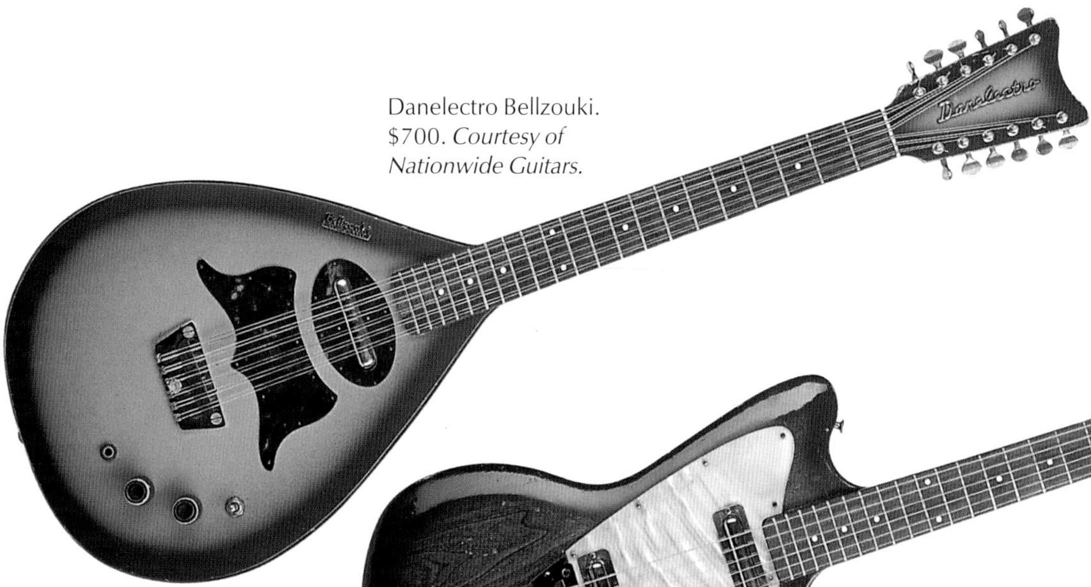

Danelectro Bellzouki. $700. *Courtesy of Nationwide Guitars.*

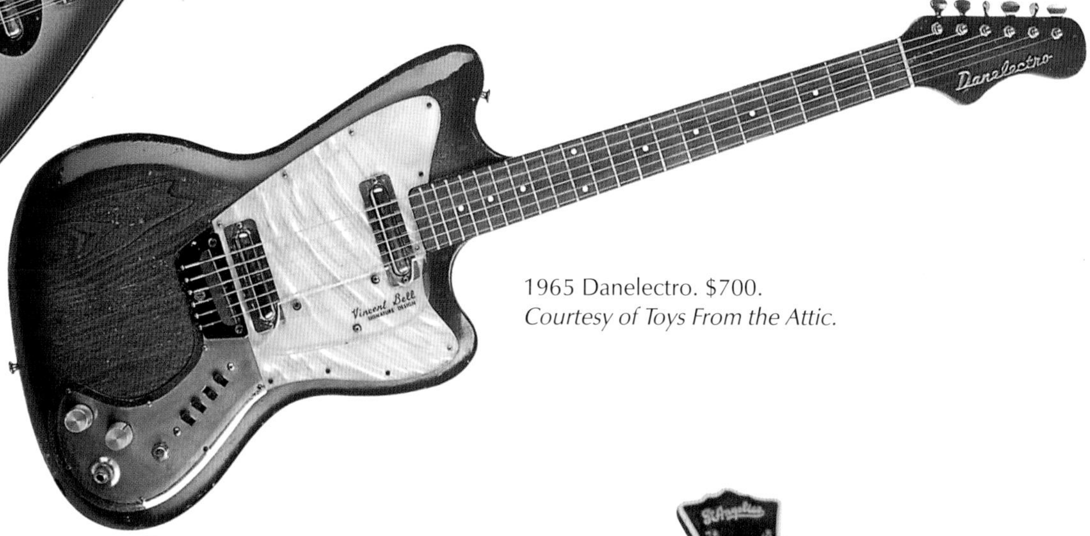

1965 Danelectro. $700. *Courtesy of Toys From the Attic.*

D'Angelico/D'Aquisto

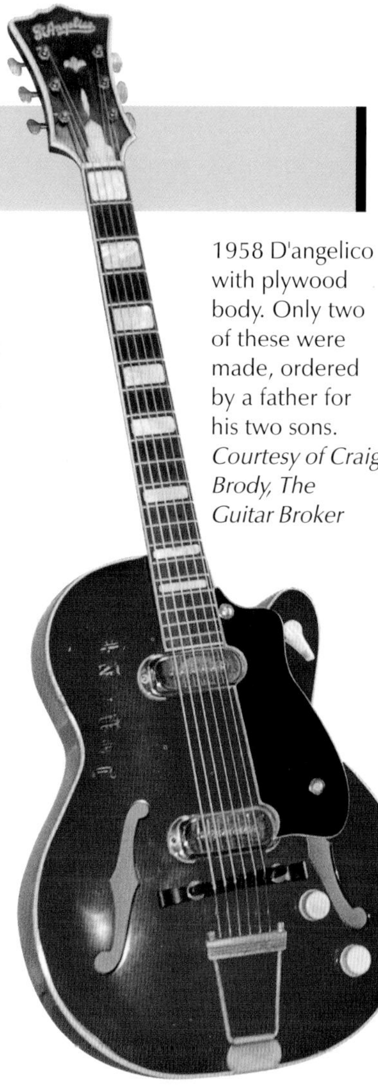

John D'Angelico was a New York City native born in 1905. In 1914 he was apprenticed by his uncle, a Mr. Ciani, who built guitars and mandolins in the Italian style. After the death of Ciani, John took over the supervision of the approximately fifteen employees in the shop.

In 1932 D'Angelico started the business that bore his name and introduced the carved top orchestra style guitars that would make him famous.

James L. D'Aquisto, a jazz guitarist, was apprenticed by D'Angelico in 1952. D'Angelico took a special interest in "Jimmy," and when his health began to fail in the late 1950s, D'Aquisto took over some of the more strenuous tasks, including carving the tops and backs of the instruments. After surviving two heart attacks, D'Angelico succumbed to pneumonia in 1964 at the age of 59.

D'Aquisto acquired D'Angelico's wood stocks and tools, as well as the right to claim that his company was the "successor to D'Angelico," though he lost that right in 1965. Jimmy started his own company in New York, first in Huntington and later, in 1973, in Farmingdale, where he built guitars in the tradition of D'Angelico. His first guitars were built in the styles of D'Angelico's New Yorker and Excel models, but soon he started to employ his own styles and designs.

In the late 1980s D'Aquisto moved to what would be his final location, Green Port, New York. During this time he would break away from traditional archtop styling and start producing some stunning and very modern looking instruments. D'Aquisto continued these concepts of modern design combined with old world craftsmanship until his untimely death in April, 1995.

During the careers of John D'Angelico and Jimmy D'Aquisto, they produced electric guitar models. John's were all hollow bodies, utilizing his necks attached to imported bodies. Jimmy produced both solid and hollow body models, all entirely by hand in his shop. Any instrument by either of these luthiers is extremely valuable and several independent appraisals should be acquired before any sales transaction takes place.

1958 D'angelico with plywood body. Only two of these were made, ordered by a father for his two sons. *Courtesy of Craig Brody, The Guitar Broker*

Dean

In 1977, after a successfully accredited work studies program repairing and building guitars, Dean Zelinsky founded Dean Guitars in Evanston, Illinois. Dean's early guitars were patterned after Gibson designs, showing his fondness for the Marque. They departed from the originals though in that they sported Dean's outrageous oversized "V" shaped headstock.

In 1980, Dean moved to Chicago, Illinois, enjoying a strong increase in production. Deans Gibson inspired guitars were aimed at the Rock-N-Roll market. But in the early 1980s the superstrat was becoming the preferred instrument in this genre of music. Dean accommodated this by designing a line of instruments to fill this void. These instruments were manufactured overseas and didn't have the quality or unique personality of the American-made instruments. Dean ended production of the U.S.A.-made guitars in 1986 and in 1990 Zelinsky sold Dean to Tropical Music. Dean guitars are currently produced in the U.S.A. and overseas. The early, made in U.S.A. instruments are currently the only models of interest to collectors, and of these the figured maple top versions carry the highest premiums.

1978 Dean Z. Pat. Pending stamp. SN: 7800811. $1000.

1981 Dean Z. SN: 8109091. $1200.

1981 Dean ML. SN: 8103227. $1000.

1980 Dean V. SN: 8001919. $1000. *Courtesy of Amanda's Texas Underground.*

1980 Dean Elite. SN: 8002270. $800. *Courtesy of Guitar Shelter.*

1981 Dean ML Bass. SN: 8102937. $900. *Courtesy of Outlaw Guitars.*

1981 Dean ML. Changed pickups. SN: 8103772. $1200.

1983 Dean Baby V Bass. SN: 8305398. $500.

Dean Serial Numbers

U.S. made instruments are quite easy to date. On the back of the headstock, the guitars are stamped with Made In U.S.A. along with a seven digit number. The first two numbers, which are spaced apart from the rest, represent the year of manufacture. Early models will also have patents pending stamped under the number.

78 00811	Pats. Pend 1978 "Z" Model
81 03227	1981 "ML" Model
83 05398	1983 Baby V Bass

Eko

Eko was the guitar line conceived in 1961 by the Italian based accordion manufacturer, Oliviero Pigini and Company. Pigini anticipated the guitar boom of the mid-1960s and wanted to capitalize on this. Eko used construction aspects that were used on their accordions of the time and their early guitars featured molded plastic bodies in all colors of the imagination and push button tone and pickup selectors which were labeled the same as an accordion. Eko was not alone in this styling exercise, with many Italian companies, like Bartolini, Crucianelli, and Gemelli, making similar styled instruments.

By the late 1960s, all of this craziness came to an end and Eko turned to more conventional styling and construction. Many of the late 1960s Vox instruments were made by Eko. Eko's 1970 instrument line shrank with the guitar market in general. By the late 1970s, Eko opened a custom shop making neck-through designs that featured DiMarzio pickups. Eko's final in-house made instruments were set-neck Alembic-inspired designs. Eko closed its doors and the company holdings were sold off in 1987.

The Eko name has been recently revived and the trademark is being used on a line of Asian built entry level guitars. Early Italian-made guitars that possess the accordion styling, like the Ekos, are of interest to certain collectors. Values seem to be directly linked to gaudiness, the number of switches, the coolness factor, and the number of pickups.

1964 Eko 700 4V. $695. *Courtesy of Rockohaulix.*

Early 1960s Eko Model 500 IZ. $600. *Courtesy of Rockohaulix.*

Early 1960s Eko Model 500 4V. $600. *Courtesy of Rockohaulix.*

Epiphone

Anastasios Stathopoulo established the House of Stathopoulo in New York City in 1873 where the company built a wide variety of high quality stringed instruments. In 1923 the newly incorporated business focused its production on banjos and related instruments. Some of these banjos carried the name Epiphone, which was a combination of Epi, the nickname of Anasasios' son Epaminondas, and phone, the Greek translation of sound.

In July of 1925 the House of Stathopoulo purchased the Fairovon Banjo Manufacturing facilities and a month later moved its operation to the Long Island location. In 1928, the company changed its name to the Epiphone Banjo Corporation.

Epiphones' already well established Master Built guitar line was officially introduced in 1930 and by the end of the decade their archtop guitars were considered to be some of the finest instruments of that type made.

In 1935, Epiphone relocated to 142 W. 14th Street in New York City, increasing the factory size twofold a year later. In 1936, Epiphone introduced their first electric, the Electar Hawaiian, a lap steel model.

In 1937, Epiphone doubled in size again and introduced their first Spanish style electric, the Electar Spanish model. Around this time, inventor and salesman Herb Sunshine was employed at Epiphone. He was the key man responsible for designing much of Epiphone's early electric guitars as well as the Frequensator tailpiece. He also contracted Nathan Daniel, of Danelectro fame, to build Epiphone's Electar series of amplifiers.

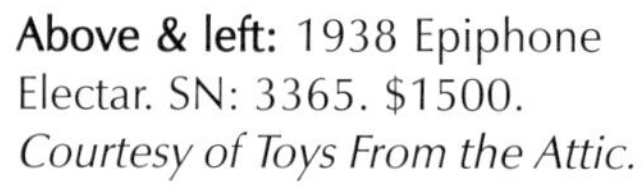

Above & left: 1938 Epiphone Electar. SN: 3365. $1500. *Courtesy of Toys From the Attic.*

Right: 1942 Epiphone Zephyr. SN: 25173. $1400. *Courtesy of Toys From the Attic.*

c. 1946 Epiphone Zephyr. SN: 25522. $1000. *Courtesy of Guitar Express.*

1947 Epiphone Zephyr Deluxe. SN: 75168. $2200

In 1939, the Electar Spanish was replaced by the Zephyr which was joined by a lower priced Century model. Epaminondas passed away in the early 1940s and was succeeded by his brother Orpheus (Orphie) as President. Their other brother, Frixo, took Orphie's position as Vice President , and in 1948 sold his share of his company to his brother Orphie.

By the mid-1940s, Epiphone's electric line had grown to include more models. These were based on the acoustic models of the time. Epiphone's upper end models shared the names of their acoustic counterparts, with the prefix "Zephyr" to denote an electric version. In 1949, when cut-away versions were introduced, Epiphone ended the name with "Regent" to show this feature. Epiphone's electrics, although sharing ornamentation, trim features, and looking like their acoustic equivalents were actually very different instruments. While acoustic versions were carved out of solid woods, the electric versions were made with laminated woods.

By 1953, Epiphone was feeling some financial pressures and Orphie decided to sell the company to their long time distributor, C.G. Conn. Conn, the large band instrument manufacturer, moved the company to Philadelphia to avoid impending union pressures. In 1955, the Stathopoulo family regained a controlling interest in the company, but never really got instrument production up to speed. In 1957, Gibson's parent company, CMI (Chicago Musical Instrument Co.) bought Epiphone at the suggestion of Gibson's then president Ted McCarty. McCarty only wanted to acquire Epiphone's tooling and the equipment that produced their upright acoustic basses, but in the deal they ended up with Epiphone's entire holdings, including the name, and all for only $20,000!

Epiphone was reincorporated under CMI as a subsidiary of Gibson, and all of the equipment and unfinished instruments were moved to Gibson's factory in Kalamazoo, Michigan. All of the pre-Gibson Epiphone electric models which included the Electar,

1951 Epiphone Zephyr Deluxe SN: 61672. $2200. *Courtesy of Pro Frets.*

Zephyr, Century, Coronet, Broadway, Harry Volpe, Deluxe, and Emperor were full-depth archtop based guitars, but after the acquisition the Broadway remained the only full depth model in the Epiphone line. The other models that were in production during this time, the Emperor, Zephyr, and Century, all went to a thin depth body and of these only the Emperor and Zephyr kept their original body outline, while the Century took the shape of Gibson's non-cut ES 125 T.

Gibson used all of the Epiphone parts they had acquired, and between 1958, when Gibson started Epiphone production, to about 1963, many of the guitars were assembled with both Gibson and New York-made Epiphone parts.

1958 also was the year Epiphone started solid body production. Epiphone revived the Coronet name for the bottom of the line model and the Crestwood rounded out this line. These guitars had symmetrical double cut-away bodies and 3 & 3 headstocks. First year models had squared-off body edges, while later ones were more rounded. 1958 models used leftover New York made Epiphone pickups exclusively; they were phased out during the next two years. In 1959, the line was expanded to include the Coronet with one P-90 or New York pickup, the Wilshire with two P-90 or New York pickups, and the renamed Crestwood Custom with two mini-Humbucker or two New York made pickups, gold hardware, and oval fingerboard inlays.

In 1960, this line expanded again to include the Olympic which became the least expensive model in the line. It was basically a mirror image of Gibson's single cut Melody Maker of the time. A three quarter size model and a 2 pickup model, The Olympic Double, were also offered. As for the other models in the line, the New York pickups became a much rarer sight.

The solid body line went under some major renovations in 1963. The body shape, which would be shared by all models, went to an asymmetrical double cut-away shape with a slightly longer horn on the bass string side of the instrument. A new model was added at the top of the line during this year. The Crestwood Deluxe featured three mini-Humbuckers, a block inlay, Ebony fingerboards, and a new six on a side headstock that resembled the

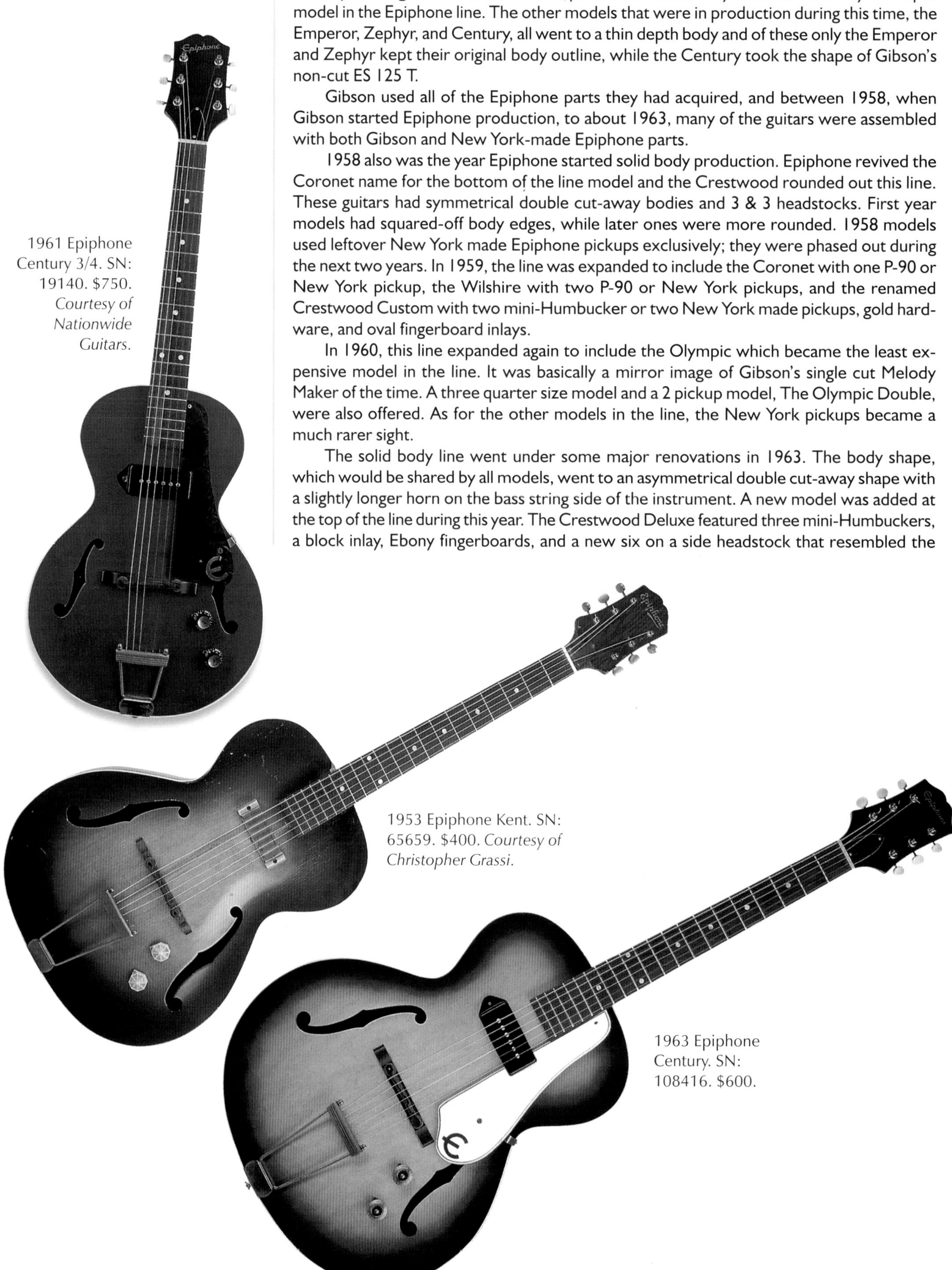

1961 Epiphone Century 3/4. SN: 19140. $750. *Courtesy of Nationwide Guitars.*

1953 Epiphone Kent. SN: 65659. $400. *Courtesy of Christopher Grassi.*

1963 Epiphone Century. SN: 108416. $600.

shape of a batwing. The batwing headstock would be reserved for the upper line models until 1965, when it was used on all models. From 1965 until 1970, when Gibson ceased U.S. Epiphone production, the solid body line remained pretty much unchanged with the exception of the addition of the rare Wilshire 12 string that was made from 1966 to 1968.

The other big news for Epiphone after Gibson's takeover was the 1958 introduction of the Sheraton. Based on Gibson's own ES 335 guitar, the Sheraton featured gold hardware, two New York style pickups, Frequensator tailpiece and a Emperor style fingerboard and headstock inlay. These appointments would make the Epiphone Sheraton Gibson's fanciest thin line model.

Through the early 1960s, Epiphone would introduce many new models of hollow and semisolid guitars with some of them having a Gibson equivalent. The Casino was introduced in 1961. It was basically a Gibson ES330 available with one or two black P-90 pickups and a dot inlaid neck. In 1963, these features would change to chrome P-90s and a single parallelogram inlaid neck.

The Riviera model debuted in 1962 as the sister to Gibson's ES 335. It featured two mini-Humbuckers, Frequensator tailpiece, and a single parallelogram inlaid neck like the Casino, the Riviera was made until 1970. A twelve string version of the Riviera was available from 1965 to 1969.

Other Epiphone guitars are the Al Caiola Custom (1963-1970), the Al Caiola Standard (1966-1970), the Howard Roberts (1964-1970) model, which looked like a Gibson ES 175 with an oval sound hole and a single mini-Humbucker in the neck position, and the Professional (1962-1966) which was meant to go as a set with a matching Professional amp. The amplifier which had no controls except an on-off switch, was connected to the guitar through a multi-din-pin cord. The guitar's front featured the controls for the amplifier, as well as the standard guitar control. The 1/4" jack on the front allowed hook up to any amp for standard use.

Epiphone also marketed a couple of basses. One was called the Rivoli. It paralleled Gibson's own EB2 models and was made from 1959 to 1970. The other was the Newport Bass (1961-1968), which followed the design trend of Epiphone's own solid body series.

Gibson ended Epiphone's U.S.A. production in 1970 and moved it to Japan until 1983, at which time it was moved to Korea, where they are currently produced. There have been a few exceptions to this, though, like the U.S.A.-made map-shaped guitars and the Spirit series of 1982 and 1983.

1963 Epiphone Cassino. $900. *Courtesy of Rumble Seat Music.*

1969 Epiphone Casino. SN: 858404. $1800 *Courtesy of Mimosa Music.*

1964 Epiphone Riviera. Nickel hardware. SN: 179203.

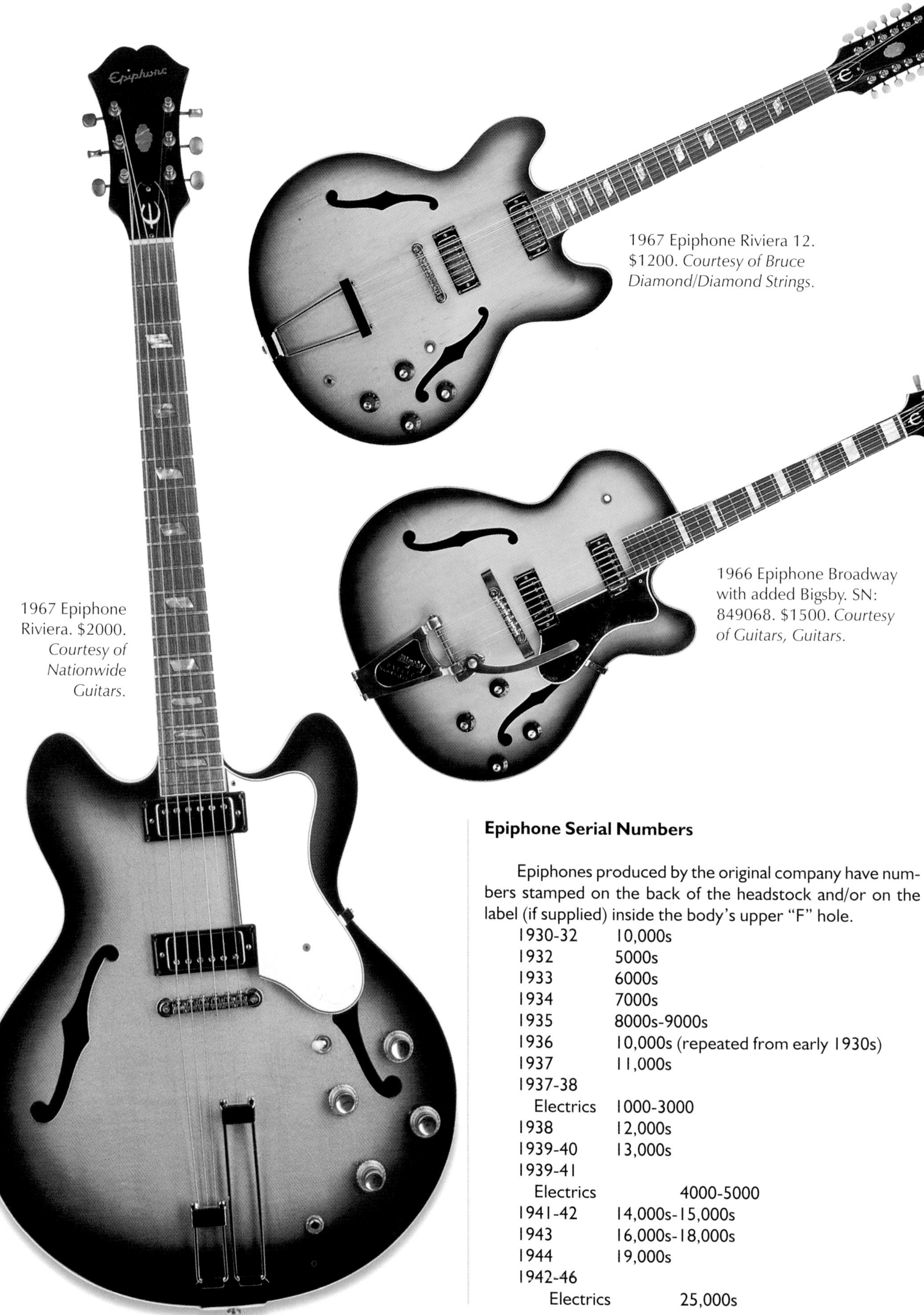

1967 Epiphone Riviera 12. $1200. *Courtesy of Bruce Diamond/Diamond Strings.*

1966 Epiphone Broadway with added Bigsby. SN: 849068. $1500. *Courtesy of Guitars, Guitars.*

1967 Epiphone Riviera. $2000. *Courtesy of Nationwide Guitars.*

Epiphone Serial Numbers

Epiphones produced by the original company have numbers stamped on the back of the headstock and/or on the label (if supplied) inside the body's upper "F" hole.

1930-32	10,000s
1932	5000s
1933	6000s
1934	7000s
1935	8000s-9000s
1936	10,000s (repeated from early 1930s)
1937	11,000s
1937-38	
Electrics	1000-3000
1938	12,000s
1939-40	13,000s
1939-41	
Electrics	4000-5000
1941-42	14,000s-15,000s
1943	16,000s-18,000s
1944	19,000s
1942-46	
Electrics	25,000s

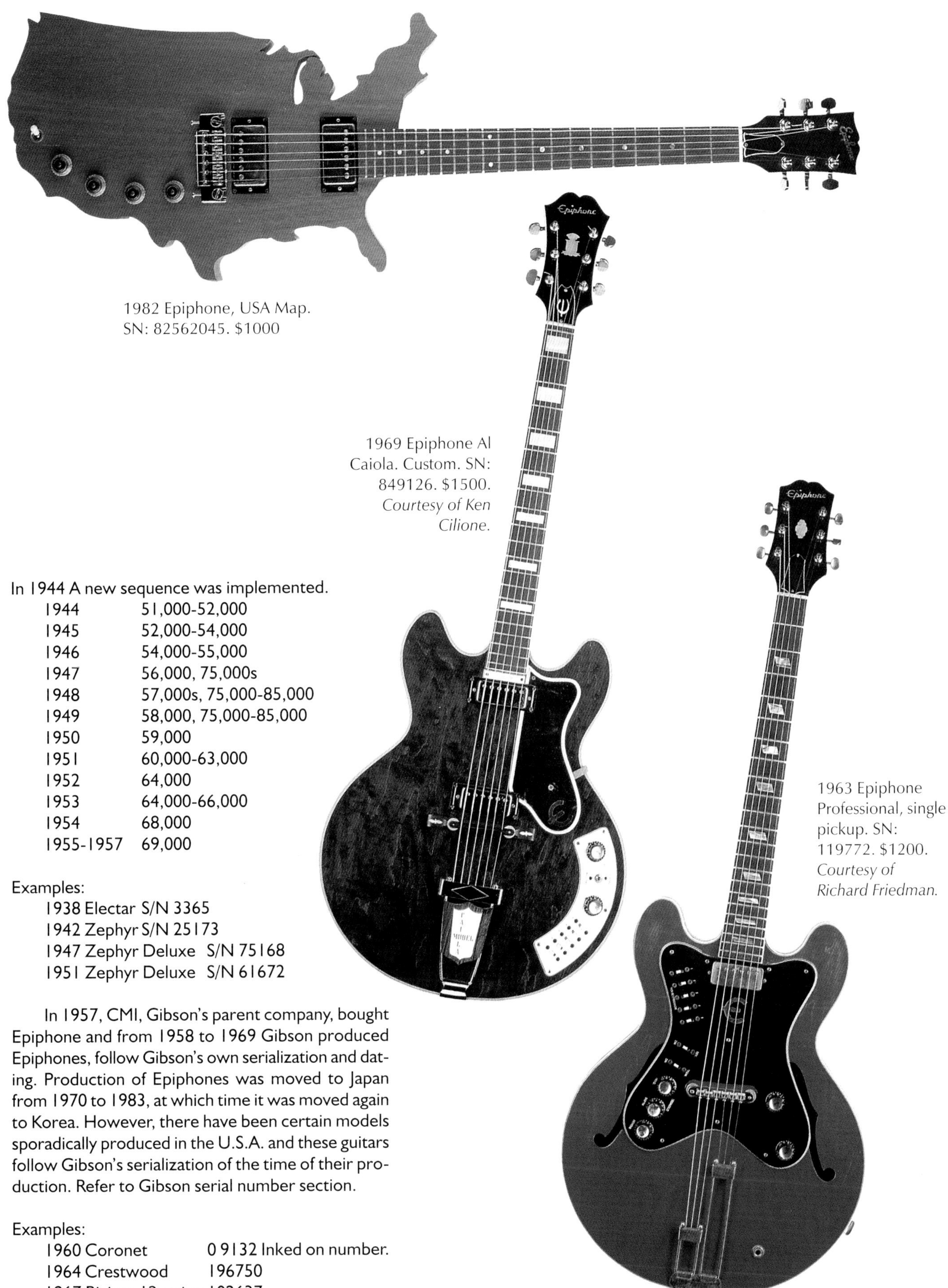

1982 Epiphone, USA Map. SN: 82562045. $1000

1969 Epiphone Al Caiola. Custom. SN: 849126. $1500. *Courtesy of Ken Cilione.*

1963 Epiphone Professional, single pickup. SN: 119772. $1200. *Courtesy of Richard Friedman.*

In 1944 A new sequence was implemented.

1944	51,000-52,000
1945	52,000-54,000
1946	54,000-55,000
1947	56,000, 75,000s
1948	57,000s, 75,000-85,000
1949	58,000, 75,000-85,000
1950	59,000
1951	60,000-63,000
1952	64,000
1953	64,000-66,000
1954	68,000
1955-1957	69,000

Examples:

1938 Electar S/N 3365
1942 Zephyr S/N 25173
1947 Zephyr Deluxe S/N 75168
1951 Zephyr Deluxe S/N 61672

In 1957, CMI, Gibson's parent company, bought Epiphone and from 1958 to 1969 Gibson produced Epiphones, follow Gibson's own serialization and dating. Production of Epiphones was moved to Japan from 1970 to 1983, at which time it was moved again to Korea. However, there have been certain models sporadically produced in the U.S.A. and these guitars follow Gibson's serialization of the time of their production. Refer to Gibson serial number section.

Examples:

1960 Coronet	0 9132 Inked on number.
1964 Crestwood	196750
1967 Riviera 12 string	102637
1982 Map of USA	82562045

Epiphone 1960 Coronet. SN: 0 9132 (inked).
Courtesy of Nicky Skopelitis.

1966 Epiphone Coronet. California Coral. SN: 560638. $2200.
Courtesy of Pat Murray.

1964 Epiphone Crestwood. Pacific Blue custom color. SN: 196750.
Mike's Music, Cincinnati, Ohio.

1965 Epiphone Olympic.

Fender

1954 Fender Esquire. SN: 8654. $6000. *Courtesy of Rumble Seat Music.*

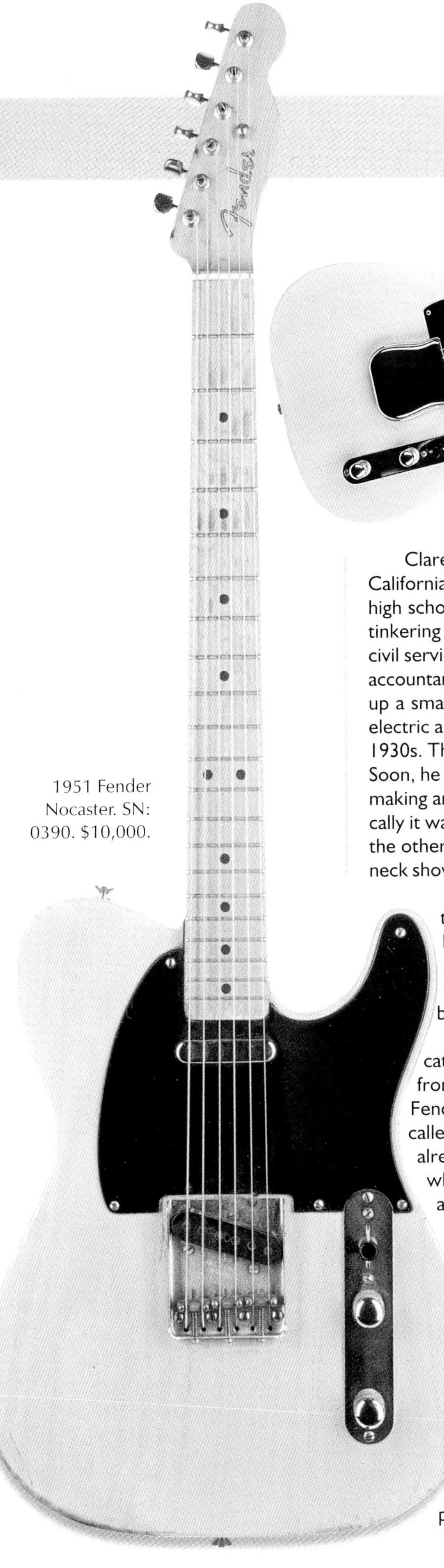

Clarence Leonidas Fender (1909-1991) was born and raised in Orange County, California. As a youth, Fender had a strong interest in electronics. After graduating high school, he held down a bookkeeping job, all the while doing radio repair and tinkering with electronics at home. From 1932 to 1933, he worked with California's civil service in the motor vehicle department and from 1934 to 1938 he became an accountant for the state. In 1939, Fender pursued his love for electronics and opened up a small radio repair shop. The shop soon became a retail store for household electric appliances too. Fender was also doing repairs for local musicians during the 1930s. These acquaintances gave Fender a finger on the pulse of the music industry. Soon, he was building his own pickups instead of repairing them and he also started making amplifiers. In 1943, Fender built a prototype solid body electric guitar. Basically it was a neck with sting anchors, bridge, and pickup on one end, and tuners on the other. Although the instrument looked like a lap steel, the rounded and fretted neck showed otherwise, that this guitar was meant to be played as a standard guitar.

1951 Fender Nocaster. SN: 0390. $10,000.

In 1941, Fender met Claton Orr (Doc) Kauffman, a guitarist and inventor, who designed and built some early vibrato units for guitars. Four years later in 1945 Kauffman and Fender formed the K & F Company, building lap steels and small amps. The venture lasted less than a year. Kauffman ended the partnership, for fear of failure of the company, and sold his half of the business to Fender.

In 1946, Fender formed the Fender Electric Instrument Company. Located on South Pamona Avenue, Fullerton, California, the company carried on from where K & F left off, making refined versions of lap steels and amps. Fender sold his instruments in his electronics store and through a distributor called Radio and Television Equipment Company (Radio-Tel), a company that already had involvement in the music industry. It was owned by Francis Hall, who later purchased Rickenbacker, . Donald Randal, Radio-Tel General Manager, would be recognized as the driving force that expanded Fender's sales territory from their home in Southern California to complete world wide distribution.

In 1948, George Fullerton came to work for Fender and during the course of that year they worked out the specifics for a new instrument. By 1949, Fender built his second prototype for a standard style solid electric guitar. The body shape was that of an Esquire with one pickup mounted at the bridge position in what was to become the classic Tele/Esquire bridge and pickup assembly. The neck, made of a solid piece of maple, had no truss rod and a plain 3 & 3 headstock.

In 1950, Fender announced their first production electric, the Fender Esquire. The single cut ash body had a see through blonde finish, one pickup, a black Bakelite pickguard and a chrome tongue depressor-shaped plate for the volume and tone controls. The one-piece maple neck featured the classic 6 on one side "Tele" headstock shape, but it still had no truss rod.

The guitar's introduction at the 1950 NAMM show was less than receptive, and even ridiculed by some at the time. The "Plank Bodied" guitar was laughed at by Gibson and others in that with its basic construction, it took no skill to make.

At the end of 1950 Fender temporarily stopped production of the Esquire because of neck warping problems, and introduced a new version with two pickups and a truss rod, called the Broadcaster. (A very few two pickup original issue Esquires were built). The Broadcasters addition of a truss rod came about after Don Randall convinced Fender that a professional caliber instrument should be so equipped, and that it would make the instrument much more marketable. The Broadcaster's name was soon under attack by Gretsch for copyright infringements over the name of their Broadkaster drum sets, so Fender complied and stopped putting the name on their guitar. Don Randall coined the name Telecaster from the explosive popularity of television in the late 1940s and the guitar's original name. By April of 1951 it was made official, and the Broadcaster became the Telecaster. Fender, not being a wasteful person, wanted to use up the remaining Broadcaster decals and simply cut the name off of the Fender decal before applying it to the guitar. These instruments have earned the nickname "No-Casters" by collectors. This went on until about August of 1951 when the old decals ran out even though the instruments new name, the Telecaster, was approved 4 months earlier. From this point on the Telecaster would be marketed as the 2 pickup version and the Esquire would have a single pickup. The latter's body, though, would have the neck pickup route in it.

In 1952 the Tele's wiring would be modified to include a tone control instead of the pickup blending control on the original.

In 1951 Fender changed the look of Rock-N-Roll forever with the introduction of the precision bass. Prior to this, a bassist's only choice of instrument was the "Doghouse" upright bass. The Fender bass was revolutionary not because it was electric or fretted, but because it combined both of these traits in a sleek, compact package. With it's double cut-away solid body, single coil pickup, fretted neck, and 34 inch scale, the bass was intended to be played in the same position as a guitar. This freed the bass player to be able to move around with the instrument. Obviously the other advantage it had over the old Doghouse was that it was not susceptible to feedback and therefore could be played at higher volumes, and with its fretted fingerboard, notes could be played with "precision."

It is interesting to note that for decades after the introduction of the precision, the term "Fender Bass" almost took on a generic status. A bassist, no matter what brand of bass he was playing, was often said to be playing a "Fender Bass", instead of an electric bass.

1968 Fender Paisley Telecaster. SN: 240332. $3000. *Courtesy of Buck Sulcer's Guitar Network.*

1969 Fender Telecaster. Blonde. SN: 283847. $1600

1960 Fender Custom Esquire. SN: 58327. $5500. *Courtesy of Larry Henrikson, Ax in Hand.*

1981 Fender Black & Gold Telecaster. SN: CE11777. $1000

1971 Fender Telecaster. Candy Apple Red custom color. Factory Bigsby tremolo. SN: 317016. *$3500. Courtesy of Steve Senerchia, The Music Man.*

1960 Custom Telecaster. SN: 57760. $6000. *Courtesy of Gary's Classic Guitars.*

1968 Fender Thinline Telecaster. Mahogany. SN: 279362. $2500. *Courtesy of Buck Sulcer's Guitar Network.*

1970s Fender Telecaster Deluxe. SN: 581823. $800. *Courtesy of Mike's Music.*

1955 Fender Stratocaster. SN: 7186. $17,000. *Courtesy of Pro Frets.*

1959 Fender Stratocaster. SN: 36954. $8000. *Courtesy of George Alessandro.*

1954 Fender Stratocaster. SN: 0114. $16,000. *Courtesy of Axe-zactly.*

Fender's business began to outgrow the current facilities and in the spring of 1953 Fender acquired another lot of land in Fullerton on East Valencia Street to erect 3 new production facilities. Fender also began to outgrow their distributor, Radio-Tel, which was still also involved with the electronics industry. To rectify the distribution problem, Radio-Tel's Francis Hall, Don Randall, and Charlie Mayes, a sales rep, along with Leo Fender set up Fender Sales Incorporated with each of them owning equal shares.

By mid-1953 Fender had a new guitar on the drawing board and with the help of musician Bill Carson and new Fender employee Freddie Tavares, the design was perfected and by spring of 1954, the Stratocaster was born. The guitar was like nothing else that came before. Its sleek contoured double cut-away body was fitted with three single coil pickups that had staggered polepieces to even out string response. There was a chrome scoop that housed the input jack and, of course, there was Fenders "synchronized tremolo." This vibrato system, which was compact and operated on principles of a

1959 Blonde Strat. SN: 38633. $25,000. *Courtesy of Buck Sulcer's Guitar Network.*

Above: 1961 Fender Strat. Daphne Blue. $14,000.

Right: 1962 Fender Strat, lefthanded. Olympic White. $13,500. *Both courtesy of Craig Brody, The Guitar Broker*

fulcrum, disappeared into the body of the guitar. The icing on the cake was the headstock shape which echoed Bigsby's elegant design of 6 years earlier. Fender's head was more streamlined, though, and this shape would be copied the world over. The Stratocaster featured a two-color sunburst finish, white single layer Bakelite pickguard and a maple neck.

By 1955 the Tele's see-through butterscotch yellow color became whiter and the pickguard changed from black to white.

In June of 1955 Charlie Mayes was killed in a car accident. Fender and Randall bought his share of Fender Sales Inc. from his widow, and at the same time they bought out Francis Hall's shares in the company.

New in 1955 was Fender's announcement of a deluxe Strat. This model had an ash body finished in blonde with gold parts. The guitar would become known as the Mary Kaye model from its association with the entertainer.

Fender's Precision Bass went through a couple of changes. The body received contouring like the Strat, and it also took the Strat's sunburst and white guard color scheme, replacing its previous blonde with black pickguard.

Although Fender had moved into its new factories, production still lagged behind, and Fender went about to rectify the problem by hiring Forrest White, and industrial engineer, and appointing him plant manager.

By 1956 Fender's line would be refined and expanded. Bakelite gave way to plastic, hardware underwent changes, ash gave way to alder on the Strat, and Fender would introduce two student guitars, the single pickup MusicMaster, and the two pickup Duo-Sonic. But the big news was that players could order a guitar in any Dupont Ducco color they chose.

In 1957 Fender's Precision Bass went through another change. The pickup went from a single coil to a split single coil, and the headstock went from Tele-shaped to Strat-shaped. The body's two-tone sunburst remained, but the old white pickguard was traded in for a new gold anodized aluminum one.

In 1958 Fender introduced the JazzMaster, introducing the rosewood fingerboard which would be used across the complete Fender line by the end of the following year.

The JazzMaster also debuted the vibrato with the Trem-Lock system, which was intended to keep the guitar in tune if the player broke a string, the offset waisted body, and wide single coil pickups.

In 1959 Fender phased in the three-color sunburst, with added red, and the rosewood fingerboards. The Telecaster and Esquire customs were introduced with their bound sunburst bodies, and by this time the standard Telecaster and Esquire finish had become even whiter and more opaque than the 1955 change. Late in 1959 plastic pickguards replaced the metal ones where applicable. The pickguards also now used multi-layer material made of celluloid. The white guards

1963 Fender Stratocaster. Shore Line Gold custom color. SN: L18294. $13,000. *Courtesy of Mike's Music, Cincinnai, Ohio.*

1962 Fender Strat. Sparkle Red. *Courtesy of Craig Brody, The Guitar Broker*

1966 Fender Stratocaster. Olympic White, custom color. Hard Tail. SN: 144897. *$6000. Courtesy of Amanda's Texas Underground.*

1964 Fender Stratocaster. Lake Placid Blue, custom color. *$10,000. Courtesy of Ryland Fitchett, Rockohaulix.*

1964 Fender Stratocaster. Candy Apple Red, custom color. SN: L15250. $8000. *Courtesy of Pro Frets.*

often took on a greenish tint. Tortoise shell colored pickguards also made their appearance this year.

In 1960 Fender published its first custom color chart. The 14 colors available were Lake Placid Blue, Daphne Blue, Sonic Blue, Burgundy Mist, Sherwood Green, Foam Green, Surf Green, Inca Silver, Shoreline Gold, Fiesta Red, Dakota Red, Shell Pink, Black, and Olympic White. Blonde was also considered a custom color on the Strat as sunburst was on the Tele.

1960 also saw the introduction of Fender's second bass. The Jazz Bass featured JazzMaster styling, two single coil picks, two sets of stacked tone and volume controls, and a narrower neck width.

Late in 1961 Fender introduced the Bass VI. This instrument combined aspects of a standard guitar, combined with a 30 inch scale neck that allowed the instrument to be tuned to bass guitar registers. The instrument resembled a Jaguar with an elongated body and a third pickup.

In 1962 the Jaguar was introduced at the top of Fenders guitar line. Basically it was a fancier JazzMaster with two narrow single coil pickups and a shorter 24 inch scale neck.

By 1963 Fender changed the fingerboard construction on their complete line of instruments. The thick slab rosewood board was replaced by a much thinner curved veneer. Also changing this year was neckplate serialization with numbers starting with an "L." The other news for 1963 was the new custom color Candy Apple Red, which replaced Shell Pink. The end of this year also saw the change over from a clay like fingerboard position markers to pearloid ones.

1964 saw the introduction of the Mustang, an upscale student model with two pickups and a newly designed vibrato system. Fender's other student models followed the styling cues of the new Mustang. But the major news for 1964 was the sale of Fender Electric Instrument Co. Leo's health had been deteriorating due to a recurring strep infection and he felt that the pressures of running Fender were to the detriment of his health. Don Randall negotiated the sale of Fender, first, unsuccessfully, to Baldwin Piano & Organ Co., and then, successfully, to CBS (Columbia Broadcasting Systems, Inc.). Fender Electric Instruments and Fender Sales Inc. were sold for 13 million dollars on Jan. 5, 1965.

The year 1965 is considered a major and enthusiastic turning point for guitar collectors. Instruments produced prior to this would become known as pre-CBS models, and these guitars now carry a much bigger price tag. CBS manufactured Fenders were rumored to be of inferior quality with corner cutting production methods, and this may be partially true. But truly poor quality instruments did not hit the market until the mid 1970s.

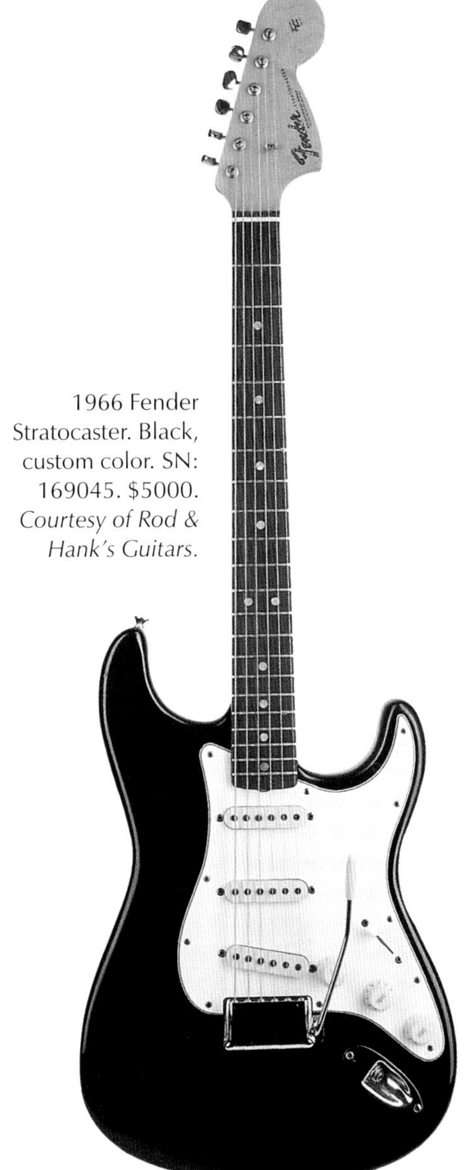

1966 Fender Stratocaster. Black, custom color. SN: 169045. $5000. *Courtesy of Rod & Hank's Guitars.*

1970 Fender Stratocaster. SN: 283914. $7000. *Courtesy of Lou Gatanas.*

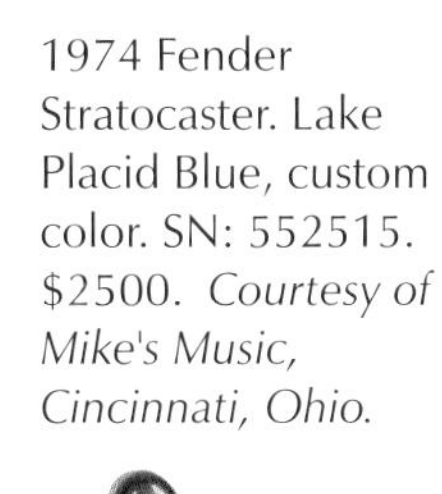

1974 Fender Stratocaster. Lake Placid Blue, custom color. SN: 552515. $2500. *Courtesy of Mike's Music, Cincinnati, Ohio.*

1974 Fender Stratocaster in custom see through blonde finish. SN: 653271. $1,400.

1979 Fender Stratocaster. SN: S935504. $800. *Courtesy of Mike's Music, Cincinnati, Ohio.*

1979 Fender Stratocaster 25th Anniversary. SN: 258048. $1000. *Courtesy of New Jersey Guitar & Bass Center.*

1979 Fender 25th Anniversary Stratocaster, Pearl White. SN: 251035. $900. *Courtesy of Carl Thomas.*

1979 Fender Stratocaster. International Color, Monaco Yellow. $1200. *Courtesy of Rumble Seat Music.*

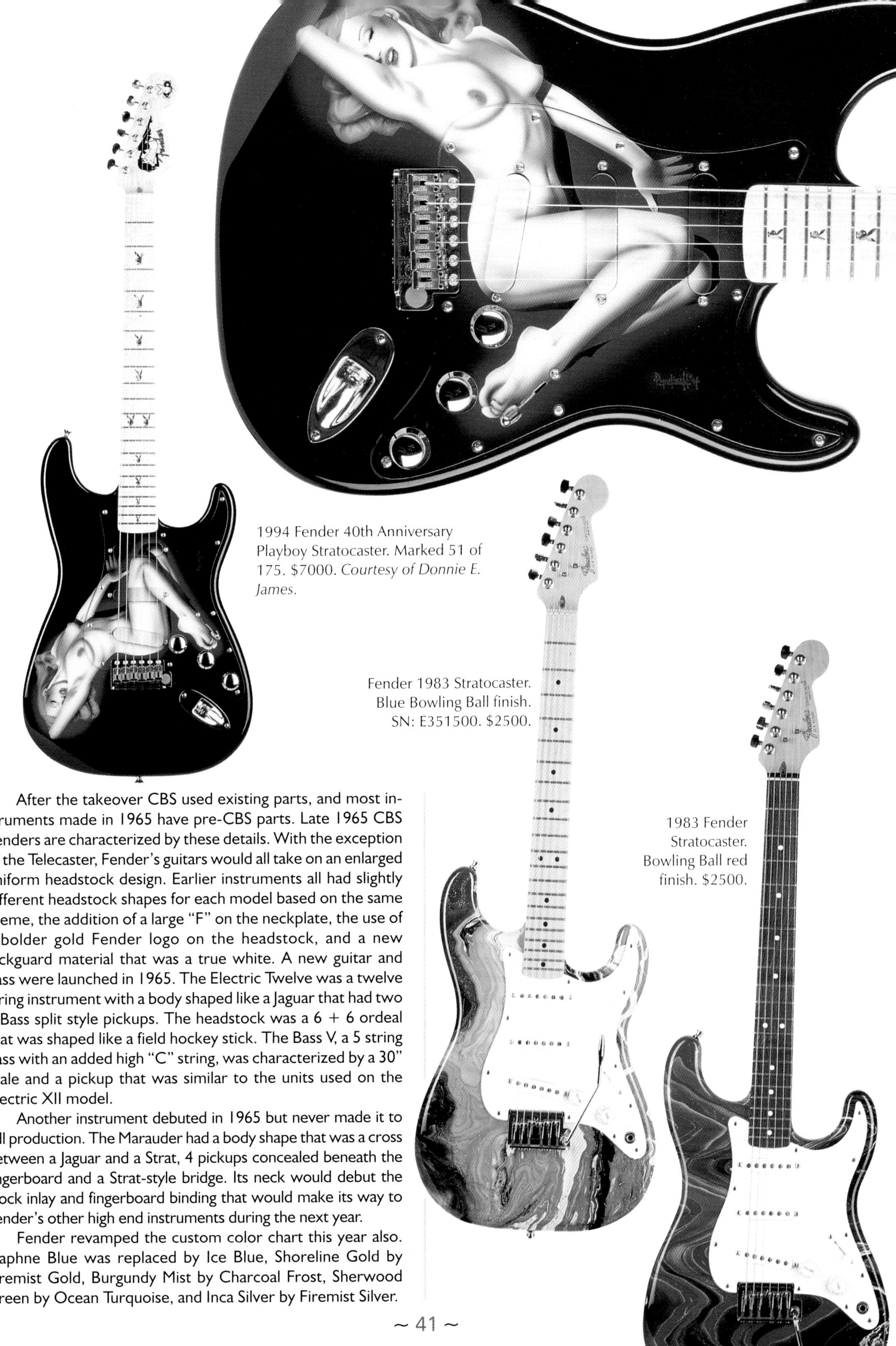

1994 Fender 40th Anniversary Playboy Stratocaster. Marked 51 of 175. $7000. *Courtesy of Donnie E. James.*

Fender 1983 Stratocaster. Blue Bowling Ball finish. SN: E351500. $2500.

1983 Fender Stratocaster. Bowling Ball red finish. $2500.

After the takeover CBS used existing parts, and most instruments made in 1965 have pre-CBS parts. Late 1965 CBS Fenders are characterized by these details. With the exception of the Telecaster, Fender's guitars would all take on an enlarged uniform headstock design. Earlier instruments all had slightly different headstock shapes for each model based on the same theme, the addition of a large "F" on the neckplate, the use of a bolder gold Fender logo on the headstock, and a new pickguard material that was a true white. A new guitar and bass were launched in 1965. The Electric Twelve was a twelve string instrument with a body shaped like a Jaguar that had two P-Bass split style pickups. The headstock was a 6 + 6 ordeal that was shaped like a field hockey stick. The Bass V, a 5 string bass with an added high "C" string, was characterized by a 30" scale and a pickup that was similar to the units used on the Electric XII model.

Another instrument debuted in 1965 but never made it to full production. The Marauder had a body shape that was a cross between a Jaguar and a Strat, 4 pickups concealed beneath the fingerboard and a Strat-style bridge. Its neck would debut the block inlay and fingerboard binding that would make its way to Fender's other high end instruments during the next year.

Fender revamped the custom color chart this year also. Daphne Blue was replaced by Ice Blue, Shoreline Gold by Firemist Gold, Burgundy Mist by Charcoal Frost, Sherwood Green by Ocean Turquoise, and Inca Silver by Firemist Silver.

1981 Fender the Strat, Walnut. SN: CC10828. $1250. *Courtesy of Mimosa Music.*

1995 Fender Stratocaster. SN: N566060. $650. *Courtesy of Retro Music.*

1997 Fender Diamond Custom Shop. Jimi Hendrix's Monterey Stratocaster. SN: 5. $10,000. *Courtesy of Jim Heflybower.*

1996 Fender SRV. SN: 6944848. $900. *Courtesy of Guitars Etc.*

The end of 1965 saw the addition of bound fingerboards on high end models. This would include the JazzMaster, Jazz Bass, Jaguar, Bass VI, Bass V, and the Electric XII. A very few Strats were made with a bound neck. By mid 1966 the high end models would also get large block fingerboard markers instead of the dots. In 1966 Fender entered the student bass market with the Mustang Bass, a scaled-down version P-Bass. The Coronado Thinline models were also introduced by 1966. These included the Model One guitar, with two pickups and dot inlay; and the Model Two guitar, with two pickups, block inlays. Both were available with or without vibrato. There was also a twelve string version and two bass models, the Model One with one pickup and dot inlays, and the Model Two with two pickups and block inlays.

In 1967 Fender introduced the Bronco guitar, an entry level instrument that was available with a matching Bronco amp, and the dye injected wildwood finishes on its Coronado series.

1968 saw a change in finishes and hardware. Nitrocelluoise lacquer gave way to polyester resin and the Kluson tuners were replaced by Schaller-made ones, with the Fender "F" stamped on the back casing. New guitars included the Telecaster Thinline and the Telecaster Bass. The latter, along with the standard Tele were available in two finishes, Blue Floral Print and Pink Paisley. The Tele Bass was basically a re-issue of the early 1950s Precision. Headstock decals became a bold black with gold border font.

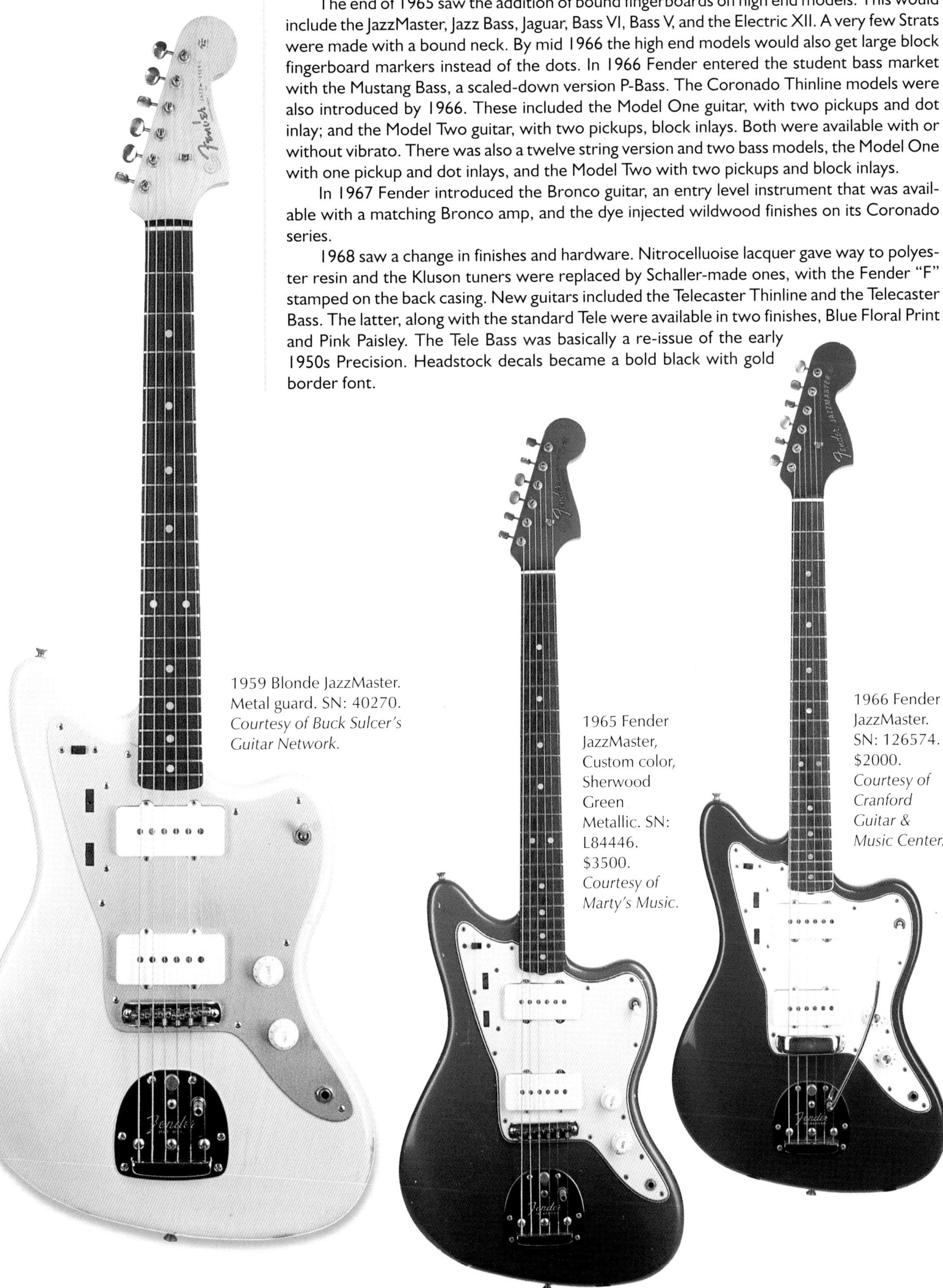

1959 Blonde JazzMaster. Metal guard. SN: 40270. *Courtesy of Buck Sulcer's Guitar Network.*

1965 Fender JazzMaster, Custom color, Sherwood Green Metallic. SN: L84446. $3500. *Courtesy of Marty's Music.*

1966 Fender JazzMaster. SN: 126574. $2000. *Courtesy of Cranford Guitar & Music Center.*

1965 Fender JazzMaster.
SN: L87983. $1800.

1966 Fender JazzMaster. Ocean Turquoise Metallic, custom color. SN: 178614.

1969 brought the deletion of the Duo-Sonic and Electric XII models and the introduction of a couple of "parts" guitars. The Swinger was composed of a Mustang neck with the headstock recut to resemble the point of an "arrow," a commonly used nickname. The body was recut from Electric XII body blanks, and the electronics and hardware were from the Music Master model. This guitar lasted for about one year.

The other model was the Custom which was also marketed under the much rarer name "The Maverick." This model utilized 12 string necks with a shortened headstock (these were often stamped with mid 1960s dates), a recut 12 string body blank, 12 string electronics, and a vibrato/bridge from the Mustang. This model lasted until 1971.

A new Telecaster model was released this year. The Rosewood Tele was based on standard model but made entirely out of Rosewood.

More guitar and bass models were deleted from the line in 1970. The Coronado line was history, as was the Bass V. The paisley and floral finishes were no longer available, nor were many of the other custom color options. The single pickup Esquire and Esquire Custom were also discontinued. The Music Master Bass, a new student model was added. It took the Mustang's spot at the bottom of the line.

In 1972 the bound body Telecaster Custom and the Rosewood Tele were discontinued. The Thinline Tele now was equipped with 2 Humbuckers. A new Tele, the Custom Telecaster was introduced with its Humbucking pickup in the neck position. The Telecaster Bass was also revamped with the addition of a large Humbucking pickup mounted near the neck.

1972 also saw the introduction of the infamous 3 Bolt Micro-Tilt Neck Attachment first installed on the Strat and the upper line Telecaster models. This often hated feature dictates a huge price drop from earlier models.

Another Telecaster model, The Deluxe, was introduced in 1973. It featured a Strat-style headstock, 2 Humbuckers and a Strat-style fixed bridge. A very few were produced with a Strat-style tremolo.

By 1975 the tilt neck feature would find its way onto the Jazz Bass. During 1975 the Bass VI, the Jaguar, the Bigsby vibrato option, (used on some earlier Teles), and custom colors option were all discontinued.

In 1976 Fender introduced the Starcaster, a new Thinline model with an offset waisted body. It lasted for 2 years until 1978.

In 1979 Fender introduced the 25th anniversary Strat. The first 500 made were painted pearl white, but after finish cracking problems, the finish was changed to a metallic silver.

By 1980 the JazzMaster, Telecaster Bass, and Musicmaster guitars were history and by 1981 the Mustang guitar and bass, the custom and deluxe Telecasters, the Bronco, and the 3 Bolt Microtilt Neck Attachment all disappeared from the Fender line.

In 1984 CBS sold Fender to a group of investors led by William Shultz for 12.5 million dollars. The new Fender company would be called Fender Musical Instruments Corporation which would relocate to Corona, California. Since this time Fender has released countless domestic and imported versions, and vintage reissues, as well as introduced many new models.

Fender also has a custom shop that can cater to the buyer's wildest dreams.

1964 Fender Jaguar. Lake Placid Blue Metallic, custom color. SN: L31149. *$2000. Courtesy of Guitar and Amp Center.*

1964 Fender Jaguar. Olympic White, custom color. SN: L54118. $2000.

1969 Fender Jaguar. Candy Apple Red, custom color. SN: 271997. $1700.

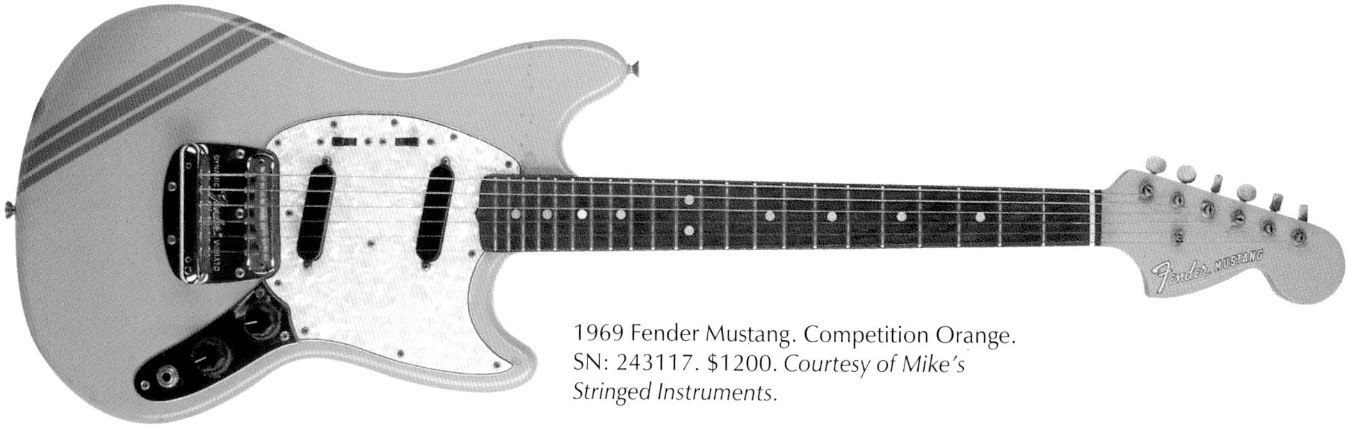

1969 Fender Mustang. Competition Orange. SN: 243117. $1200. *Courtesy of Mike's Stringed Instruments.*

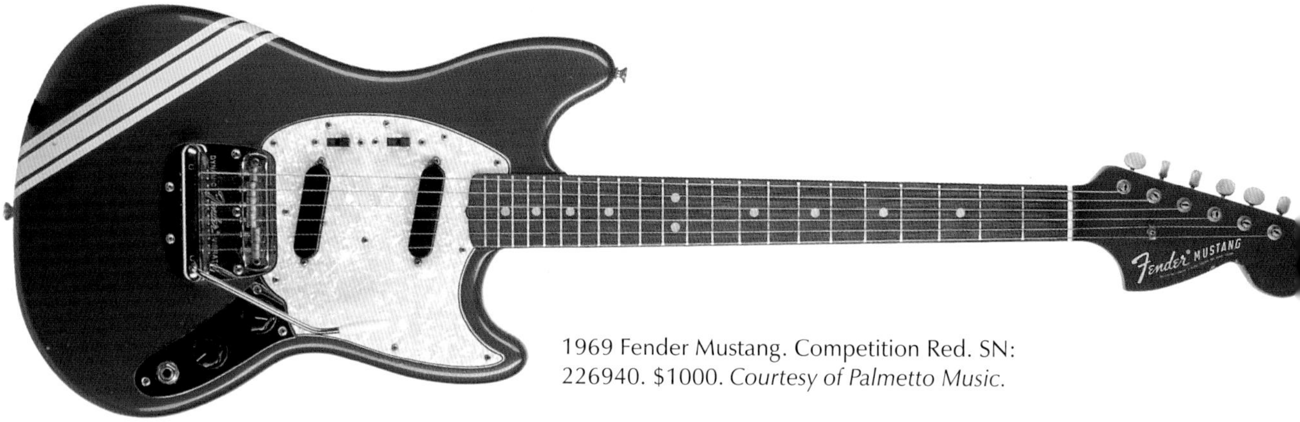

1969 Fender Mustang. Competition Red. SN: 226940. $1000. *Courtesy of Palmetto Music.*

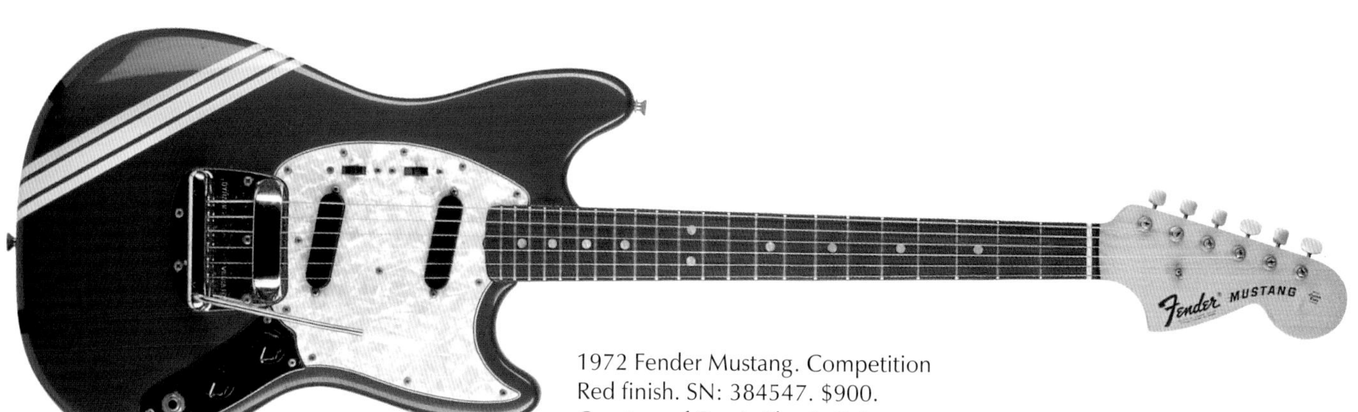

1972 Fender Mustang. Competition Red finish. SN: 384547. $900. *Courtesy of Gary's Classic Guitars.*

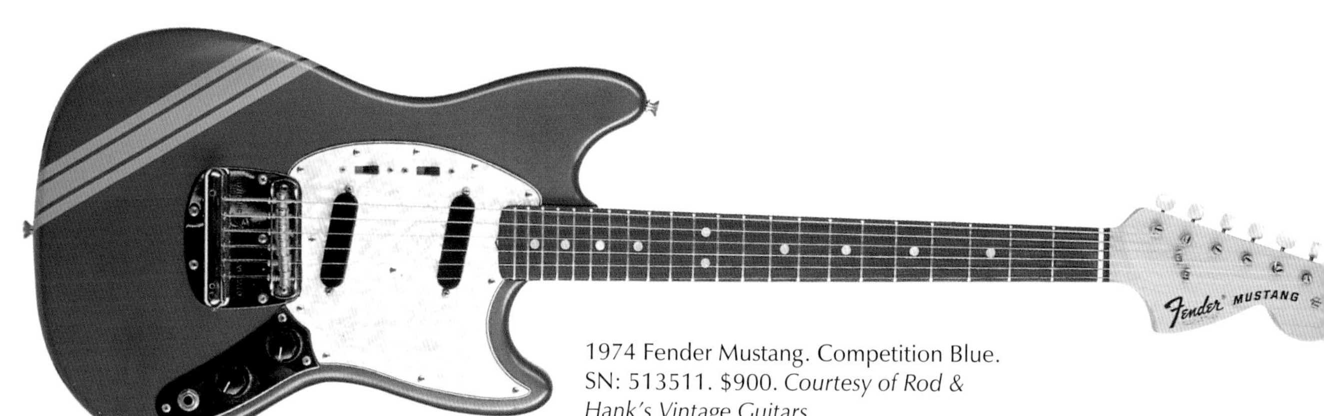

1974 Fender Mustang. Competition Blue. SN: 513511. $900. *Courtesy of Rod & Hank's Vintage Guitars.*

1957 Fender Music Master. SN: 18073. $900. *Courtesy of Blair Loughrey.*

1965 Fender Duosonic II. SN: 108508. *Courtesy of Palmetto Music.* $600

1960 Fender Music Master. Brown Metallic Custom Color. 48869. *$900. Courtesy of Norm Moren.*

1964 Fender Music Master. L33487. $550

1967 Fender Bronco. 212654. $500 *Courtesy of Norm Moren.*

Fender Music Lander. Daphne Blue. SN: 272968. $1000. *Courtesy of Mike Coulson Vintage Guitars.*

Fender Music Lander. Dakota Red. SN: 260792. *$1000. Courtesy of Mike Coulson Vintage Guitars.*

1969 Fender Custom. SN: 253473. $1800.

Fender Serial Numbers

From 1950 to 1976 Fender's Serial Numbers can be used to only generalize the time of production. Numbers for 1950 to 1954 models are found on the bridge plate or on the vibrato spring cover plate on models so equipped. From 1954 to 1976 all numbers can be found on the neckplate. From 1976 to date serial numbers have been applied to the front of the peghead with a decal. Some recent issues however, have the number applied to the back of the peghead.

Earlier instrument often have production dates stamped or penciled on one or more of its parts. Numbers can be found on the neck, heel, in the body's cavity routes, or on the bottom of the pickups.

Vintage Fender guitars can be very valuable and any disassembly should be done by a knowledgeable person, however, it is often the most accurate way to date these instruments.

1950-54 4 digits up to 6000
1954-55 4-5 digits up to the low 10,000s
1956 5 digits from low to mid 10,000s
1957 5 digits from mid 10,000s to low 20,000. A — sign may appear in front of the number on a 1957 neckplate.
1958 5 digits in the low 20,000s
6 digits beginning with 0 in the 20,000s
5 digits in the low 30,000s
1959 5 digits from the 30,000s to low 40,000s
1960 5 digits from the 40,000s to 50,000s
1961 5 digits in the 50,000s, 60,000s, and low 70,000s
1962 5 digits from the 60,000s to 90,000s
1963 5 digits in the 90,000s

From 1963 to 1965 numbers were prefixed with the letter "L"

1963 Low 00000s to 20,000s
1964 Low 20,000s to low 50,000s
1965 Low 80,000s to low 90,000s

1967 Fender Electric 12. SN: 149355. $1200. *Courtesy of Palmetto Music.*

1965 Fender Marauder. SN: 128454. *Courtesy of Guitar and Amp Center.*

At the end of 1965, following the CBS takeover, neckplates were also stamped with a large Fender style "F" in the center of the plate.

Serial Numbers are all 6 digits. F series plates are:

1965	100,000s
1966	100,000s
1967	100,000s to 200,000s
1968	200,000s
1969	200,000s
1970	200,000s to 300,000s
1971	300,000s
1972	300,000s
1973	300,000s to 400,000s
1974	400,000s to 600,000s
1975	400,000s to 600,000s
1976	500,000s to 700,000s

In 1976 Fender moved the serial number to the headstock of the guitar. Early decals from 1976 start the seven digit number with "76". Later ones would start with the letter "S" followed by a six digit number beginning with 6.

On standard USA production guitars this system of serialization is still current, with the letter stating the decade (S=Seventies, E=Eighties and N=Nineties), and the first numerical digit stating the year. As with previous Fender these numbers can overlap as much as 2 or 3 years.

Examples:

1951	No Caster	0390
1952	P-Bass 0976	
1954	Stratocaster	7186
1957	Musicmaster	18073
1959	P-Bass 35449	
1960	Custom Esquire	58327
1962	Bass VI 79665	
1963	Stratocaster	L 18294
1964	Jaguar L 54118	
1965	JazzMaster	L 87983
1966	JazzMaster	126574
1967	Custom Tele	204850
1968	Paisley Tele	240332
1969	Tele 283847	
1971	Tele Bass	302354
1972	Mustang 384547	
1973	Tele Bass	401607
1974	Stratocaster	653271
1975	Starcaster	668056
1978	P-Bass S889922	
1980	Lead II E016951	
1983	P-Bass Elite II	E327382
1995	Stratocaster	N566060

1966 Fender Coronado XII. Custom color, marked "special" on the back of the head set. *Courtesy of Action Music.*

1967 Fender Coronado Wildwood II. SN: 249006. $650. *Courtesy of Bruce Diamond/ Diamond Strings.*

1968 Fender Coronado II. SN: 504562. $700. *Courtesy of Action Music.*

1970 Fender Coronado II. Lake Placid Blue SN: 503383. *Courtesy of Greg Smith/ Guitar Buyer.*

1975 Fender Starcaster. SN: 668056. *Chicago Music Exchange.*

1980 Fender Lead II. See-thru Cherry Finish. SN: E016951. $400. *Courtesy of Mimosa Music.*

1994 Fender Custom Shop Crown Royal Guitar. Number 3 of 3 made. SN: CR03. *Courtesy of Guitars, Guitars.*

1952 Fender P. Bass. SN: 0976. *Courtesy of Buck Sulcer's Guitar Network.*

1957 Fender Precision Bass. Refinished in Sherwood Green. SN: 21134

1959 Fender Precision Bass. SN: 35449. $4500. *Courtesy of Greg Juliano.*

1966 Fender Precision Bass. Ice Blue Metallic, custom color. SN: 128573. $4000. *Courtesy of Gordy's Music.*

1978 Fender P-Bass, Fretless. Antigua. SN: S889922. $800. *Courtesy of Flashback Guitars.*

1983 Fender Precision Elite II, Candy Apple Green. SN: E3 27382. $800.

1966 Fender Jazz Bass. Shore Line Gold, custom color. SN: 133346. *$7000. Courtesy of Gordy's Music.*

1969 Fender Jazz Bass. SN: 252157. $2000. *Courtesy of Gordy's Music.*

1965 Fender Jazz Bass. Burgundy Mist Metallic, SN: L91109. $9000. *Courtesy of Chicago Music Exchange.*

1974 Fender Jazz Bass. Candy Apple Red, custom color. $2300. *Courtesy of Neal's Guitars, Broomall, Pennsylvania.*

1965 Fender Jazz Bass. Original Silver Sparkle finish. *Courtesy of Craig Brody, The Guitar Broker.*

1978 Fender Jazz Bass. $1200. Antigua finish.

1971 Fender Telecaster Bass. Black, custom color. SN: 302354. $1400.

1973 Fender Telecaster Bass. SN: 401607. $800. *Chicago Music Exchange.*

1962 Fender Bass VI. First year production. SN: 79665. $3000. *Courtesy of Dave Bush.*

1963 Fender Bass VI. 95201. *$2500. Courtesy of Gordy's Music.*

1974 Fender MusicMaster Bass. SN: 629255. $350. *Courtesy of Neil's Guitars.*

1969 Fender Mustang Bass. Competion Orange. SN: 262240. $1000 *Courtesy of Mike's Stringed Instruments.*

1980 Fender USA Bullet Bass Deluxe. $450.

Framus

Framus was established in 1946 by Frederick Wilfer. Primarily producing violins and cellos, it wouldn't be until the 1950s that the West German company entered into the guitar business. Framus built many medium quality acoustic and electric guitar models throughout its history, with many of these being loosely based on American designs. Framus production stopped in the early 1980s, but in 1996 the name was revived by Frederick's son, Hans-Peter Wilfer.

Framus Serial Numbers

Framus instruments have a split serial number. The second half of this number is two digits plus a letter, and it is this pair on numbers which indicate the instruments of manufacture.

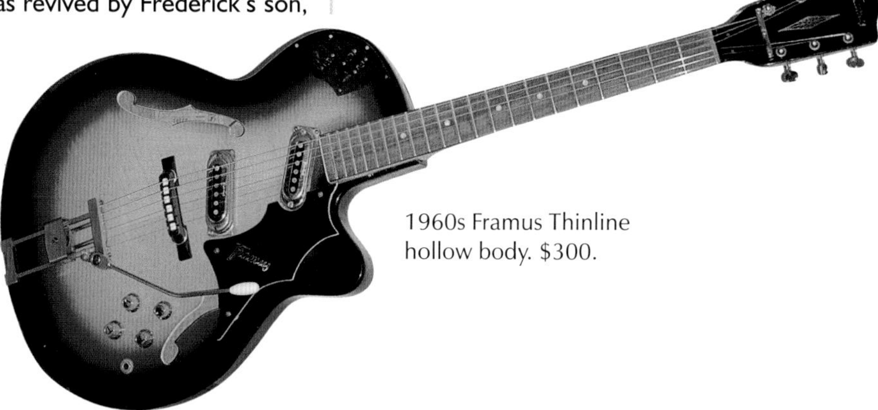

1960s Framus Thinline hollow body. $300.

G&L

After fulfilling a non-competition agreement with CBS, Leo Fender was ready to get back into the guitar business and in 1975 he started up his new company, CLF Research.

Throughout the mid- to late 1970s CLF was under an exclusive agreement with the Music Man Co. to manufacture their guitars and basses. After a conflict of business during the late 1970s, CLF stopped building instruments for Music Man.

In April, 1980, George Fullerton and Leo Fender established a new company, G & L, which stood for George and Leo. From 1980 to 1991 G & L kept refining their idea of what an electric guitar should be.

In 1991 Leo Fender passed away and the company was sold to John McLaren on December 5th . Even with Leo gone, the company continues to carry on the legacy that Fender started half a century ago.

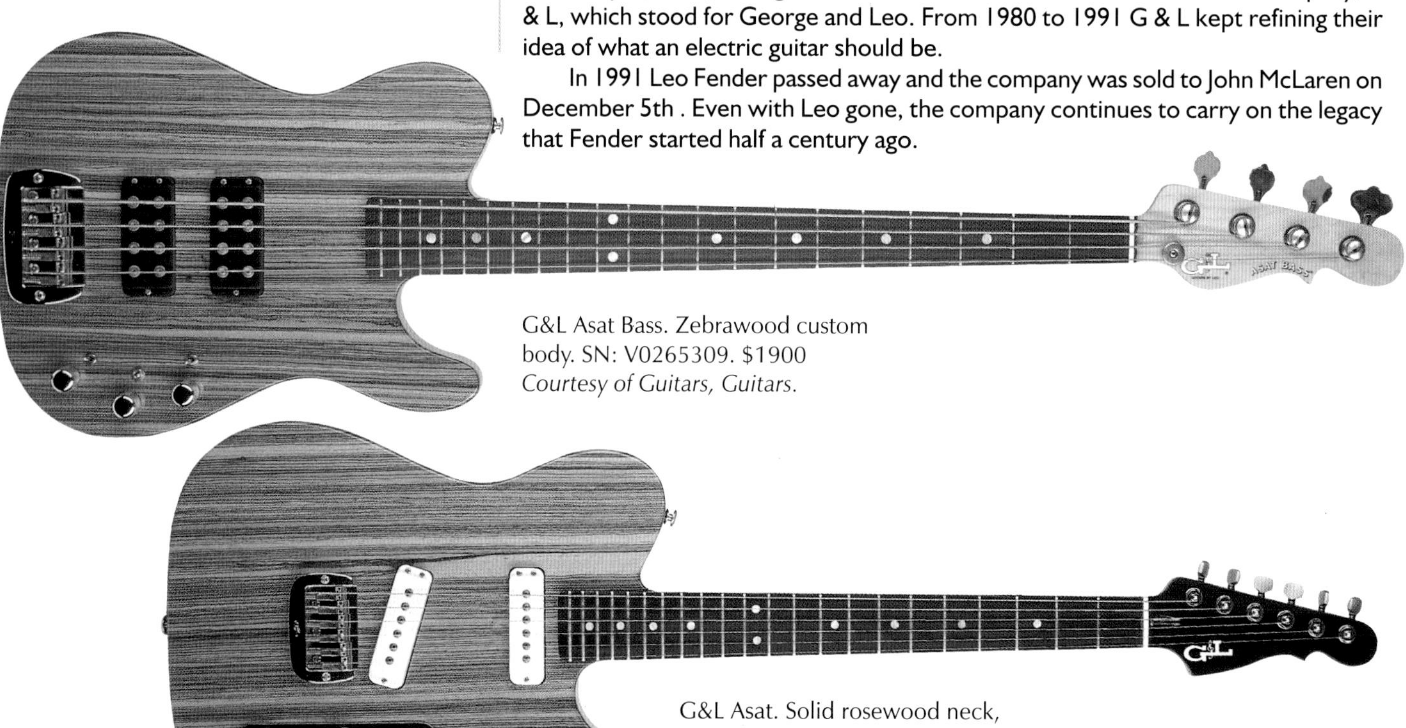

G&L Asat Bass. Zebrawood custom body. SN: V0265309. $1900 *Courtesy of Guitars, Guitars.*

G&L Asat. Solid rosewood neck, zebrawood custom body. SN: B038640. $2500. *Courtesy of Guitars, Guitars.*

Gibson

In 1856, Orville H. Gibson was born to English immigrant John Gibson in Chateaugay, New York. Orville moved to Kalamazoo, Michigan and as a young man took several menial jobs. His lifelong interests in woodworking and music eventually led to the purchase of a small woodworking shop. From 1896 until 1902 the "O.H. Gibson, Manufacturer, Musical Instruments" Co. built highly ornamented, high quality fretted stringed instruments based on the idea that an unstressed piece of wood would give the best acoustic properties.

Gibson's instruments were all made from solid pieces of wood that were either cut or carved for the top, back, and sides.

On October 11, 1902 "The Gibson Mandolin Guitar Manufacturing Co., Ltd." was established through a financial agreement between a group of five investors and Orville Gibson. By 1904 the newly located Kalamazoo company became incorporated and dropped "Ltd." from its name.

In 1906 the renamed Gibson Mandolin-Guitar Co. relocated to a larger facility in Kalamazoo, on the south side of East Exchange Place. In 1915 Orville Gibson, now playing the guitar professionally, negotiated a new contract with the Gibson Co., in which he would receive monthly royalties for the rest of his life. Orville passed away on August 21, 1918.

In 1917 Gibson moved again to 225 Parsons St., Kalamazoo, Michigan. Throughout this period the Gibson Co. proudly refined their violin inspired archtop stringed instruments. Company literature of the period would commonly state the superiority of their products and proclaim all others to be inferior. The archtop guitar that Gibson invented was now evolving into its own class of guitars among flat-tops and classicals.

1953 Gibson ES 125. $800

1958 Gibson ES125T. $700. *Courtesy of Groovy Guitar.*

1957 Gibson ES125D. *Courtesy of Steve Peck.*

1960 Gibson. ES125TC. $950.
Courtesy of Luccesi Vintage Guitars.

Lloyd Loar joined Gibson in 1919. An acoustic engineer and accomplished musician, Loar brought many innovations to the company of which included the elevated finger rest and fretboard, adjustable bridge, and the "F" hole design. The latter of these would become a feature of Gibson's highly esteemed Style 5 line. These instruments, which featured Loar's signature from 1922 to 1924, are considered one of the greatest accomplishments attributed to his legacy. During his five year tenure, Loar also experimented with electrical amplified instruments.

Loar, along with company official Lewis A. Williams, believed that the next logical step in the development of Gibson's instruments was to electrically amplify them. Gibson, even though they had working prototypes, did not share this view of a marketable electric instrument. Gibson's decision not to enter this market led Williams, who also had interests in the loudspeaker and sound reproduction field, to resign in 1923. Loar stayed on for another year before leaving in 1924.

Gibson went through another name change in the mid 1920s, dropping the word Mandolin from their name. Gibson Incorporated would still continue to experiment with electric instruments through the late 1920s and early 1930s. However, it would not be until 1935 that Gibson would introduce an electrical guitar for public consumption.

In 1935, after Rickenbacker's success with their pioneering lap steel or "Hawaiian" guitar, Gibson entered the market with a similar model. Like Rickenbacker's model, the "Gibson Electric Hawaiian" guitar sported an aluminum body and an electro-magnetic pick up.

Gibson's pickup however differed in design, with its bar-shaped magnets made from cobalt and steel. This "bar" pick would later acquire the nickname "The Charlie Christian Model" from its use by Benny Goodman's legendary guitarist. Gibson would use this pickup in its many applications until 1940.

1961 Gibson ES125TDC. $1250.
Courtesy of Luccesi Vintage Guitars.

1965 Gibson ES125TDC. SN: 350768.

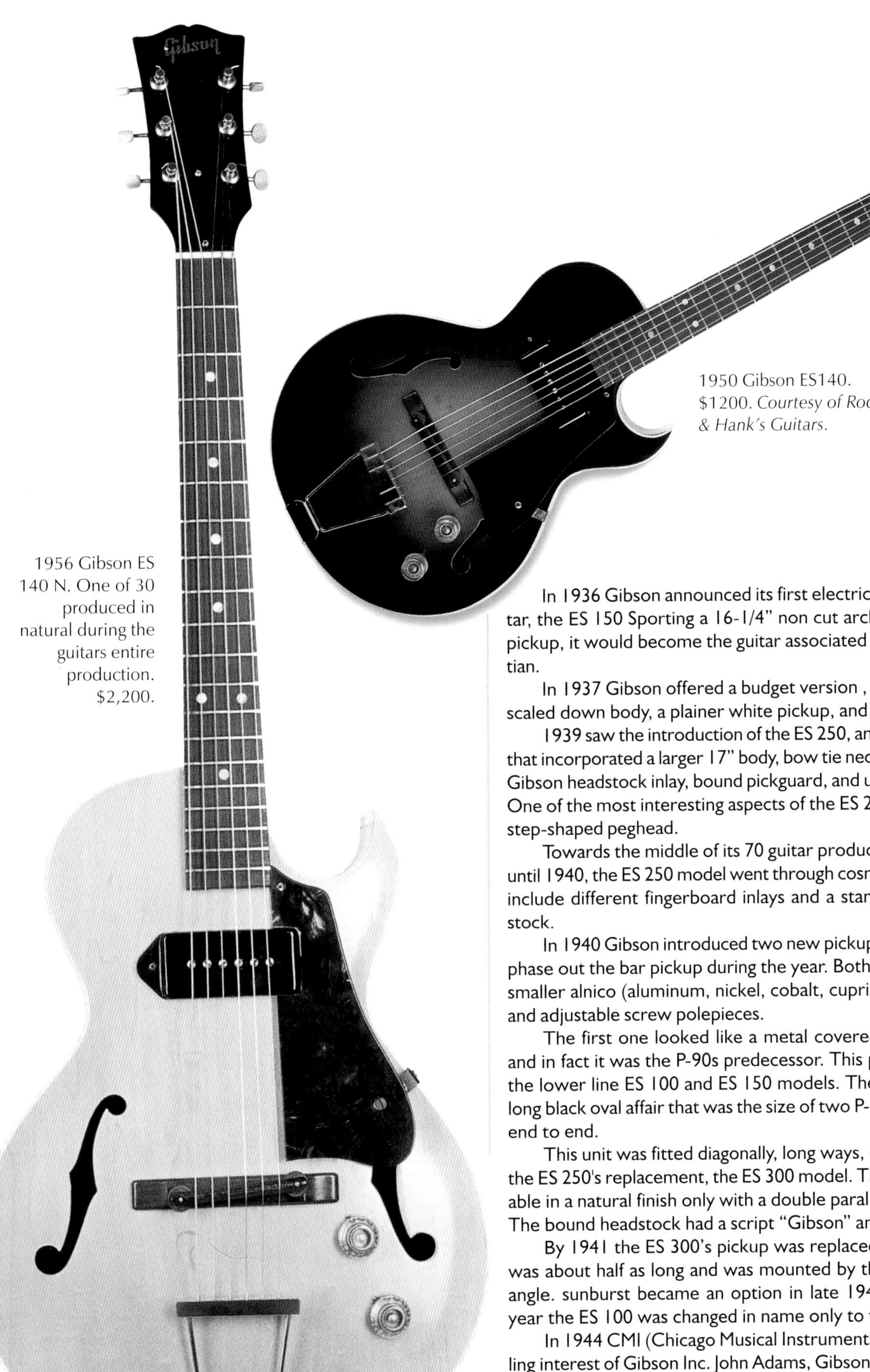

1950 Gibson ES140. $1200. *Courtesy of Rod & Hank's Guitars.*

1956 Gibson ES 140 N. One of 30 produced in natural during the guitars entire production. $2,200.

In 1936 Gibson announced its first electric Spanish model guitar, the ES 150 Sporting a 16-1/4" non cut archtop body, and one pickup, it would become the guitar associated with Charlie Christian.

In 1937 Gibson offered a budget version , the ES 100. It had a scaled down body, a plainer white pickup, and cheaper hardware.

1939 saw the introduction of the ES 250, an upper grade model that incorporated a larger 17" body, bow tie neck inlays, pearl script Gibson headstock inlay, bound pickguard, and upgraded hardware. One of the most interesting aspects of the ES 250 design is its stair step-shaped peghead.

Towards the middle of its 70 guitar production run that lasted until 1940, the ES 250 model went through cosmetic changes which include different fingerboard inlays and a standard shaped headstock.

In 1940 Gibson introduced two new pickup designs that would phase out the bar pickup during the year. Both designs used much smaller alnico (aluminum, nickel, cobalt, cuprite, ferrite) magnets and adjustable screw polepieces.

The first one looked like a metal covered P-90 style pickup and in fact it was the P-90s predecessor. This pickup was used on the lower line ES 100 and ES 150 models. The second one was a long black oval affair that was the size of two P-90 style pickups put end to end.

This unit was fitted diagonally, long ways, under the strings to the ES 250's replacement, the ES 300 model. The ES 300 was available in a natural finish only with a double parallelogram neck inlay. The bound headstock had a script "Gibson" and crown inlay.

By 1941 the ES 300's pickup was replaced with a model that was about half as long and was mounted by the bridge at a slight angle. sunburst became an option in late 1941. Also during this year the ES 100 was changed in name only to the ES 125.

In 1944 CMI (Chicago Musical Instruments) acquired controlling interest of Gibson Inc. John Adams, Gibson's president since its initial buy out in 1902, retired at the age of 85 and was succeeded by former general manager Guy Hart. CMI president and founder Maurice H. Berlin became the company's secretary and treasurer.

1946 Gibson ES 150. $1,500.

1952 Gibson ES150. *Courtesy of Steve Peck.*

1953 Gibson ES150N. Rare. $2500. *Courtesy of Mike's Stringed Instruments.*

In 1945 with financial banking now provided by CMI, Gibson was able to expand their production facilities by 15,000 square feet and prepare for the much anticipated post-war boom for stringed instruments. CMI also took over Gibson's Sales and Marketing departments. Headed by Clarence E. Havenga, formerly a Gibson sales rep, the department aggressively set up franchises and advertising compaigns.

In 1946, Gibson updated its line of guitars. The ES 125's body was enlarged to 16-1/4" wide and featured laminated construction as opposed to the solid wood construction of the earlier versions. This would hold true for Gibson's other electrics also.

The 125 was also equipped with Gibson's newly introduced P-90 lookalike pickup with non-adjustable polepieces. The fingerboard now featured trapezoid style inlays, a feature that would only last a few years, when the inlays would revert back to dots.

The ES 150 now had a 17" wide body, a new single P-90 pickup mounted near the neck, and dot inlays on the neck. The dots would end up giving way to the trapezoid style that was used on the earlier ES 125 model.

The ES 300 remained 17" wide though it was now laminated. It sported a single P-90 pickup with adjustable poles mounted at the neck, and was available in natural and sunburst finishes.

In 1947 Gibson introduced the modern slanted headstock logo that replaced the earlier script logos. The ES 350 P made its debut in 1947 at the top of the electric line. The model was essentially an ES 300 with a venetian (rounded) cut-away.

In 1948 Guy Hart would appoint Theodor M. McCarty as the General Manager of Gibson. McCarty wasted no time and within a few months developed a pickguard that had one or two pickups, the controls, and the input jack built into it, and was designed to be able to be retrofitted to Gibson's acoustic archtops easily.

Gibson marketed their L7 model acoustic with this unit factory installed under the names L7E (single pickup), L7E D (Double pickup), L7CE (single pickup with cut-away), and L7CED (double pickup with cut-away).

Called the "Fingerest" pickup, the two pick up versions were, in effect, Gibson's first multi-pickup electric instrument. By the end of 1948, though, the ES 300 and ES 350 P were available in double pickup versions, and with this change the ES 350 P became the ES 350.

1950 Gibson ES175N. SN: A5720. $3500. *Courtesy of Joey Colonna.*

1969 Gibson ES150DN. SN: 542947. $1500. *Courtesy of Amanda's Texas Underground.*

1952 ES 175 Prototype. Only three made. SN: A10365. $5800. *Courtesy of Norm Moren.*

1955 Gibson J160E. Rare double pickguard. *Courtesy of Neal's Guitars, Broomall, Pennsylvania.*

1959 Gibson ES175. SN: A29698. $3500. *Courtesy of Steve Peck.*

1955 Gibson ES175D. SN: A21526. $3000. *Courtesy of Mike Coulson Vintage Guitars.*

1973 Gibson ES175. SN: 132857. $1800.

1957 Gibson ES225TD. $1750. *Courtesy of Fred Schrager.*

In the early part of 1949 the single pickup versions of the ES 300 and ES 350 were dropped. Gibson introduced the ES 5 by mid-1949. Available in natural (ES5-N) and sunburst, the ES5 is considered the world's first 3 pickup guitar. The ES 175 made its debut in this year as Gibson's first Florentine (pointed) cut-away electric. The body, based on the size and shape of the acoustic L4C, was made of laminated maple and was available in sunburst or natural. The guitar featured one P-90 pickup mounted near the neck.

In 1950 the ES 140 was introduced as a 3/4 size ES 175. It featured a 12-3/4" wide body with a scale length of 22-3/4".

The ES 125 went through some updates with an adjustable P-90 pickup replacing the non-adjustable one and the body material changing from laminated mahogany to laminated maple.

In 1951 the CF 100E was introduced. This flat-top Florentine cut-away electric was based on the CF 100 acoustic model that was introduced one year earlier. The 14-1/8" body followed the general outline of the non-cut-away LG series acoustics. The instrument was much fancier, though, with its pointed cut-away, trapezoid fingerboard inlays, and a crown and Gibson headstock inlay in pearl. The P-90 pickup was mounted under the guitar's top at the end of the fingerboard with the polepieces protruding through holes and a plastic bezel mounted on the guitar's top. Gibson's top of the line acoustic archtop models, the L5C and Super 400C, both received electrified brothers available in sunburst and natural. (The S-400 CSN wasn't produced until 1952.)

Unlike Gibson's other electrics that were made from plywood laminates, these were both constructed from the same solid woods as their equivalent acoustic models, although the tops are thicker and more heavily braced to support the electronics. Both guitars featured two P-90 pickups and they would both introduce Gibson's classic two pickup wiring circuitry that included separate volume and tones for each pickup plus a pickup selector switch.

The big news for 1951, though, was Gibson's approval by their upper management to develop and market a solid body electric Spanish guitar. Gibson was no stranger to this concept, having produced many varieties of solid lap steel model electrics. They had also been watching Fender to see if their standard solid electrics would be accepted by the public, and with Fender's apparent success, it was time to jump on the solid body bandwagon. Gibson, a company rich in tradition, and still skeptical about gambling their name on such a novel idea, needed a celebrity guitarist to endorse the new guitar to get

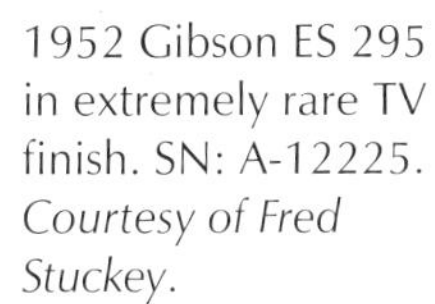

1952 Gibson ES 295 in extremely rare TV finish. SN: A-12225. *Courtesy of Fred Stuckey.*

1954 Gibson ES-295. SN: A18295. *Courtesy of Larry Henrikson, Ax in Hand.*

1962 Gibson ES330TDC. *Courtesy of Jim Stephenson, Courtesy of Lucchesi Vintage Instruments.*

the public's approval. Lester William Polfuss (1915-), better known as Les Paul, was the man that they found, or actually found them about 10 years earlier.

Les Paul, an innovator in multi track recording and in overdubbing had been experimenting with the idea of solid electrics since 1941, by mutilating a couple of Epiphone archtops by putting solid blocks of wood through the center of the guitars bodies in search of more sustainability.

The experiments, nicknamed The Log, and The Clunker, though crude in execution were successful. Les Paul proposed the idea to Gibson in the early 1940s and was promptly turned down. But by 1951 the time was right and Les Paul was the right man for the public to associate the new guitar to. It is uncertain how much input Les Paul made to the design of the guitar, but it was no doubt developed with his ideas and his needs as a musician in mind. Aspects of the original instrument can be traced to their sources. The general outline of the instrument's body, the carved top, and the design of the pickups definitely came from Gibson. Les Paul designed the one piece bridge and tailpiece design. It is interesting to note that when Gibson put the guitar into production, the neck set angle would not allow the strings to run over the bridge the way it was designed. Instead they had to run underneath into facilitate decent string to fingerboard action, but this inhibited the players ability to palm mute the strings and made the guitar hard to play. It would only last for two years on the Les Paul guitar. But, properly installed, it would later make its appearance on two hollow archtop models through the decade .

Gibson's first prototypes were flat mahogany bodies cut in the shape of an ES 140 with a 16th fret neck joint. The maple cap came out of the search for more sustain and a brighter sounding instrument. Carving an arch in the maple cap came from Gibson wanting to make their guitar different and harder to copy. The pickups and electronics had been in use on their top-of-the-line L-5CES and S-400 CES.

The general body outline was slightly modified in the cutaway horn area, with the sharp point of the prototypes shortened and rounded out. According to Les Paul, the gold finish on the guitar was used because "gold means rich," and, according to Gibson, it was used to hide the

1950 Gibson ES300. SN: A5626. $2400. *Courtesy of Frank Ash.*

1967 Gibson ES330TD with Tremolo. *Courtesy of Freedom Guitars, Inc.*

1968 Gibson ES330, Sparkling Burgundy. SN: 972703. $1700. *Courtesy of Nationwide Guitars.*

1961 Gibson ES335TDC. Dot neck. SN: 10001. $9000. *Courtesy of Gary's Classic Guitars.*

1964 Gibson ES335TDC. Stop tail piece. SN: 177467. $7500. *Gary's Classic Guitars.*

Gibson ES335-12. $1400. *Courtesy of Mimosa Music, Nashville, Tennessee.*

1969 Gibson ES335TDC. 807085. $2200. *Courtesy of Gary's Classic Guitars.*

construction of the guitar. There is some question whether Gibson intended to call the guitar a Les Paul or a Gibson Les Paul, although we all know the outcome. One thing that is known for sure is that Gibson agreed to pay Les Paul a 5% royalty on any guitar that had his name on it, and an additional royalty on any other electric instrument that Gibson produced.

In 1952 Gibson unveiled what would become their most popular electric guitar design to date, the Les Paul model. The first 50 or so made have an unbound fingerboard with trapezoid inlays. Later ones have binding. Early versions also have two diagonally located screws holding the bridge pickup to the body. (The P-90 pickups used on the Les Pauls have been nicknamed soapbars due to their cream plastic rectangle covers.) Some guitars display an all gold finish while others have only the tops painted gold.

A matching all gold painted ES 175 style guitar also made its debut. Sporting two cream P-90 pickups, the ES 295 also used gold plated hardware, including a correctly used Les Paul-style tale piece. A cream pickguard with a gold vine design finished things off.

In 1953 Gibson would introduce double pickup versions of the ES 175 and ES 175N. A new pickup, the Acnico V, would debut on Gibson's L-5CES and Super 400 CES. The Gibson electric bass was introduced to complete with Fender's Precision Bass. Gibson's version, though, would have a solid mahogany body that resembled the shape of a violin and a shorter 30.5" scale neck topped with a peghead that carried banjo style tunnels. The huge single coil pickup was mounted on its side at the neck position. This instrument debuted the stop style tailpiece that would, in one form or another, find its way onto every other Gibson electric solid body guitar.

In 1954 Gibson's Les Paul line expanded with the addition of two new models. The upper line Les Paul Custom had a carved top solid mahogany body finished in black. It featured a Super 400 headstock inlay, ebony fingerboard with block markers, and thin low frets, the Acnico V pickup in the neck position, and all gold hardware, including a stop tailpiece and the newly introduced Tune-o-Matic bridge. This bridge, one of Ted McCarty's many revolutionary patents, allowed precise string to string intonation and string height adjustments. It was debuted on the L-5CES, S-400 CES, ES 5, and ES 350 models.

1967 Gibson EB2DC Bass.

1968 Gibson EB2 Bass.

The lower line model utilized a flat mahogany single cutaway body stop tail and bridge unit, one P-90 pickup, and plain appointments. It was available in sunburst and a color called the TV finish or limed mahogany.

This finish, along with some short scale versions that were built, wouldn't be listed as separate models until 1956 when they would be referred to as the Les Paul TV and the Les Paul JR 3/4 respectively.

The original Les Paul model was updated to include the new stop tail/bridge tailpiece. The ES 130 was introduced as a fancy ES 125 with fingerboard binding, trapezoid inlays, and a beveled 5 ply pickguard. Also introduced in 1954 was Gibson's second electric flat-top. The J-160E basically was a CF 100-E with a 16-1/4" wide J-45 style body.

1961 Gibson ES-345 TD. SN: 37111. *$5000.*
Courtesy of Mike's Music, Cincinnati, Ohio.

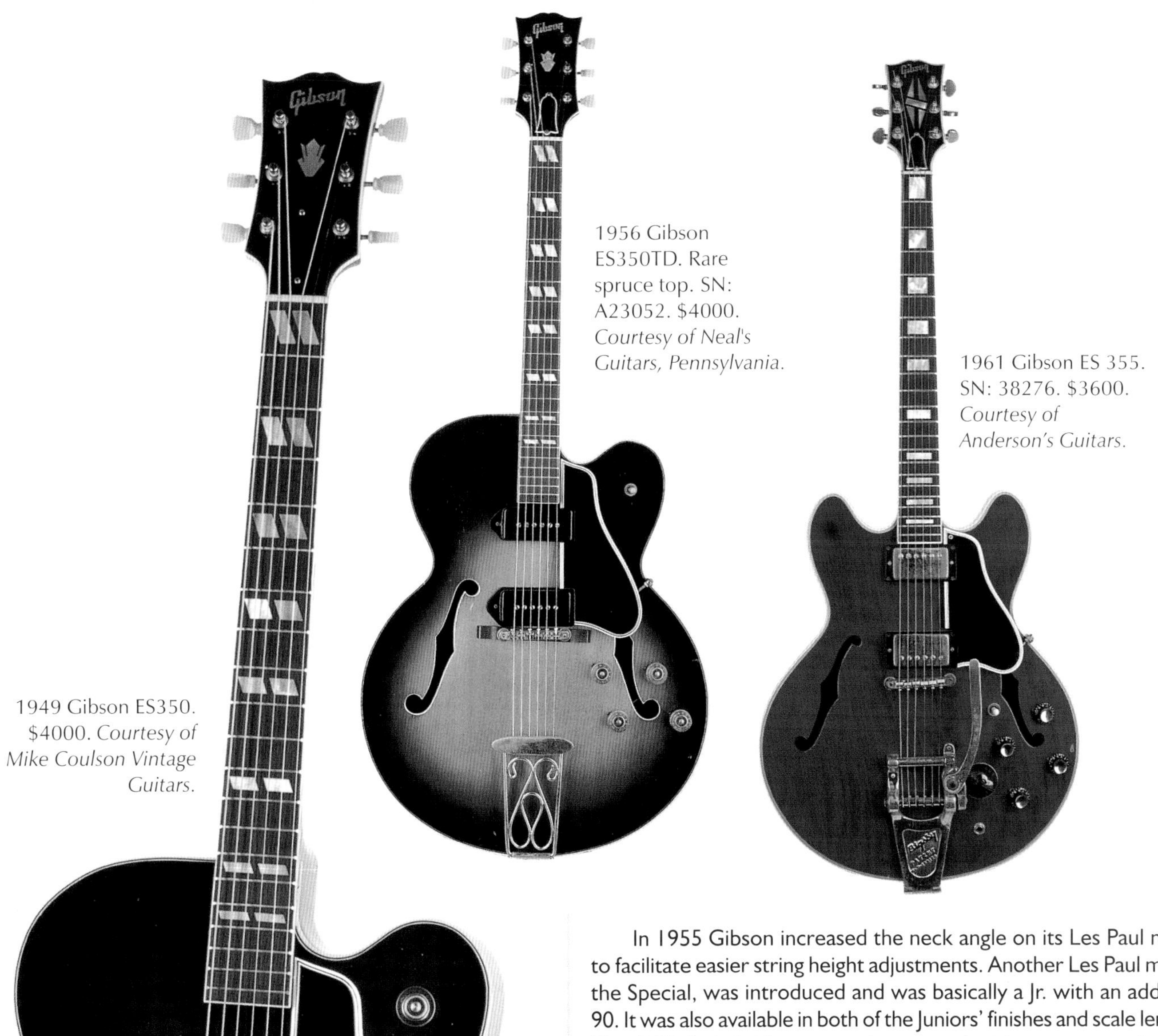

1956 Gibson ES350TD. Rare spruce top. SN: A23052. $4000. *Courtesy of Neal's Guitars, Pennsylvania.*

1961 Gibson ES 355. SN: 38276. $3600. *Courtesy of Anderson's Guitars.*

1949 Gibson ES350. $4000. *Courtesy of Mike Coulson Vintage Guitars.*

In 1955 Gibson increased the neck angle on its Les Paul model to facilitate easier string height adjustments. Another Les Paul model, the Special, was introduced and was basically a Jr. with an added P-90. It was also available in both of the Juniors' finishes and scale lengths. The E-S5 Switch Master was introduced with more versatile electronics than the soon to be discontinued ES-5. Gibson would introduce the first Thinline model hollow bodies during this year. The ES 350 TD and ES 350 TDN were introduced as 2-1/4" thick versions of the full depth 3-3/8" models.

The ES 225 T was a thin 1-3/4" thick hollow body with a silhouette of an ES 175. The guitar debuted with one P-90 in the middle position, a bound, dot inlaid fingerboard, pearl Gibson headstock inlay and an original Les Paul style bridge/trapeze tailpiece unit.

In 1955 Gibson discontinued the L7 series guitars that were fitted with the Fingerest pickguard/pickup assembly. The Byrdland would debut at the top of Gibson's new line of thin hollow body electrics. Named after Billy Byrd and Hank Garland, the guitar was basically a short 23-1/2" scale L-5CES with a thinner 2-1/4" thick body.

1956 saw the introduction of a thin version of the ES 125 (ES 125T) and of the ES 140 called the ES 140T. Gibson also introduced natural versions of the ES 140, but only 30 thick body and 57 thin body examples were built, throughout their entire production runs. Gibson also introduced a double pickup version of the ES 225T, the ES 225TD, and these were also now available in natural. Also new in name only was the ES 135 that replaced the ES 130. The ES 150, their first production electric, was discontinued this year, but a tenor version soldiered on. The ES 350, was also history, being replaced by its thinner counterpart. The big news in 1956 was the introduction of

1951 Gibson L7 with McCarty pickup. SN: A6677. $2000. *Courtesy of Toys From the Attic.*

1955 Gibson ES5. Changed pickups. SN: A20853. $2800. *Courtesy of Norm Moren.*

1960 Gibson ES5. SN: A33693. $8500. *Courtesy of McPeake's Unique Guitars.*

Gibson's Humbucking pickup, although only on a pedal steel guitar, the Gibson Electra Harp. This pickup, designed by Gibson engineer Seth Lover, would change the sound of Gibson and years later start a whole new off-shoot industry, the Boutique Pickup Manufacturer. During the early 1950s Gibson wanted a new pickup to raise the bar so to speak over their competition.

Seth Lover, a Gibson engineer was appointed to head the project in 1954. His main goal was to build a pickup that reduced or canceled the hum that all of the single coil units out on the market at the time produced. He discovered that a twin coil pickup would achieve his goals. Lover then experimented with coil positions in relation to each other, and his patents that were filed on June 22, 1955 show some of the different ideas. Gibson produced only one of them, the classic side-by-side coil. It is interesting to note that the Vega Company designed and produced a hum-canceling pickup almost 2 decades earlier that shared a very similar design.

In 1957 this "Humbucking" pickup would make its debut on a Spanish style guitar on the ES 175. Throughout the rest of the year all of Gibson upper line models would be fitted with the new pickup model. Early model Humbuckers had a sticker applied to the bottom that read "Patent applied for." These early "PAF" pickups have gained a strong cult following and now fetch prices of between $500 to $1000 for a single pickup. In 1962 Gibson's patent was granted and the "patent applied for" sticker was replaced by a patent number sticker. 1957 also brought out the addition of more thin hollow bodies with the ES 125 T 3/4 and the two pickup ES 125TD and the deletion of the ES 140.

1958 has to be considered Gibson's finest moment. The introduction of the Flying "V" and Explorer, although a commercial failure at the time, demonstrated Gibson's commitment to introduce futuristic ideas to the guitar playing public. The production versions came from three different design exercises that Ted McCarty filed patents for in 1957. The first one, the Futura, was a radical pointed hour-glass shaped affair with a split headstock design. From patent drawing to production, the body's same general outline was retained although slightly modified for aesthetic and production reasons. The headstock design was changed to an angled down 6 on a side affair that would become the model for just about every superstrat model guitar of the 1980s. Although some of the earliest explorers utilized the split headstock design of the Futura prototypes, the name would be changed from Futura to Explorer. The body and neck material would change from the mahogany used on the prototypes to African limba wood that resembled a light mahogany. Gibson would coin the term "Korina" to use for their new instruments body material.

The Flying V made it from its original conception to prototype to production with very little change except for the neck heel area, which, in the patent drawings, extends out to the 15th fret. This instrument was also produced in Gibson's new and exotic Korina.

1961 Gibson L-5 CES. Custom pickguard. Note custom made placque beneath the neck. SN: 16675. *Courtesy of Philip Lang.*

1974 Gibson L5S Prototype. SN: 122820 featuring a Tal Farlow type Viceroy Brown Sunburst, thicker than normal neck binding, stock Grover tuners, and patent sticker number pickups. $2,400.

The final design of this trio was the Modern. Shaped like half of a flying "V" and a crescent moon fused together in the middle, this design never made it past the drawing board, until it was "re-issued" in 1982. The original issue Flying V's and Explorers were made in very limited quantities, about 120 for the V and maybe 40 for the Explorer, making these instruments extremely valuable today. Some of these original issue instruments were finished and released as late as 1962, with the final units sporting nickel hardware instead of the earlier gold hardware.

Gibson also took the gold paint off the Les Paul model guitar, which now would be referred to as the Les Paul Standard, and replaced it with a cherry sunburst finish. This move revealed the two-piece figured (usually) maple top. This feature has earned these legendary guitars the nicknames Flame Tops and Sunbursts. The Les Paul Custom, which now had three Humbuckers, was left unchanged, although a few 2 pickup versions were made, and even fewer were finished in dark cherry red. The Les Paul Jr.'s and Specials got a new double cut-away body and the new cherry finish, though they were still available in the TV finish.

A completely new instrument was unveiled in 1958. The revolutionary semi solid ES 335T (The "D" suffix would be added the following year). This instrument would debut a new rounded double cut-away body shape that would find its way onto many Gibson and Gibson-made Epiphone electrics.

The thin hollow body featured a solid block of maple down the center of it, to which all of the hardware and neck were attached to. This feature gave it sonic similarities to a solid body with the aesthetics of a hollow body. The guitar featured nickel hardware, two Humbuckers, an unbound dot inlaid neck, and a pearl Gibson and crown inlaid headstock. A bass version, the EB2, would also make its debut this year. Another first for Gibson was the introduction of the double neck instrument with the guitar-mandolin called the Double Mandolin and the 6 and 12 string guitar called the Double Twelve. These instruments both featured a hollow maple laminate sharp double cut-away body, with a carved spruce top.

Discontinued during this year was the ES 135 model, the ES 295, and the EB1 (Gibson's violin-shaped electric bass.)

1959 brought about more changes. The EB1's replacement, the EB0 debuted with a cherry red mahogany body in the shape of the Les Paul Jr.

Two upper line ES 335-TD models were introduced, the ES 345 and 355 TD. The 345 featured double parallelogram neck inlays, gold hardware, and a Vari-tone circuit with stereo wiring. The 355 featured neck and headstock appointments as found on the Les Paul Custom. The guitar was available with standard wiring or with the Stereo Vari-tone wiring (SV suffix). An all hollow version was introduced as the ES 330, available with one or two P-90 pickups and aesthetic appointments of the ES 335, minus the crown headstock inlay. It would be the replacement for the ES 225 models that were discontinued during this year. Also discontinued was the CF 100 E. The Les Paul Special was renamed the SG Special with no other changes.

Gibson introduced a new entry level line of solid bodies called Melody Makers. These featured a flat single cut body and one or two thin single pickups.

1960 would mark the end of the Sunburst Les Paul Standard which would be replaced by a SG-shaped model in 1961. The SG Special's neck pickup would be moved slightly back to facilitate a stronger neck joint. The EB 6 was introduced as a 6 string bass or baritone guitar and shared the body of the EB2 bass. A cut-away version of the ES125 T and ES 125 TD became available. A new flat-top electric made its debut. The C-1E was an electrified version of the C-1 Classical guitar.

1961 saw big changes at Gibson with the huge addition added to the Gibson plant. The entire line of Les Paul

1958 Gibson Super 400 CES. SN: A27884. $12,500. *Courtesy of David W. Musselwhite.*

1958 Gibson Super 400CES. SN: A28321. $12,500. *Courtesy of M.K. Music, David Comtois.*

Guitars were transformed from either the classic single cut-away or double cut-away shape to the pointed double cut body shape that is now associated with the SG series guitars. The EB3 electric bass was introduced with the new SG body style. Gibson also started to release its artist endorsement series of hollow electrics. The Barney Kessel Custom and Regular debuted with a new body style that utilized a double Florentine (sharp) cut-away.

The Johnny Smith was Gibson's most expensive "artist" model. The Venetian cut-away body utilized all solid wood construction with one or two floating mini-Humbucking pickups. The neck and fingerboard shared appointments with the Super 400. Gibson's other high end carved top electrics, including the L-5CES, S-400CES, and Byrdland, now went to the single Florentine cut-away body style.

The Melody Maker line went to a double cut-away body that had a shape unique to this line of guitars.

In 1962 another artist model was introduced the Tal Farlow model. This highly ornamented guitar featured a maple ply Venetian cut-away body with a scroll inlay.

Also in 1962 the ES-5 Switchmaster was discontinued. The EB6 went to a solid SG shaped body. The budget ES 120 with Melody Maker pickup was introduced, the ES 330 and 335 received small block inlays. The EB 2's production was temporarily put on hold, and the Humbucker equipped guitars started to get patent sticker models. Gibson also expanded the factory again with the acquisition of a 20,000 square foot building on East Ranson Street in Kalamazoo, MI.

1963 saw the end of the use of the Les Paul name on Gibson's solid body line. The sideways vibrato Bigsby, or ebony tail block short Vibrolas that were used on the standard and custom model was replaced by the long Vibrola with a lyre engraved cover plate. The new designations for this line of guitars would be the SG Jr., the SG Special, the SG Standard, and the SG Custom. The single pickup models in the ES 330 series were discontinued, as were the ES 350T guitars. Gibson's double necks went to the current style solid mahogany "SG style" body.

1961 Gibson Super 400 CES. SN: 61189. $11000. *Courtesy of Mechanicland Guitars.*

In 1963 Gibson also unveiled a new line of electric guitars, the Firebird series. These instruments feature a neck-through body construction that was emphasized with the ridges between the neck center piece and body wings. This feature was a first for Gibson. The shape of the body was designed by Ray Dietrich, an automotive designer. It was something of a cross between a rounded Explorer and a flipped over Fender JazzMaster. The headstock shape also resembled that of an upside down Fender. The guitars were conceived and built to compete more directly with Fenders electrics. To do this more thoroughly, Gibson also introduced their first custom color chart to accompany the guitars. The colors included Frost Blue, Pelham Blue, Kerry Green, Inverness Green, Cardinal Red, Ember Red, Heather, Silver Mist, Golden Mist, and Polaris White. Of course the customer could also order black or cherry red.

The Firebird guitars all featured banjo style tuners and a version of the mini-Humbucker that Gibson was using on their Epiphone line of guitars. The Firebird I was the budget version equipped with one pickup, a stop bar/bridge tale piece, and a dot inlaid fingerboard. The Firebird III featured an added pickup, fingerboard binding, and a short based Vibrola. The Firebird V featured trapezoid fingerboard inlays, Tune-o-Matic bridge, and the long lyre engraved Vibrola. The top-of-the-line Firebird VII sported block inlays in a bound ebony fingerboard. A third pickup was added and all the hardware was gold plated. A bass version, called the Thunder Bird II, was also launched during this year featuring standard style tuners, a single pickup, and an intonateable bridge, a first for Gibson. A two pickup version, the Thunderbird IV would join the line within a year.

The year 1964 brought about few changes for the new model year. Gibson's only new electrics were the Trini Lopez Deluxe and standard models.

Both guitars featured diamond shaped "F" holes, split diamond fingerboard inlays and variations of the Firebird headstock design, but that's where the similarities end. The Deluxe's body was based on the full depth Barney Kessel Regular while the standard's was based on the ES 335. Gibson also brought back the EB2 during this year.

The third plant expansion in four years also took place with the acquisition of a two story

1992 Gibson ES775. SN: 93022534. $2000. *Courtesy of John SanGiacomo.*

1998 Gibson Tal Farlow Model. (Historic Collection. Tal's Personal Guitar for Inspection) SN: 9052-8003. $3000. *Courtesy of Mike Larko.*

1969 Gibson Super 400 CES. Repro pickguard. SN: 538500. $9500. *Courtesy of Mike Larko.*

1963 Gibson Byrdland. SN: 61560. $3700

Gibson 1963 Barney Kessel Regular. SN: 61842. $2000. *Courtesy of Amanda's Texas Underground.*

1965 Gibson Byrdland. SN: 346321. $3600. *Courtesy of Steve Peck.*

1967 Gibson Byrdland. SN: 891894. $3500. *Courtesy of Gary Gene Overman.*

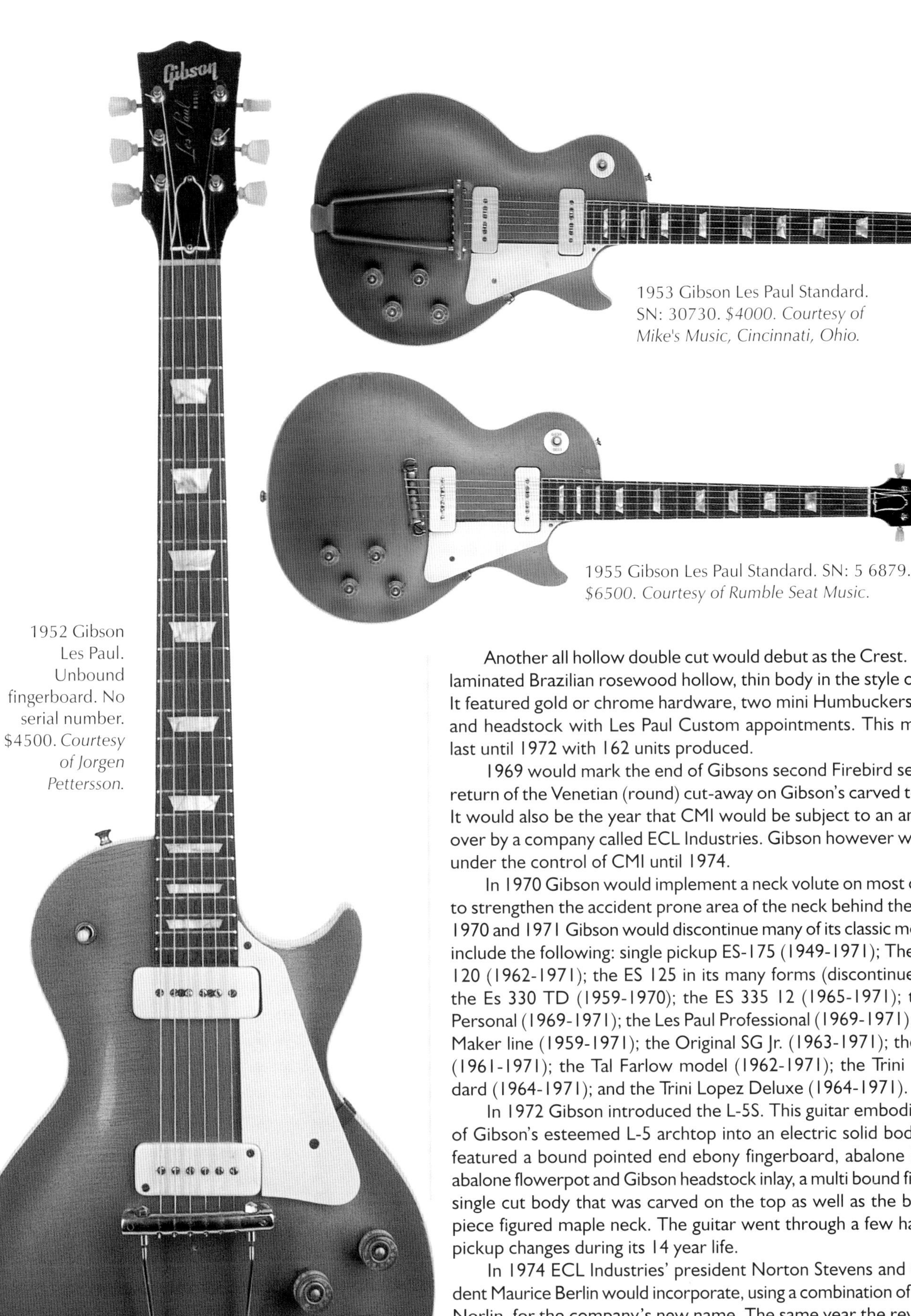

1953 Gibson Les Paul Standard. SN: 30730. $4000. *Courtesy of Mike's Music, Cincinnati, Ohio.*

1955 Gibson Les Paul Standard. SN: 5 6879. $6500. *Courtesy of Rumble Seat Music.*

1952 Gibson Les Paul. Unbound fingerboard. No serial number. $4500. *Courtesy of Jorgen Pettersson.*

Another all hollow double cut would debut as the Crest. It featured a laminated Brazilian rosewood hollow, thin body in the style of an ES 330. It featured gold or chrome hardware, two mini Humbuckers, and a neck and headstock with Les Paul Custom appointments. This model would last until 1972 with 162 units produced.

1969 would mark the end of Gibsons second Firebird series and the return of the Venetian (round) cut-away on Gibson's carved top electrics. It would also be the year that CMI would be subject to an amicable take over by a company called ECL Industries. Gibson however would remain under the control of CMI until 1974.

In 1970 Gibson would implement a neck volute on most of its models to strengthen the accident prone area of the neck behind the nut. During 1970 and 1971 Gibson would discontinue many of its classic models. These include the following: single pickup ES-175 (1949-1971); The Budget ES-120 (1962-1971); the ES 125 in its many forms (discontinued by 1970); the Es 330 TD (1959-1970); the ES 335 12 (1965-1971); the Les Paul Personal (1969-1971); the Les Paul Professional (1969-1971); the Melody Maker line (1959-1971); the Original SG Jr. (1963-1971); the SG Special (1961-1971); the Tal Farlow model (1962-1971); the Trini Lopez Standard (1964-1971); and the Trini Lopez Deluxe (1964-1971).

In 1972 Gibson introduced the L-5S. This guitar embodied the ideas of Gibson's esteemed L-5 archtop into an electric solid body version. It featured a bound pointed end ebony fingerboard, abalone block inlays, abalone flowerpot and Gibson headstock inlay, a multi bound figured maple single cut body that was carved on the top as well as the back, and a 5 piece figured maple neck. The guitar went through a few hardware and pickup changes during its 14 year life.

In 1974 ECL Industries' president Norton Stevens and CMI's president Maurice Berlin would incorporate, using a combination of their names, Norlin, for the company's new name. The same year the revived Gibson Company would open a new production facility in Nashville, Tennessee.

Gibson would remain under Norlin's control until 1986. Throughout the often maligned 1970s Gibson released countless versions of their classics, and a few re-issues, including the 1972 Firebird V Medallion, the 1976 Bicentennial Firebird and Thunderbird, and the 1976 Limited (Hah!) Edition Explorer. Some new designs also came and went.

Below: 1956 Gibson Les Paul Standard. SN: 614467. $8500. *Courtesy of Lou Gatanas.*

Right: 1957 Gibson Les Paul Standard Gold Top. SN: 7 7666. $23000. *Courtesy of Gary's Classic Guitars.*

Below right: 1958 Gibson Les Paul. SN: 8 2786. $25,000. *Courtesy of Joe Menza.*

By the early 1980s Gibson realized that the public wanted accurate re-issues of their late 1950s electric models. The Heritage series Les Pauls came close, but Gibson got the cutaway shape wrong. In 1982 Gibson unleashed a trio of Korina bodied instruments that were meant to be exact reproductions of the originals. They were also very close, but, among other things, construction details were not correct. These re-issues were well made guitars, though, and they showed the public that they company was headed in the right direction.

Norlin decided to sell Gibson in 1980 but it would take six years for a transaction to happen. In the meantime Gibson's manufacturing and day-to-day business continued, but it was being consolidated and moved to the Nashville factory. By 1983 the Kalamazoo plant was used only for special edition and custom ordered instruments. In June, 1984, the final instruments were produced in Kalamazoo and by September the plant was closed. Gibson's Kalamazoo plant manager at that time, Jim Deurloo, with some of his Gibson associates, decided to stay in Kalamazoo and start the Heritage Guitar Co. The former Gibson plant would become Heritages new home.

In 1986 Norlin sold Gibson to Gibson's president, Henry Juszkiewicz, David Berryman, and Gary Zebrowski for 5 million dollars. The newly revived company worked hard to restore the production quality that made Gibson famous in the 1950s and 1960s. Gibson focused on their classic models and started producing high quality modern interpretations as well as accurate reproductions.

In 1989 Gibson opened the Bozeman, Montana facility for acoustic guitar production. In 1991 Gibson introduced their historic collection which focused on duplicating certain vintage instruments exactly. Gibson's custom shop would be responsible for these as well as special and truly limited production instruments.

Gibson closed the Bozeman plant in 1996 and moved acoustic guitar production to a new plant in Nashville. The Gibson Guitar Corporation today is building instruments that are of equal or better quality than anything that the company has produced during its highly esteemed past.

1960 Gibson Les Paul Standard. Renecked by Gibson. SN: 0 7446. $25,000. *Courtesy of Steven Segal.*

1960 Gibson Les Paul. SN: 08353. *Courtesy of Joe Menza.* $40,000

1960 Gibson Les Paul Standard. SN: 0 7632. $50,000. *Courtesy of Lou Gatanas.*

1959 Gibson Sunburst Les Paul. SN: 9 1086. $40,000. *Courtesy of Gary's Classic Guitars.*

Gibson Serial Numbers

Gibson has used many different serial number sequences up to the present and some of the sequences use numbers twice, as in the late 1960s. Numbers don't always pinpoint the date of manufacture, but with factory order numbers (FON's) and different construction features, fairly accurate dating is possible from 1902 to 1961. Gibson used serial numbers only on its upper line instruments. From 1908 to 1961 all hollow instruments however were produced with a FON stamped inside the body. Gibson used this number for manufacturing purposes and it can be used to date the instrument. Solid body instruments from 1952 (Gibson's initial year of production) and early 1953 do not have any serial numbers, with the exception of a few stamped with a three digit number on the top of the headstock. All solid bodies from 1953 to 1961 however are stamped on the back of the headstock with their own number sequence. From 1961 to 1971 Gibson's serial number were again changed and now covered all instrument lines.

Beginning in 1970 "Made in the USA" was stamped in the back of the headstock along with the number. Number sequences changed as well in 1970, and again in 1975, and also in 1977 to the current method. Recent exceptions would be with the historic re-issues which mimic the numbering system used on the original models series.

1961 Gibson Les Paul/SG Standard. Extremely rare black. SN: 15570.*Courtesy of Larry Henrikson, Ax in Hand.*

Gibson 1963 Les Paul SG Standard. Rare White finish. SN: 98834. *Courtesy of Larry Henrikson, Ax in Hand.*

1968 Gibson Les Paul Standard Gold Top. SN: 522142. $3500.

Numbers on White Oval Label

Year	Range
1902-1903	100-1150
1904	1151-1850
1905	1851-2550
1906	2551-3350
1907	3351-4250
1908	4251-5450
1909	5451-6950
1910	6951-8750
1911	8751-10850
1912	10851-13350
1913	13351-16100
1914	16101-20150
1915	20151-25150
1916	25151-32000
1917	32001-39500
1918	39501-47900
1919	47901-53800
1920	53801-62200
1921	62201-69300
1922	69301-71400
1923	71401-74900
1924	74901-80300
1925	80301-82700
1926	82701-83600
1927	83601-85400
1928	85401-87300
1929	87301-89750
1930	89751-90200
1931	90201-90450
1932	90451-90700
1933	90701-91400
1934	91401-92300
1935	92301-92800
1936	92801-94000
1937	94001-95000
1938	95001-95500
1939	95501-96000
1940	96001-96600
1941	96601-97300
1942	97301-97600
1943	97601-97800
1944	97801-98150
1945	98151-98600
1946	98601-99300
1947 (Jan-Apr)	99301-99999
1947 (Apr-Dec)	A 100-A 1305
1948	A 1306-A 2665
1949	A 2666-A 4410
1950	A 4411-A 6595
1951	A 6595-A 9420
1952	A 9421-A 12460
1953	A 12461-A 17435
1954	A 17436-A 18665

At this point Gibson used orange oval.

1955	A 18666-A 21910
1956	A 21911-A 24755
1957	A 24756-A 26820
1958	A 26821-A 28880
1959	A 28881-A 32285
1960	A 32286-A 35645
1961	A 35645-A 36150

Gibson started solid body production in 1952. 1952 and early 1953 models generally have no numbers, with the exception of a few that were stamped with a 3 digit number on the top of the headstock. 1953 to 1961 solid bodies are numbered as follows in stamped ink on the back of the headstock.

1953	3+ 4 digits
1954	4+ 4 digits
1955	5+ 4 or 5 digits
1956	6+ 4 or 5 digits
1957	7+ 4 or 5 digits
1958	8+ 4 or 5 digits
1959	9+ 4 or 5 digits
1960	0+ 4 or 5 digits
1961	1+ 4 or 5 digits

In 1961 Gibson's new numbering system includes all instruments and are impressed into the wood on the back of the headstock.

1961	100-41199
1962	41200-61180
1963	61450-64222
1964	64240-70501
1962	71180-95846
1963	95849-99999
1963, 1967	100000-106099
1963	106100-108999
1963, 1967	109000-109999
1963	110000-111549
1963, 1967	11550-115799
1963	115800-118299
1963, 1967	118300-120999
1963	121000-139999
1963, 1967	140000-140100
1963	140101-144304
1063, 1967	144305-144380
1963	144381-145000
1963, 1964	147001-149891
1963	148892-152989
1964	152990-174222
1964, 1965	174223-179098
1964	179099-199999
1964	200000-250199
1965	250540-290998
1965	300000-305999
1965, 1967	306000-306099
1965	311000-320149
1967	320150-320699
1965	320700-325999
1965, 1966	326000-326999
1965	327000-329999
1965, 1967-68	300000-330999
1965	331000-346119
1965, 1966	346120-347099
1966	348000-349100
1965	349101-368639
1966	368640-369890
1967, 1968	370000-370999
1966-68	380000-380999

1966	381000-385309
1967	390000-390998
1965-68	400001-400999
1966	401000-408699
1966, 1967	408800-409250
1966	420000-438922
1965-66, 1968-69	500000-500999
1965	501009-501600
1968	501601-501702
1965, 1968	501703-502706
1968	503010-503109
1965, 1968	503405-520955
1968	520956-530056
1966, 1968, 1969	530061-530850
1968, 1969	530851-530993
1969	530994-539999
1966, 1969	540000-540795
1969	540796-545009
1966	550000-556909
1969	558012-567400
1966	570099-570755
1969	580000-580999
1966, 1967, 1968, 1969	600000-600999
1969	601000-606090
1966, 1967	700000-700799
1968, 1969	750000-750999
1966, 1967, 1968, 1969	800000-800999
1966, 1969	801000-812838
1969	812900-819999
1960, 1969	820000-820087
1966	820088-823830
1969	824000-824999
1966, 1969	828002-847488
1966, 1969	847499-858999
1967	859001-895038
1968	895039-896999
1967, 1969	897000-898999
1968	899000-972864

In 1970 the next series of numbers was implemented along with the serial number. The words "Made in USA" were impressed into the back of the headstock. The oval orange label previously used on Gibson's hollow bodied instruments was replaced by a white and orange rectangle label on acoustic models and a small rectangle black, purple, and white label on the electric models. Numbers in this series are very random.

1970	100000s, 600000s, 700000s, 900000s
1971	100000s, 600000s, 700000s, 900000s
1972	100000s, 600000s, 700000s, 900000s
1973	000001s, 100000s, 200000s, 800000s
1974	100000s, 200000s, 300000s, 400000s, 500000s, 600000s, 800000s
1974	A, B, C, D, E, or F prefix followed by a 6 digit number was used on a few instruments.
1975	100000s, 200000s, 300000s, 400000s, 500000s, 600000s, 800000s
1975	A, B, C, D, E, or F prefix followed by a 6 digit number was used on a few instruments.

From 1975 to 1977 Gibson applied a clear oval decal that had a 8 digit number on it. Also on the decal was "Made in USA," and on some models the actual name of the instrument was included. Also, on some series of instruments, like the mid 1970s Explorer re-issue. Gibson also put "Limited Edition" on the decal. Numbers are fairly accurate in this series with the first two digits depicting the year.

1975	99 + 6 digits
1976	00 + 6 digits
1977	06 + 6 digits

From 1977 to the present Gibson has used a very accurate 8 digit numbering system. Numbers are again impressed on the back of the headstock along with "Made in USA." The first and the fifth digit denote the year of manufacture; the second, third, and fourth digit are the day of the year; and the final three digits show the instruments rank of production during that day, as well as which plant it was made in. Instruments from 1977 to 1984 made in Kalamazoo will have a number from 001 to 499. Nashville instruments from 1977 to 1989 will have a number from 500 to 899, and from 1990 to present will have a number from 300 to 899. Instruments made in the Bozeman plant starting in 1989 will have numbers from 001 to 299. Instruments with a number higher than 900 are prototypes. There are exceptions to this system though, as in the "Lonnie Mack Limited Edition Flying V" whose first two digits of the 8 digit number denote the year of manufacture.

Gibson's factory order numbers (FON) from 1935 to 1961 can also be very useful in dating an instrument. It should be noted that the FON was stamped at the beginning of the instruments manufacture, and the serial number was stamped toward the end. FONs can be found stamped in ink onto the wood inside one of the instruments sound holes, or in the case of lower grade instruments, made between 1938 and 1940, on the back of the headstock. The FON consists of numbers and one or more letters. It is the letter or first letter in the FONs number sequence that denotes the year of manufacture. From 1943 to 1948 there were no FONs and from 1949 to 1952 they were number sequences only.

1935	A
1936	B
1937	C
1938	D
1939	E
1940	F
1941	G
1942	H
1943	N/A
1944	N/A
1945	N/A
1946	N/A
1947	N/A
1948	N/A
1949	100s - Low 2000s
1950	High 2000s - Low 5000s
1951	High 5000s - Low 9000s
1952	Z or High 9000s
1953	Y
1954	X
1955	W
1956	V
1957	U
1958	T
1959	S
1960	R
1961	Q

1969 Gibson Les Paul. SN: 539266. $2700. *Courtesy of Darryl Agler.*

1980 Gibson Les Paul Heritage 80 Elite. SN: 82371579. $2200. *Courtesy of New Jersey Guitar and Bass.*

1981 Gibson Les Paul. Leo's commissioned 59 reissue. SN: L1 0147. $5500. *Courtesy of Outlaw Guitars.*

1982 Gibson Les Paul Guitar Trader. First guitar off the production line. SN: 90901. $6000. *Courtesy of Groovy Guitar.*

1982 Gibson Guitar Trader Les Paul Prototype. SN: B1 0001. $6000. *Courtesy of Rhoads Music.*

1990 Gibson Les Paul Standard. SN: 91910364. *$1200. Courtesy of John M. Sangiacomo.*

1993 Gibson Les Paul Standard. 1960 re-issue. SN: 3 1023. $2,200.

1994 Gibson Les Paul Classic Premium Plus. SN: 4 0067. $2000. *Courtesy of John SanGiacomo.*

1953 Gibson Les Paul Custom. Prototype. *Courtesy of Larry Henrikson, Ax in Hand.*

1956 Les Paul Custom. SN: 612371. $5000. *Courtesy of Rumble Seat Music.*

1961 Gibson Les Paul/SG Custom. SN: 18803. *$3800. Courtesy of Mike's Music, Cincinnati, Ohio.*

1968 Gibson Les Paul Custom. SN: 519269. $4000. *Courtesy of Gary's Classic Guitars.*

1974 Gibson Les Paul Custom. Brazilian rosewood top. SN: 377162. *Courtesy of Dave Leibert.*

1997 Gibson Reissue of 1957 Les Paul Custom. Historic Collection. SN: 7 7118. *$2000. Courtesy of Kevin Lapekas.*

1979 Les Paul Custom. SN: Unknown. Priceless. *Courtesy of Pittsburgh Guitars.*

1959 Gibson Les Paul Junior. SN: 9 7408. *$2200. Courtesy of Outlaw Guitars.*

1962 Les Paul Jr. SG Shape. SN: 113384. *Courtesy of Coleman Music.* $900

1958 Gibson Les Paul Jr. SN: 8 2854. $2000. *Courtesy of Brian McCombs & Greg Platzer/ BCR Music.*

1959 Gibson Les Paul Jr. 3/4. SN: 9 9562. $1600.

1958 Gibson Les Paul Special. SN: 84894. $2500. *Courtesy of Joe DiJiosia Jr.*

1958 Gibson Les Paul Special. TV finish. SN: 8 6891. $3000. *Courtesy of Gary's Classic Guitars.*

1960 Gibson Les Paul Special. TV finish. SN: 09981. $4000. *Courtesy of Rick Rybinski, Outlaw Guitars.*

1958 Gibson Les Paul Special. TV finish. SN: 8 1344. *Courtesy of Mike Coulson Vintage Guitars.*

1969 Gibson Les Paul Jumbo.
$2500. Courtesy of Joe's Guitars.

1961 Gibson EBO Bass. SN: 10187.
Courtesy of *Chicago Music Exchange.*

Les Paul Signature. SN: 120393. $1800.
Courtesy of Rod & Hank's Guitars.

1973 Les Paul Signature Bass (wrong pickguard). SN: 114596. $1500 as is.
Courtesy of Mimosa Music.

1971 Gibson Les Paul Deluxe. Rare See Through Cherry. SN: 179215. $2000. *Courtesy of Outlaw Guitars.*

1971 Gibson Les Paul Deluxe in Tobacco Sunburst finish. SN: 688791. $1,300.

Gibson Les Paul Artisan SN: 06204091. Stamped "second". $1500 *Courtesy of Pittsburgh Guitars.*

1974 Gibson Les Paul Deluxe. SN: 302203. $1,200.

1980 Gibson Les Paul Artist. SN: 80780573. $1600. *Courtesy of Joe's Guitars, Langhorn, Pennsylvania.*

1998 Gibson Les Paul Ultima Butterfly Edition. Custom Shop. SN: 8 9223. $9875.

1985 Gibson Kenny Burell Prototype. SN: 82565501. *Photo: Stan Jay/Mandolin Bros.*

1963 Gibson SG Standard. SN: 121495. $3500. *Courtesy of Ed Smith.*

1964 Gibson SG Special in White. SN: 189041. $1600.

1968 Gibson SG Special. SN: 909483. $1000. *Courtesy of Philly Guitar.*

1963 Gibson SG Junior. SN: 144016. $850.

Gibson EDS 1275 in rare Inverness Green. *Courtesy of Rumble Seat Music*

1972 Gibson SG2. SN: 967054. *$450.Courtesy of Jim Morrissey.*

1968 Gibson SG Custom. SN: 899760. $2500. *Courtesy of Chicago Music Exchange.*

1970 Gibson SG Standard in rare black finish. SN: 954349. $1,800.

1969 Gibson SG Standard. SN: 898222 . *$1600. Courtesy of Ed Smith.*

1972 Gibson SG Standard. SN: 138629. $750. *Courtesy of The Music Shop.*

1974 Gibson SG Custom. $900.

1993 Gibson SG Korina. Marked: 113 of 236. $2500. *Courtesy of Flashback Guitars.*

1988 Gibson SG90. SN: 82528540. $650

1978 Gibson SG Standard. $700.

1968 Gibson EB, Pelham blue. SN: 940924. $600. *Courtesy of Flashback Guitars.*

1970 Gibson EB3. $700.

1972 Gibson EBO Bass. SN: 733200. $550. *Courtesy of Mike's Music.*

1972 Gibson EB3. SN: 176099. $1200. *Courtesy of Gary's Classic Guitars.*

1959 Gibson Melody Maker 3/4. SN: 927033. $600. *Courtesy of Brian Borel.*

1963 Gibson Melody Maker. SN: 135562. $600. *Courtesy of Nationwide Music.*

1968 Gibson Melody Maker. 12-string, Sparkling Burgundy; SN: 909080. Rare, $1,100.

Gibson Melody Maker in Pelham Blue finish. 550341. $550. *Courtesy of Mimosa Music, Nashville, Tennessee.*

1965 Gibson Melody Maker. SN: 286531. $550. *Courtesy of Rod & Hank's Vintage Guitars.*

1967 Gibson Flying V. Sparkling Burgundy. SN: 920010. *Courtesy of Mars.*

1971 Gibson Flying V Medallion. SN: 321. $4000. *Courtesy of Gary's Classic Guitars.*

1979 Gibson Flying V. Silver Burst. SN: 72719154. $1400. *Courtesy of Philly Guitar.*

1980 Gibson Flying V in rare gold with registered pearl . Placque No. 46 on back of headstock. $1500.

1989 Gibson Flying V 90. SN: 80149710. $800.

1983 Gibson Flying V. Korina Reissue. SN: D124. $2500.

1980 Gibson V2. $1000. *Courtesy of Retro Music.*

1980 Gibson Explorer E2. SN: 80810087. $750.

1994 Gibson Lonnie Mack Flying V. SN: 94007191. $2500.

1983 Gibson Explorer FMT. Flame top. SN: 81113503. $850.

1998 Gibson Historic Flying V. SN: 9 8097. New: $18,000. *Courtesy of Edwin Wilson-Gibson Custom Art & Historic Shop.*

1998 Gibson Historic Futura. SN: 7 8571. New $18,000. *Courtesy of Edwin Wilson-Gibson Custom Art & Historic Shop.*

1998 Gibson Historic Explorer. New $18,000. Courtesy of *Edwin Wilson-Gibson Custom Art & Historic Shop.*

1982 Gibson Moderne. F043. $2000. *Courtesy of Buck Sulcer's Guitar Network.*

1963 Gibson Firebird I. SN: 173741. $3000. *Courtesy of Rick Rybinski, Outlaw Guitars.*

1963 Gibson Firebird III. Kerry Green custom color. SN: 131722. *Courtesy of Larry Henrikson, Ax in Hand.*

1982 Gibson Firebird. SN: 80402014. $1000.

1990 Gibson Firebird V reissue. SN: 92980720. $1000.

1991 Gibson Firebird VII. Custom shop. Frost Blue. SN: 93311705. $2500.

1964 Gibson T-Bird IV. Original Frost Blue Finish. $11,500. *Courtesy of Rockohaulix.*

1973 Gibson L5S. SN: 10621C. $1800

1974 Gibson L5S. Two piece top. SN: 395661. $2700.

1978 Gibson L5S. Burgundy finish. SN: 71388127. $2500. *Courtesy of Guitars, Guitars.*

Gibson L6-S. SN: 302612. $450. *Courtesy of Blue Note.*

Gibson 1977 RD Artist. 73017015. $750. *Courtesy of Joe's Guitars, Langhorn, Pennsylvania.*

Greco

Built in Japan from the 1960s to the 1970s, Greco guitars were generally based on other companies' guitars, although they did produce some highly original models of their own design. One of these came equipped with boomerang shaped pickups, ten years before Gibson came out with similar shaped units of their V2 Flying V model. Greco guitars were imported to the U.S. by Avnet, the electronics company that owned Guild from 1966 to 1986.

c. 1967 Greco ("the pregnant Telecaster"). Candy Apple Red. $300. *Courtesy of Flashback Guitars.*

Gretsch

1975 Gretsch White Falcon. SN: 11.5035. $3000

Born in Germany in 1856, Friedrich Gretsch immigrated to America with his family in 1872 when he was 16. In 1883 Friedrich opened a small drum, banjo, and tambourine manufacturing facility on Middleton Street in Brooklyn, New York. In April of 1895 Friedrich died during a trip to Germany, and his eldest son Fred Gretsch. found himself at the head of a prospering business. Even though he was only 15 at the time, Fred was an inspiration to the company as he took on all tasks of the business from promoting to production. By the turn of the century the expanding business was thriving and the product line grew to include mandolins. In 1916 Gretsch expanded considerably, occupying a 10 story building at 60 Broadway, in New York City. During the next 10 years Gretsch became an international company and in 1926 they acquired the K. Ziudjian Cymbal Company. In 1927 Gretsch announced its first guitar, a tenor model, and by 1929 the company expanded again opening a midwestern branch at 226 South Wabash Avenue, Chicago, Illinois. Throughout the 1930s Gretsch's guitar line grew considerably larger. In 1935 the Chicago plant was moved to a larger facility at 529 South Wabash. In 1940 Gretsch would announce its very first electric, a very plain model based on a low line archtop model. This first model would become to be known as the Electromatic Spanish model 6185.

In 1942 Fred retired from Gretsch and the company was taken over by his son, Walter William Gretsch. Walter's presidency would only last six years due to his untimely death at the age of 44. In 1948 Fred Gretsch, Jr., another son, would assume the presidency and it would be during his tenure that the classic Gretsch electric guitars would be manufactured.

With the upper models in the archtop Syncromatic line of guitars featuring slash cut "Cat's - Eye," sound holes, and their Syncromatic flat-tops that would later become the Rancher models, featuring a triangle shaped sound hole, the 1940s demonstrated Gretsch's ability to produce high quality, flashy, and innovative guitars.

In 1951 Gretsch's guitar line underwent major renovations. The acoustic archtop models that Gretsch had put so much of the company's pride into were now reduced in quantity of models and were down graded. Gretsch was finally jumping on the electric bandwagon and announced three new models of electrics to join the lone Electromatic Spanish model that had endured the previous decade.

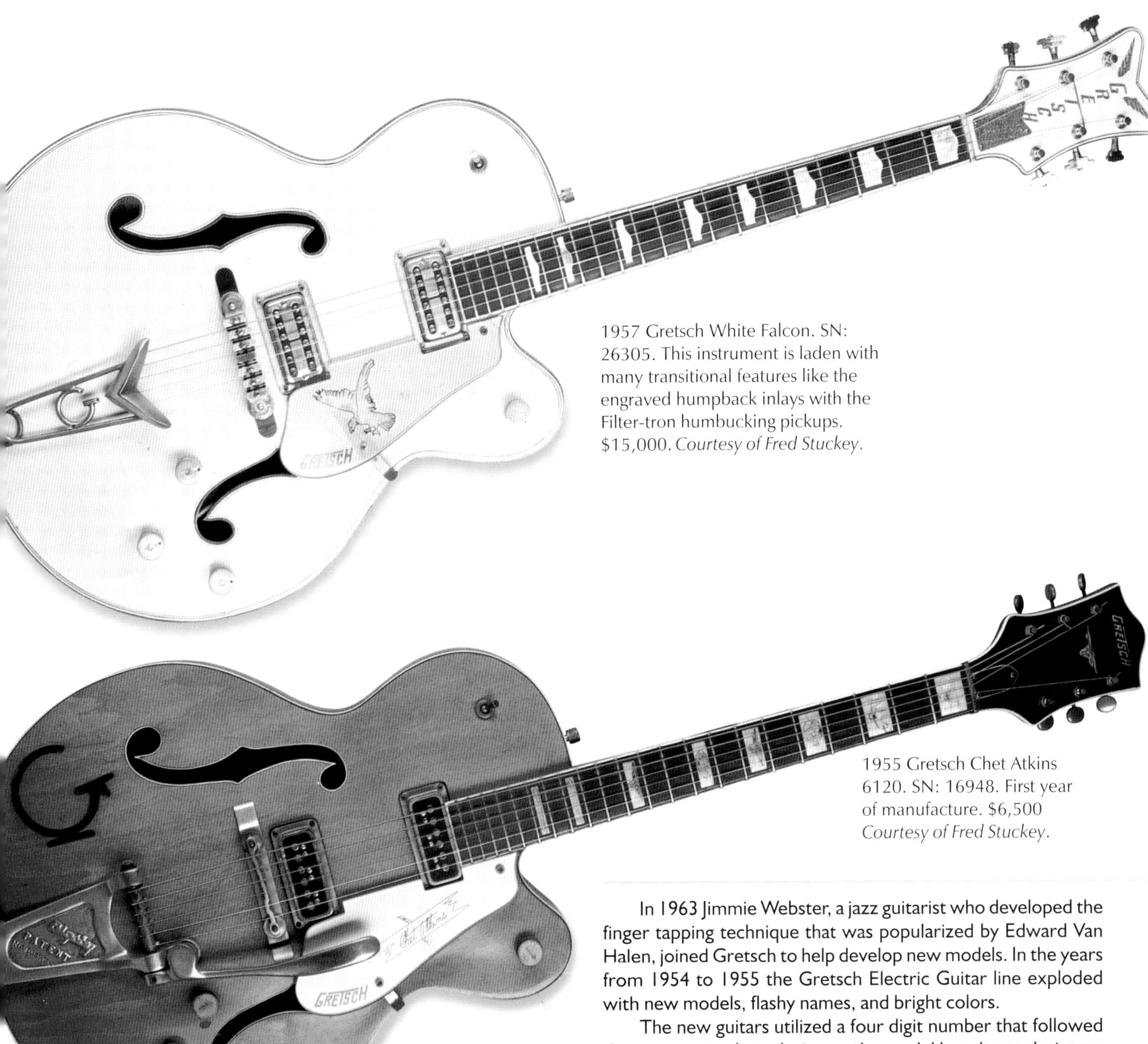

1957 Gretsch White Falcon. SN: 26305. This instrument is laden with many transitional features like the engraved humpback inlays with the Filter-tron humbucking pickups. $15,000. *Courtesy of Fred Stuckey.*

1955 Gretsch Chet Atkins 6120. SN: 16948. First year of manufacture. $6,500 *Courtesy of Fred Stuckey.*

The new line of electrics included the original Electromatic Spanish with redesigned model numbers 6182 (sunburst finish) and 6183 (natural finish). This guitar remained a 16" non cut-away full depth model with one DeArmond pickup. It also included the Electromatic model, a 16" cut-away, available with one or two DeArmond pickups, the Electro II 6187-8, a 16" non cut model that had two DeArmond pickups and available in sunburst and natural, and the top-of-the-line Electro II G192-3 (sunburst or natural), which featured a 17" cut-away body, two DeArmond pickups, a bound block inlaid fingerboard, and a bound peghead that was labeled Synchromatic.

In 1963 Jimmie Webster, a jazz guitarist who developed the finger tapping technique that was popularized by Edward Van Halen, joined Gretsch to help develop new models. In the years from 1954 to 1955 the Gretsch Electric Guitar line exploded with new models, flashy names, and bright colors.

The new guitars utilized a four digit number that followed the name not only to designate the model but also to designate the color that the instrument was finished in. The Corvette, 6182 (sunburst), 6183 (natural), and 6184 (Gold), was the same basic instrument as the Electromatic Spanish. The Streamliner, 6190 (sunburst), 6191 (natural), or 6189 (Yellow/Copper), was a 16" single cut-away with one DeArmond pickup and hump-block fingerboard inlays. The Country Club, 6192 (sunburst), 6193 (natural), 6196 (Cadillac Green), was a 17" single cut-away with two DeArmond pickups, hump-block inlays, and gold hardware. This model was actually released in 1953 with block inlays and bound pick-guard, made of tortoise shell plastic.

The Chet Atkins Hollow Body, 6120 (Amber Red, or Western Orange), was a single cut-away 16" hollow body with a "G" brand on the top lower bout. It had bound "F" holes, two DeArmond pickups, a Bigsby vibrato, block fingerboard inlays engraved with western motifs, a steer head peghead inlay, and Chet Atkins's signature on the gold pick-guard.

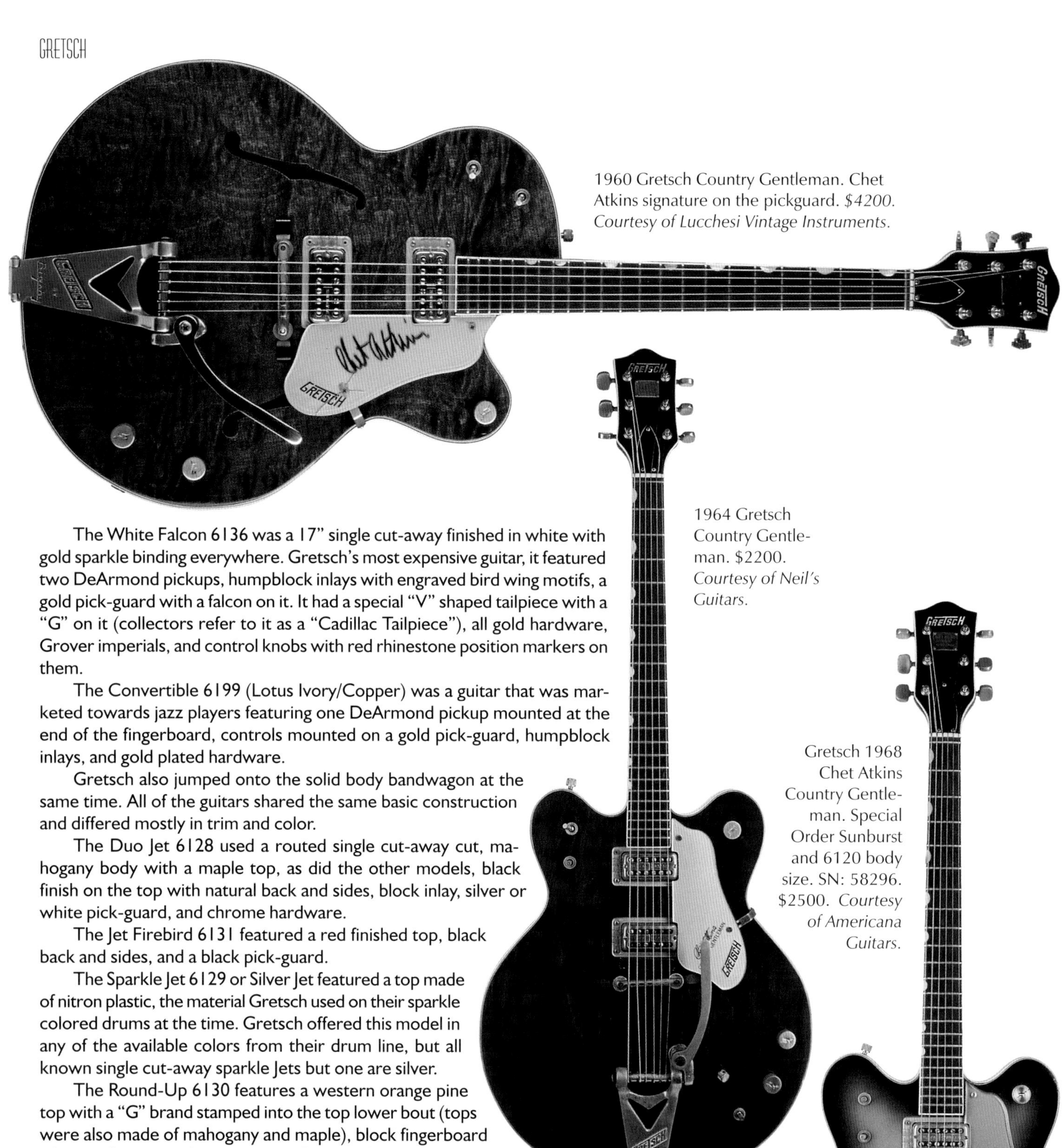

1960 Gretsch Country Gentleman. Chet Atkins signature on the pickguard. *$4200. Courtesy of Lucchesi Vintage Instruments.*

1964 Gretsch Country Gentleman. $2200. *Courtesy of Neil's Guitars.*

Gretsch 1968 Chet Atkins Country Gentleman. Special Order Sunburst and 6120 body size. SN: 58296. $2500. *Courtesy of Americana Guitars.*

The White Falcon 6136 was a 17" single cut-away finished in white with gold sparkle binding everywhere. Gretsch's most expensive guitar, it featured two DeArmond pickups, humpblock inlays with engraved bird wing motifs, a gold pick-guard with a falcon on it. It had a special "V" shaped tailpiece with a "G" on it (collectors refer to it as a "Cadillac Tailpiece"), all gold hardware, Grover imperials, and control knobs with red rhinestone position markers on them.

The Convertible 6199 (Lotus Ivory/Copper) was a guitar that was marketed towards jazz players featuring one DeArmond pickup mounted at the end of the fingerboard, controls mounted on a gold pick-guard, humpblock inlays, and gold plated hardware.

Gretsch also jumped onto the solid body bandwagon at the same time. All of the guitars shared the same basic construction and differed mostly in trim and color.

The Duo Jet 6128 used a routed single cut-away cut, mahogany body with a maple top, as did the other models, black finish on the top with natural back and sides, block inlay, silver or white pick-guard, and chrome hardware.

The Jet Firebird 6131 featured a red finished top, black back and sides, and a black pick-guard.

The Sparkle Jet 6129 or Silver Jet featured a top made of nitron plastic, the material Gretsch used on their sparkle colored drums at the time. Gretsch offered this model in any of the available colors from their drum line, but all known single cut-away sparkle Jets but one are silver.

The Round-Up 6130 features a western orange pine top with a "G" brand stamped into the top lower bout (tops were also made of mahogany and maple), block fingerboard inlays with engraved western motifs, a steel head peghead inlay, gold hardware, tortoise pick-guard, and the body's entire edge is trimmed in tooled leather.

The Chet Atkins Solid Body was basically a Round Up with Bigsby vibrato, non-adjustable bridge, metal nut, and a gold pick-guard with Chet Atkins signature on it.

The White Penguin 6134 was a white finished Duo-Jet style guitar with all of the amenities of the White Falcon guitar. Differences would be a gold pick-guard with a penguin on it, and on some examples a gold banjo style armrest.

In 1957 Gretsch introduced the Chet Atkins Country Gentleman 6122, light to dark walnut stain finish, 17" single cut-away body, two Filter-tron Humbucking pickups, thumb print fingerboard inlay, painted on "F" holes, Bigsby vibrato, and gold hardware.

The Rambler 6115 (ivory/black) was a 3/4 size single sharp cut-away hollow body with a single DeArmond pickup. This little guitar would last until 1961 with the only change being a round cut-away that was implemented in 1960.

1957 Gretsch Model 6120 Chet Atkins. SN: 25304. $5500. *Courtesy of Steve Senerchia, The Music Man.*

1960 Gretsch Chet Atkins 6120. SN: 37649. $4500. *Courtesy of Pro Frets.*

1961 Gretsch Chet Atkins Tennessean Model 6119. SN: 40615. $2000. *Courtesy of Steve Senerchia, The Music Man.*

As Gretsch updated their guitars through the years they would implement the change to all models that were in production at the time. Transition period instruments will combine features of two production periods.

Changes that were implemented in 1958 are the use of Filter-tron pickups, the thumb print inlay, the replacement of the Melita bridge with a roller bridge unit, and thinner body depths.

Guitars that were introduced this year included the Chet Atkins Tennessean 6119 (cherry red), which was a stripped down Nashville with one Filter-tron pickup and chrome hardware.

The Single Anniversary 6124 (sunburst) 6125 (two tone green, or two tone tan) was a 16" single cut-away, single pickup guitar that was launched to celebrate Gretsch's 75th anniversary.

The Double Anniversary 6117 (sunburst) 6118 (two tone green) was the two pickup version of the Single Anniversary.

The Sal Salvador model was the 1958 version of the Convertible utilizing the new changes for that year in a sunburst finish. It was also available with a Bigsby vibrato.

The Clipper 6186 (sunburst) 6187 (beige/gray) 6188 (natural) had a single cut-away 16" body with one DeArmond pickup.

The Project-O-Sonic 6101 (sunburst) was basically a Country Club with two closely spaced Filter-trons that are specially

1962 Gretsch Tennesean Model 6119. $1200. *Courtesy of Mimosa Music.*

1961 Gretsch Model 6193 Country Club. Unusual thin body. SN: 39387. *Courtesy of Steve Senerchia, The Music Man.*

designed to be wired in stereo, with the neck pickup picking up the signals from the three-bass strings and the other pickup picking up the signals from the other strings. The system was meant to utilize two separate amplifiers.

The White Falcon was offered with this wiring system as model 6137.

In 1959 the stereo wiring utilized pickups that allowed switching from the normal mono mode to stereo.

In 1960 the White Falcon got double string mutes and a round snap on back pad.

In 1961 Gretsch updated its line of guitars again, with some of the changes being radical redesigns. Double round cut-aways were implemented on all of the upper line hollow bodies, with the exception of the White Falcon which would hold out for another year.

Round snap-on back pads were fitted to these guitars covering up an electronics access panel. The lower line guitars would get a new pickup called the "Hi-Lo Tron." The solid bodies would also go to a symmetrical double cut-away body shape. String mutes would find their way onto many models. The Chet Atkins models would get painted "F" holes, and standby switches would appear. The Round Up model would disappear and Gretsch would introduce some new models.

The Corvette 6132 (natural) 6133 (platinum gray) had nothing to do with the earlier model, with this one having an offset double cut-away solid mahogany body. It featured one Hi-Lo Tron pickup and a symmetrical 3+3 headstock.

The Bikini 6023 (black guitar neck assembly) 6024 (black bass neck assembly) 6025 (complete double neck instrument), was a double cut-away solid body that had sliding detachable neck/centerpiece assemblies that fit onto a folding main body. The bass and guitar neck assemblies each contained its own set of controls and one Hi-Lo Tron pickup. These could actually be played separately, they could also be purchased separately.

1960 Gretsch Double Anniversary Model 6117. SN: 34360. $1500. *Courtesy of Rockohaulix.*

1962 Gretsch Single Anniversary Model 6124. SN: 45515. $1000. *Courtesy of Brockton Music Works, Inc.*

1963 Gretsch Anniversary Model 6124. Left handed. SN: 53441. $1100. *Courtesy of Brockton Music Works, Inc.*

In 1962 Gretsch introduced their second bass (second to the Bikini). The Country Gentleman Bass 6070 (amber or sunburst) was a 17" double cut-away model with one pickup and a symmetrical 2+2 headstock.

The Princess 6106 (blue, pink, orwhite) was a Corvette-style solid body with gold accents and a back pad and was marketed to the female segment of the guitar playing community. The upper line solid bodies were offered with a Burns-style vibrato.

In 1963 the Chet Atkins Solid Body was discontinued and the Sparkle Jet was absorbed into the Duo Jet. The Duo Jet was now available in black, silver sparkle, gold sparkle, champagne sparkle, burgundy sparkle, and tangerine sparkle.

The Corvette's cut-aways became sharper and it was now available with a second pickup and either a Burns-style or Bigsby vibrato.

The White Penguin would become extinct during this year.

In 1964 Gretsch introduced the Viking 6187 (sunburst), 6188 (natural), 6189 (Cadillac green) near the top-of-the-line, being second only to the White Falcon. This 17" double cut-away body featured the T-Zone fingerboard that utilized slightly angled frets in an attempt to give perfect intonation. Other features debuting on this guitar were the tuning fork bridge, that actually had an A440 tuning fork extending into the body which would supposedly improve the guitar's resonance, and the Super-Tron pickups.

The biggest news for Gretsch in 1964 was probably George Harrison's appearance on the Ed Sullivan Show with a Country Gentleman.

The Corvette Solid Body got a new asymmetrical 4+2 headstock and models that were equipped with Grover Imperials started to get Grovers with a large kidney shaped button.

In 1965 Gretsch introduced the Astro-Jet 6126 (red/black). This eccentric double cut-away solid body featured the new Super-Tron pickups and a asymmetrical 4+2 headstock.

1966 was an active year for Gretsch. By now many of the maligned features of the Viking would make their way onto the White Falcon.

There were new models to choose from too.

The Monkees Rock-N-Roll model (6123) made to capitalize on the made for television pop band. It featured a 16" double cut body painted red with two Super-Tron pickups, chrome hardware, a Bigsby, white trim with the Monkees logo on the pickguard and truss rod cover, and double thumb print inlays on the fingerboard.

The Gold Duke 6135 (gold metal flake) was a two pickup Corvette with a Bigsby, finished in this special paint.

The Silver Duke 6135 (silver metal flake) was a silver version of the Gold Duke. Both models sported chrome hardware and black plastic pick-guards.

The sparkle finish Duo-Jets would be discontinued by year's end.

1967 would mark an end of an era for Gretsch. Fred Gretsch Jr., the company's president since 1948, decided to sell the business to the D.H. Baldwin Piano and Organ Company. Baldwin had previously tried to acquire Fender but was outbid by CBS. So in 1965, desperately wanting to take advantage of the guitar boom, they acquired Burns of London's manufacturing facilities. Since then they had been assembling the Baldwin/Burns guitars in their Booneville, Arkansas plant from imported Burns parts. Gretsch guitars would carry on their business in New York with Fred Jr. becoming a director at Baldwin. Through all of these happenings the company still managed to put out new products.

The Rally 6104 (rally green) 6105 (bamboo yellow/copper) was a 16" double cut-away model with chrome hardware and two Hi-Lo Tron pickups. The pick-guard sported racing stripes.

The Blackhawk 6100 (sunburst) 6101 (black) was a 17" double cut-away sharing many of the features of the Viking. It also featured two SuperTron pickups, chrome hardware, and a silver pick-guard.

Model feature changes for 1967 were the use of SuperTron pickups on the high end, solid bodies, and the Chet Atkins 6120 hollow body being renamed the Chet Atkins Nashville.

In 1968 double pickup versions of the two bass models were offered. Model 6072 was the 17" version and model 6073 was the 16" version.

The Van Eps 6079 (sunburst), 6080 (walnut), was a 17" single cut-away 7 string guitar. Designed for George Van Eps, a specialist in chord melodies, it featured two special 14 pole Filter-tron pickups, tuning fork bridge, and an asymmetrical 4+3 headstock. The Van Eps 6081 (sunburst), 6082 (walnut), was the 6 string version.

The Monkees model would be discontinued by the end of the year as was the Sal Salvador model.

In 1969 a new solid body was introduced. The Roc Jet 6127 (orange), 6130 (black), returned to the single cut-away shape of the 1950s solid bodies. It featured two Super-tron pickups and chrome hardware.

In 1970 Baldwin, wanting to consolidate their guitar production, moved Gretsch to their Booneville plant in Arkansas. With the move Baldwin phased out the production of the Burns model guitars. Many Gretsch guitars from this period feature the Burns style truss rod with a key adjustment. Throughout the 1970s Gretsch introduced many new models, most of them forgettable. Some of the notable exceptions include the Deluxe Chet 7680 (wine), 7681 (walnut), a solid body introduced in 1973. Its name was changed to Super

1957 Gretsch Clipper Model 6186 Lefty. SN: 22900. $850. *Courtesy of Brockton Music Works, Inc.*

1964 Gretsch Clipper Model 6186. SN: 71221. $750. *Courtesy of Toys From the Attic.*

Axe in 1976 and it was discontinued in 1980. Another exceptional guitar was the Super Chet 7690 (wine) 7691 (walnut) was a hollow body with a single cut-away. It featured two Filter-trons, pick-guard mounted controls, fancy inlays, gold hardware, and triple edge body binding. It was made from 1972 to 1980.

Many of Gretsch classic models were discontinued during the decade and the ones that remained differed substantially from their original conceptions. Gretsch survived two fires during this time.

In the late 1970s and early 1980s, Gretsch's guitar production was moved to Chanute, Kansas, and then to Gallatin, Tennessee before returning to Arkansas. Final production of Baldwin-era Gretschs was in Mexico.

In 1985 longtime Gretsch employee Charles Kramer brokered a deal between Baldwin and Fred Gretsch III. Returning the brand name to the founding family, Kramer, who started working at Gretsch in 1935 and has been involved with Gretsch's guitars in one form or another ever since, designed a new line of guitars with Fred III. These instruments, which are based on the classic Gretsch guitars of the 1950s, are currently produced by the Terada Company in Japan.

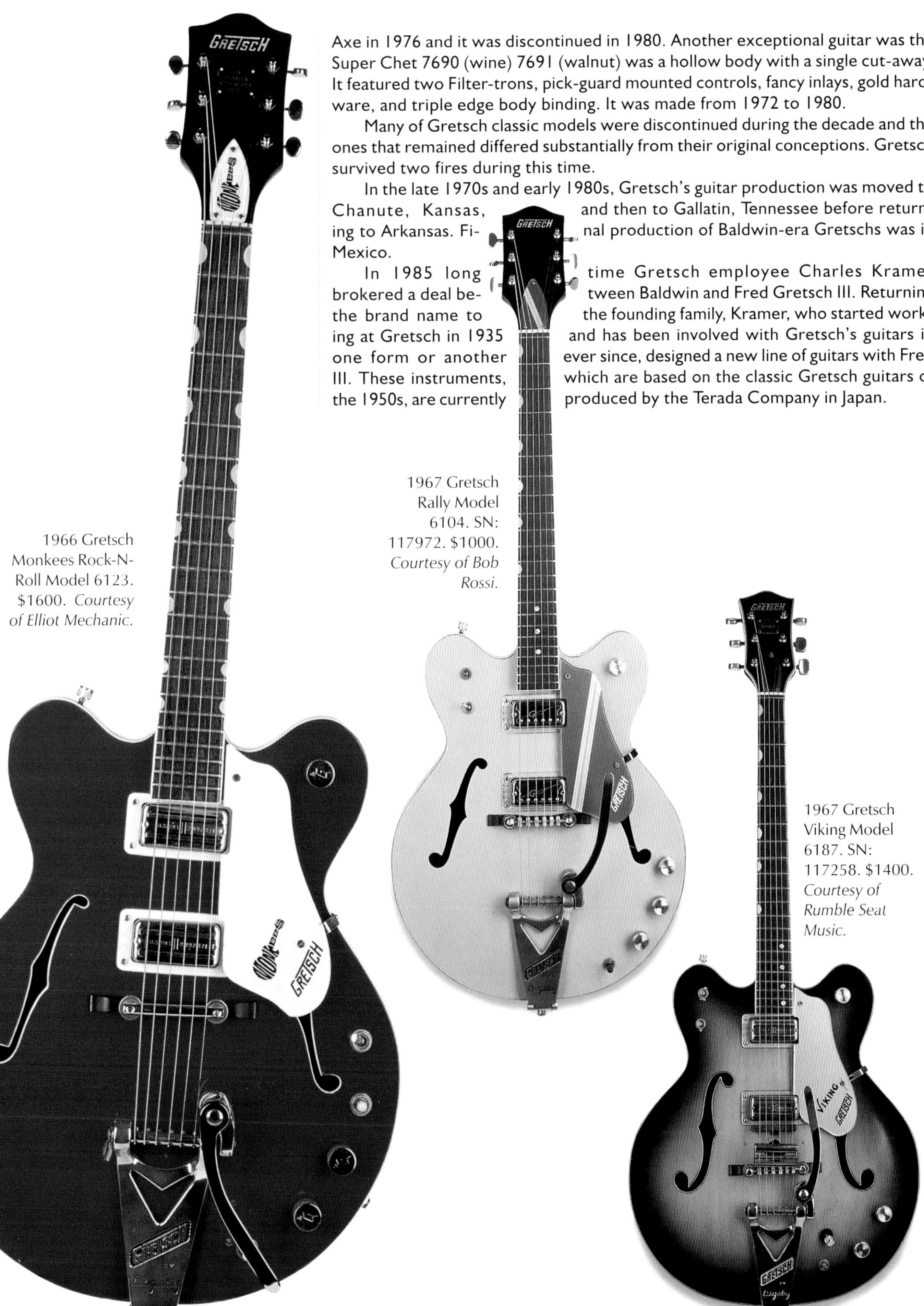

1966 Gretsch Monkees Rock-N-Roll Model 6123. $1600. *Courtesy of Elliot Mechanic.*

1967 Gretsch Rally Model 6104. SN: 117972. $1000. *Courtesy of Bob Rossi.*

1967 Gretsch Viking Model 6187. SN: 117258. $1400. *Courtesy of Rumble Seat Music.*

1955 Gretsch Duo-Jet Model 6128. $3000. *Courtesy of Rumble Seat Music.*

1956 Gretsch Jet Firebird Model 6131. $2500.

1957 Gretsch Duo-Jet Model 6128. $3000. *Courtesy of Rumble Seat Music.*

Gretsch Serial Numbers

From 1939 to 1949 numbers were handwritten in pencil inside Gretsch's higher end instruments. From 1949 to 1957 a white rectangular label with gray trim was used. The model number was stamped in black, and the serial number was stamped in red on this label. From 1957 to 1973 the label changed to a white one with orange and black trim. The model number was stamped in large black font, and the serial number was stamped in a small black font on this label. Starting in 1949 some instruments have numbers stamped into the back of the heads too. This is especially true for solid body instruments.

1939-1945	001-1000
1946-1949	1001-2000
1950	2001-3000
1951	3001-5000
1952	5001-6000
1953	6001-8000
1954	8001-12000
1955	12001-16000
1956	16001-21000
1957	21001-26000
1958	26001-30000
1959	30001-34000
1960	34001-39000
1961	39001-45000
1962	45001-52000
1963	52001-63000
1964	63001-78000
1965	78001-85000

In 1965 Gretsch changed its numbering to a system that identified the month, the year, and the number of that instrument produced that month. Numbers 1 through 12 indicate the months Jan-Dec. The next digit indicates the year, and the remaining digits were the production number.

Examples

117258: 1967 Viking, 258th instrument made in November.

58296: 1968 Country Gent. 296th instrument made in May.

In 1967 Gretsch started putting "Made in USA" on its guitars. In 1973 the label was changed to a white and black affair. The serial number had a hyphen added between the month and year on solid instruments. This number is located in the control cavity rout.

7-9229: 1979 Committee, 229th instrument made in July.

11-5035: 1975 White Falcon, 35th instrument made in November.

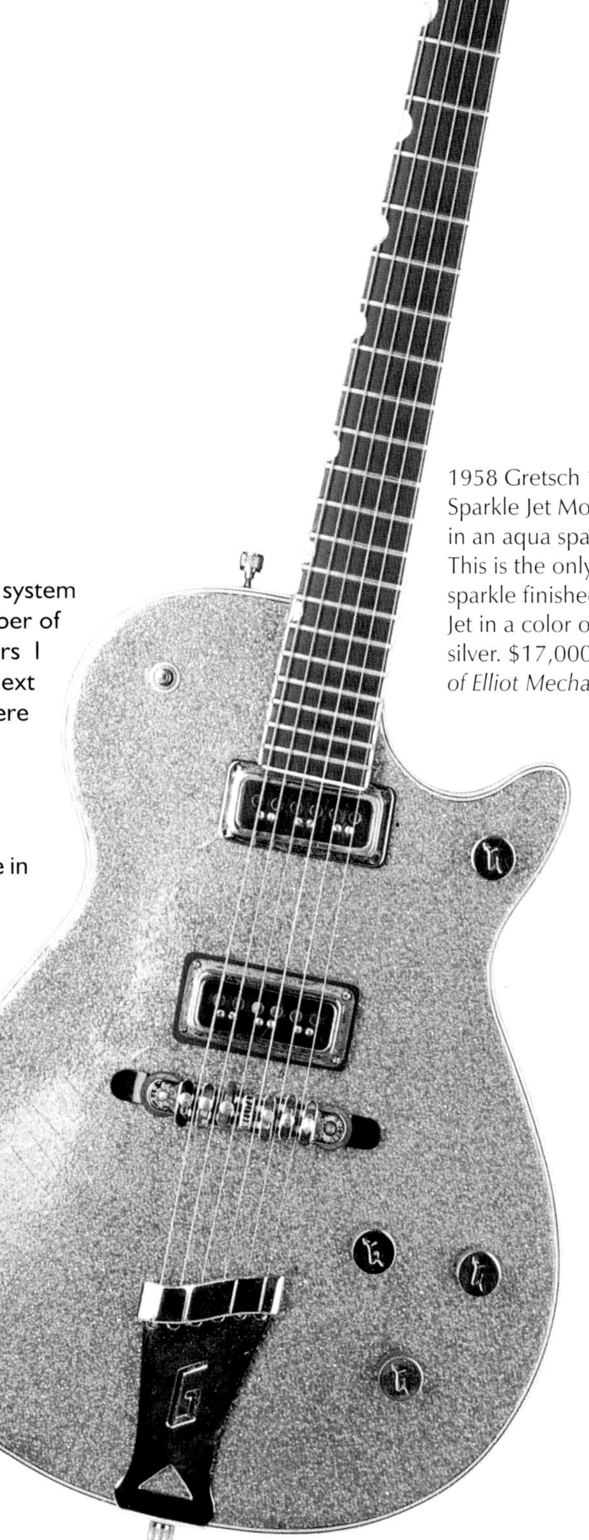

1958 Gretsch 1958 Sparkle Jet Model 6129 in an aqua sparkle finish. This is the only known sparkle finished single cut Jet in a color other than silver. $17,000. *Courtesy of Elliot Mechanic.*

1967 Gretsch Corvette Model 6132. SN: 107870. $500. *Courtesy of Mimosa Music.*

1972 Gretsch Deluxe Chet Model 7680. SN: 102037. $1200 *Courtesy of Guitars, Guitars.*

Gretsch Princess Model 6106. SN: 48762. $2000

1973 Gretsch Superchet Model 7690. SN: 103261. $2000. *Courtesy of McPeake's Unique Instruments.*

1979 Gretsch 7628. SN: (BST 5000) 7-9229. $500.

1968 Gretsch Bass Model 6073. SN: 48246. $1000. *Courtesy of Mike's Music.*

1975 Gretsch SuperAx Model 7680. $1600. *Courtesy of McPeake's Unique Instruments.*

Guild

Guild has to be considered a fairly young company when it comes to classic American made guitars. Founded in 1952 by Alfred Dronge, Guild has earned a reputation for building fine acoustic and archtop electric guitars.

Alfred Dronge immigrated from Europe to New York City where he worked at several music stores. During this time he became an accomplished guitarist and music teacher. This led him to opening his own retail music store before World War II called Sagman and Dronge Music. Following the war, Dronge left the retail business and started importing and distributing accordions. This business venture made Dronge a wealthy man, and it's with this money that Dronge was able to finance the start up of Guild Guitars.

In the early 1950s the Epiphone Company was having labor problems with New York's local unions. The company decided to move its production to Philadelphia to avoid these problems, but many of their seasoned luthiers did not want to leave their homes in New York and make the move to Philadelphia. Dronge was able to take advantage of this and attracted many of the ex-Epiphone luthiers to come work for Guild.

From 1952 to 1956 the Guild Guitar Company occupied a small New York City loft. It is here that Dronge and his five man staff started building the flap top acoustics and archtop electrics that would earn Guild a reputation for world class quality instruments.

Guild's early guitars showed their Epiphone roots in their laminated neck construction, body outlines, neck inlay designs, and with some of the electronics used. Guild guitars built until 1963 use a headstock shape that is a slight variation on Gibson's "open book" design.

Early 1980s Guild X500. SN: B100166. $1800. *Courtesy of Action Music.*

1991 Guild Artist Award Model. SN: JA100196. $3000.

1963 Guild X 175. SN: 27594. $1400. *Courtesy of Flashback.*

1981 Guild X175. SN: JC100123. $1300. *Courtesy of Jay Pilzer, New Hope Guitar Traders.*

Guild's Electric Archtop line was fairly extensive from the get-go and early models included the Johny Smith / Artist Award Model built from 1954 to date. Johny Smith was Guild's first endorsing artist and his name was used on their flagship model until the rising jazz star left for a Gibson endorsement in 1960. The Artist Award Model features a 17" single round cut-away body with a carved solid spruce top solid figured maple back and sides and laminated neck. To avoid hindering the acoustic tone of the instrument, the single gold plated pickup was mounted at the end of the fingerboard floating above the top, and the single volume control was mounted on the pick-guard. Headstock inlays for the Johny Smith variant were a "G" shield with Guild above it, and for the Artist Award Model pearl and abalone rectangle engraved with "Artist Award Model" and a trophy cup with Guild inlaid above that. Fingerboard inlays are pearl blocks with abalone wedges. Body and neck binding found everywhere including the "F" holes.

The Stuart X-500 (sunburst) X-550 (natural) was made from 1953 to 1985 and it featured the same body outline as the artist award model but was made with laminated woods. It used two cream covered single coil pickups with a selector switch and a volume and tone control for each pickup. Its trim features matched what was used on the Johny Smith model. Later models would share the X-500 number no matter what color the instrument was finished in.

The Stratford X-350 (sunburst) x-375 (natural) was made from 1952 to 1973 and it also featured a 17" body but its single round cut-away was not as deep as the X-500s. It featured three cream covered single coil pickups with a six button selector system and master volume and tone controls. It featured the same headstock inlay as the X-500, the X-350 had all gold plated hardware. The X-375 number would later be dropped and X-350 would refer to any color.

The Manhattan X-175 was made from 1954 to 1984 and was available in natural and sunburst finishes. The 16-5/8" round cut-away body used all laminated woods and had two cream covered single coil pickups. The circuitry included a pickup selector switch and a master volume and tone. The mahogany neck had a Rosewood fingerboard with block inlays, and the headstock was inlaid with the "G" shield and Guild. The body binding was plainer than that of the X-350, but as this model was refined through the years its body grew to 17" and the trim appointments were upgraded.

The Savoy X-150 was made from 1954 to 1965 and was basically a stripped down X-175 with one pickup and nickel plated hardware.

The Capri CE-100 was made from 1953 to 1985 and was available in sunburst, natural, and black. Its 16-5/8" laminated spruce and maple body featured a sharp cut-away and basically it was this feature that distinguished this guitar from the X-150.

The Aristocrat M-75 was made from 1952 to 1963 and was available in sunburst and natural. This small hollow 13-1/2" guitar featured a round cut-away and no "F" holes. The electronics utilized two cream covered single coil pickups, a selector switch, and a separate volume and tone control for each pickup. The fingerboard was inlaid with blocks and the headstock had the "G" shield and Guild inlay, the hardware on this "lightweight semi-solid midget model" as advertised by Guild was "all gold plated."

1958 Guild CE-100. SN: 7054. $900. *Courtesy of Pittsburgh Guitars.*

1966 Guild CE100D. SN: EF227. *$1100. New Jersey Guitar and Bass Center.*

The Granada X-50 was built from 1952 to 1962 and it represented the bottom of the Guild's electric guitar line. This 16" non cut-away utilized one cream covered single coil pickup mounted near the neck. The body was the only part of the guitar with binding. The fingerboard had dot inlays and the headstock had a script Guild logo silkscreened on it.

By 1956 Guild had outgrown their original location and by the end of the year they moved to a much larger facility in Hoboken, New Jersey. A new headstock emblem was introduced at this time on the mid-line models called the Chesterfield logo. It featured a column with a crown above it. The original "G" shield logo was now reserved for the upper line models only.

In 1960 Guild introduced the Slim Jim T-100, a thin hollow body, with the same body outline as the CE-100. Available in sunburst, natural, and black the single pickup guitar had dot fingerboard markers and a Chesterfield headstock inlay. Guild also produced a two pickup version, the Slim Jim T-100 D. These models lasted until 1972.

In 1961 the thriving company incorporated and became a stockholder-owned business. A new line of guitars was unveiled that would become a Guild staple. The Starfire Series in its inaugural year included the Starfire I, made from 1961 to 1966 and featured a single sharp cut-away 16-5/8" body made from either laminated mahogany or maple. The thinline guitar used one white DeArmond pickup. Trim included body and neck binding, dot fingerboard markers, and a Chesterfield and Guild headstock inlay. It was available in cherry red, black, emerald green, or honey amber with chrome hardware.

The Starfire II was made from 1961 to 1972 and it was the two pickup version.

1970 Guild CE100D. Rare D'Armond pickups. SN: EF 798. $1600. *Courtesy of Jay Pilzer, New Hope Guitar Traders.*

The Starfire III was made from 1961 until 1970 and it was basically a Starfire II with a Bigsby.

In 1962 Guild introduced a new Humbucking pickup that would replace the cream single coil units on the mid to upper line models throughout the year.

The low line models would get a new thin white single coil with chrome trim to replace their original style pickups. The DeArmonds that were introduced on the Starfire series would be replaced by the Humbuckers by 1963, but would remain available as an option on any Guild guitar.New guitars for 1962 included the Freshman M-65 which was basically the replacement model for the Savoy 150. It utilized the same body shape but it had the new style single coil pickup. The neck had dot inlays and the headstock had a silkscreened Guild logo. This model was discontinued in 1968.

The Freshman M-65-3/4 was made from 1962 until 1970 and it was a scaled down , 13-1/2" wide, 22-3/4" scale model of the regular M-65. Both models were available in sunburst finish only.

The Cordoba X-50 was made from 1962 until 1970 and was the replacement for the Granada X-50 model. Updates included a thinner 2-7/8" thick body and Guilds new style single coil pickups.

The Cordoba T-50 Slim was an even thinner 2" thick version.

By 1963 Guild had standardized a few features on their electric archtop models. These included the classic stairstep pickguard, and the harp tailpiece. The latter of which would be engraved on the high end models.

In 1963 Guild would introduce many new models including their first solid bodies, and a variety of artist endorsed models.

The George Barnes "Guitar in F" was one of Guild's more original designs. It had a 13-1/2" wide body with a single round cut-away. The general outline being that of the M-75, but that's where the similarities end. The "Guitar in F" had a solid carved spruce top, and solid mahogany back and sides. This is where things get weird. The top featured no "F" holes, only bound rectangular cutouts where the two Humbucking pickups were mounted on an internal support, protruded through it. The pickguard mounted controls continued the theme of keeping the guitars top from being inhibited with mounted hardware. The pickup selector was mounted on the guitar's cut-away horn where it wouldn't interfere with the instrument's acoustic properties. Also, by not having the pickups attached directly to the top of the guitar, feed back problems were supposed to be drastically reduced. The short 22-3/4" scale neck featured block inlays and the headstock had a stylized "F" and Guild inlaid into it. The neck, body, and headstock were all bound. Finishes available were sunburst and natural and the hardware was chrome plated. These extremely rare guitars were only made from 1963 until 1965 and very few survive today.

The George Barnes Acoustic-Electric was a 17" full size version of the "Guitar in F." Differences included a maple back

1963 Guild T100D. Black, custom color. SN: 25003. $850. *Courtesy of Thomas D. Jabour.*

1965 Guild T100. SN: EE 1188. $750. *Courtesy of Jay Pilzer, New Hope Guitar Traders*

1968 Guild ST-302. SN: ES262. $800. *Courtesy of Bruce Diamond/ Diamond Strings.*

and sides, "G" shield headstock inlay, and gold hardware. This model was made from 1963 until 1967 and is just as scarce as the "Guitar in F."

The Duane Eddy DE-500 was made from 1963 to 1967 and it featured a thin 17" single round cut-away body made of laminated spruce and maple. The electronics utilized two Humbucking pickups each with their own volume and tone controls, a pickup selector switch, and a master volume control located on the cut-away horn. The trim appointments included the pearl block with abalone wedge neck inlays and the "G" shield and Guild headstock inlays, everything had binding including the "F" holes. All of the hardware had gold plating including the mandatory Bigsby vibrato. The pick-guard featured Duane Eddy's signature and the tuners had pearl buttons. Finishes available were sunburst and natural.

The Duane Eddy DE-400 was made from 1963 until 1969 and was the down grade model of the DE-500. Differences included plainer maple for the back and sides, mahogany instead of maple for the neck, chrome hardware, plain block neck inlays, a Chesterfield headstock inlay and a wood instead of metal bridge.

The Bert Wheedon model was made from 1963 to 1965 and was basically a DE-400 with a double round cut-away, 16-5/8" Starfire style body. Other differences included Bert Wheedon's signature on the pick-guard instead of Duane Eddy's, and that this model was made for export only.

The Starfire line was expanded to include the model IV which featured a new 16-5/8" double cut-away semi-solid body. It utilized two Humbucking pickups with separate volume and gone controls for each pick up and a selector switch on the lower cut-away horn. The fingerboard had dot inlays and the headstock had a Chesterfield and Guild inlay. The body and neck were bound and the hardware was chrome plated. The Starfire IV is the only Starfire model that has been constantly in production since its introduction in 1963 though it has gone through detail changes throughout the years. From 1972 until 1980 it had a master volume and in 1980 it got an ebony fingerboard and a stop tailpiece. The many finishes used on this guitar include sunburst, natural, cherry red, walnut, emerald green, blue, and black.

The Starfire V was made from 1963 until 1972 and it was an upgraded IV model. Upgrades included a master volume, block inlays, and a Bigsby vibrato.

The Starfire VI was the top of the Starfire line and was made from 1963 until 1979. Based on the model V, its upgrades included double bound ebony fingerboard with pearl block and abalone wedge fingerboard inlays, bound peghead with "G" shield inlay, bound "F" holes and all of its hardware is gold plated.

The newly introduced solid body line included three different models.

The Thunderbird S-200 was introduced at the top of the solid body line made from 1963 until 1970. This solid mahogany guitar embodied many unique features. The shape of the instrument resembles an elongated Fender Jaguar with a concave cut out across the bottom of lower bout. This design feature was not for purely aesthetic reasons, but instead served to create the front two feet of the folding stand built into the back of the guitar. The bound neck had block inlays and the unique asymmetrical 3+3 headstock was bound with an eagle and Guild logo inlay. The two Humbucking or single coil pickups were controlled by separate volume and tone controls and a three sliding switch assembly that was similar to the Fender Jaguars. All of the hardware was chrome plating including the vibrato of Guilds own design. The palate of colors included sunburst, natural, cherry red, emerald green, and black.

The Polara S-100 was made from 1963 until 1968 and its solid mahogany body also featured the built in stand. The shape of the guitar was a tamed down version of the S-200. The neck had dot inlays and the headstock had a Chesterfield and Guild logo inlay. Electronics included two Humbucking or single coil pickups, a volume and tone control for each pickup, and a standard 3-way selector switch. All of the hardware including the vibrato was chrome plated and the finishes available included sunburst, natural, cherry red, emerald green, and black.

The Jet Star S-50, produced from 1963 until 1968 was basically a single pickup version of the Polara S-100. The only other difference was the lack of the Chesterfield headstock inlay.

In 1964 Guild introduced their first electric basses. Both models were based on Guild's Starfire IV semi-solid double cut-away guitar and featured the same trim appointments as that guitar.

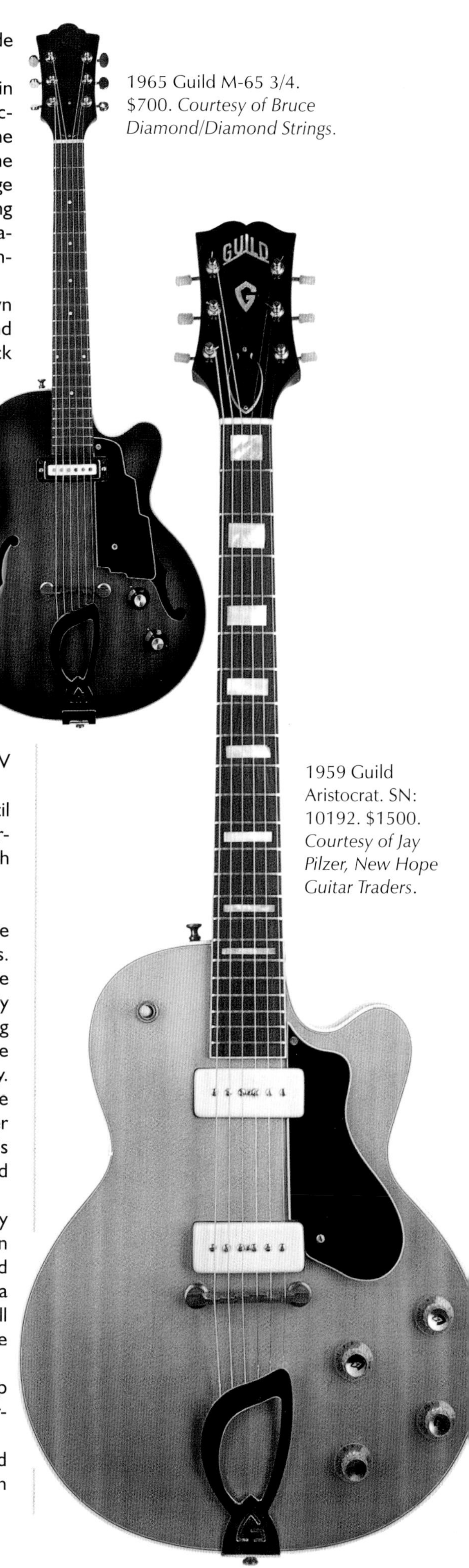

1965 Guild M-65 3/4. $700. *Courtesy of Bruce Diamond/Diamond Strings.*

1959 Guild Aristocrat. SN: 10192. $1500. *Courtesy of Jay Pilzer, New Hope Guitar Traders.*

The Starfire Bass I was made from 1964 until 1975. It featured one Humbucking pickup (in 1970 this was changed to a single coil unit), a 2+2 center peaked headstock, and thumb and finger rests.

The Starfire Bass II was made from 1964 until 1977 and it was the two pickup version of the Bass I.

By 1964 Guild had implemented its recently reshaped headstock design onto all of the instruments that previously used the open book style headstock, and this center peaked design continues today. Instruments that weren't affected by this change over at the time were the solid body guitars with their asymmetrical headstock shapes.

In 1966 Al Dronge sold Guild Musical Instruments to Avnet Incorporated, a company that is involved with consumer electronics, automotive products, and other industrial fields.

Dronge stayed on as President of Guild and the take over of his company had no effect on the conducting of Guild's daily business.

Guild introduced a twelve string electric in 1966, as did many other manufacturers. The Starfire XII was built from 1966 until 1975 and was a twelve string version of the Starfire IV.

In 1967 Guild introduced a special version of the Starfire III. The Starfire III Special was made only in 1967 and it was based on the standard model. The differences were block fingerboard inlays, two white DeArmond pickups, a Melita bridge, and Grover Roto-Matic tuners as standard equipment.

New models for 1968 included the ST series and the Blues Bird series of guitars.

The ST 301 was made from 1968 until 1972 and featured a 16-5/8" double sharp cut-away body that was 1-7/8" deep. It utilized one thin single coil pickup, a bound fingerboard with dot position markers, a headstock with the Chesterfield and Guild inlay, and chrome plated hardware. In 1970 the pickup was changed to a Humbucker model.

The ST 302 was made from 1968 until 1972 and was the two pickup version of the ST 301.

The ST 303 was made from 1968 until 1972 and was basically an ST 302 with a Bigsby vibrato.

The ST 304 was made from 1968 until 1972 and basically it was a 2-7/8" thick version of the ST 303.

The Blues Bird M-75 was made from 1968 until 1974 and it was basically the aristocrat model reincarnated with Humbucking pickups, chrome hardware, a 1/8" thicker body and a Chesterfield headstock inlay.

The Blues Bird M-75 G was the gold plated version. Both models were available in sunburst and natural finishes.

During 1968 and 1969 Guild started shifting its ever increasing production to their newly built plant in Westerly, Rhode Island. Original plans were to build the flat-top instruments in the new facility only, but because of labor and financial reasons, they decided to move Guild's entire production to the new plant. The move was completed in 1971, but many early Rhode Island guitars carry a Hoboken label which were used until they ran out.

In 1970 Guild introduced solid versions of the Blues Bird models and bass versions as well. The Blues Bird M-75 CS was made from 1970 until 1984. It featured a solid carved top mahogany body, angled stop tailpiece, two Humbucking pickups, a block inlaid fingerboard, Chesterfield headstock inlay, and chrome hardware. The Blues Bird M-75 GS was the gold plated version of the M-75 CS. The M 851 Bass was made from 1970 until 1980. It's 13-1/2" wide semi solid body had the same outline as the Aristocrat guitars but it's body was thicker at 2-7/8". It's 30-3/4" scale neck featured dot inlays and its headstock had the Chesterfield and Guild inlay. The M85 II Bass was the two pickup version with an added master volume.

Guild also introduced a new solid body that resembled a Gibson SG. The S-100 made from 1970 until 1974 was a solid mahogany double cut-away and featured two Humbuckers, slanted stop tailpiece, or Guild style vibrato, bound fingerboard with block markers and a Chesterfield headstock inlay. It had chrome hardware and was available in natural, cherry red, em-

1957 Guild X50. SN: 11712. $750.
Courtesy of Johnny's Guitars.

1967 Guild X50. SN: 45103. $650.
Courtesy of Scott Mulrooney.

erald green, black, and white finishes. Later additions to this line of guitars were the S-100C made from 1974 until 1976, which had an acorn engraving in the top, and the S-100 Deluxe made from 1973 until 1975 that featured a Bigsby vibrato.

In 1972 tragedy hit the company when their president Alfred Dronge was killed in a private plane crash. The business that he started in a small New York City loft twenty years ago was then headed by Leon Tell, who had served as Vice President since 1962.

During the mid- to late seventies Guild introduced the S-300, an odd bell-shaped double cut-away solid body. With it came different guitar and bass versions, but as with all of Guild's solid body guitars, they proved to be not overly successful.

Throughout the 1980s Guild introduced many new electronic guitar models in all kinds of crazy shapes and none proved to be very successful. Guild's solid body electric guitars were never a strong point for the company and they have yet to establish any kind of a large following.

In 1984 Guild introduced the Brian May model, based on the legendary guitarist's home made model that he used when he played with the band Queen. The Brian May model and its subsequent re-issues in the 1990s are probably considered Guild's most valuable solid body guitars to date.

In 1986 Avnet sold Guild to a group of investors from New England and Tennessee. But financial woes for the investment group caused them to sell Guild Guitars to the U.S. Musical Corporation, (formerly the FAAS Corporation) of New Berlin, Wisconsin in January of 1989.

In 1995 Fender Musical Instrument Corporation acquired Guild, and in recent years has re-issued some of Guilds classic archtop and solid body electric guitar models.

1963 Guild DE 400, Duane Eddy. $1200.

1967 Guild Starfire V. SN: EN1031. $1000.

1967 Guild Starfire 3 Special. SN: EK-2507. $1200.

Guild Serial Numbers

From 1952 to 1979 Guild's serial numbers were sequential, except for the period between 1965 and 1969 when certain models were given their own numbering scheme.

1952	001-250 Approximate
1953	250-800 Approximate
1954	800-1500 Approximate
1955	1501-2467
1956	2468-3829
1957	3830-5711
1958	5712-8347
1959	8348-12034
1960	12035-14713
1961	14714-18419
1962	18420-22722
1963	22723-28943
1964	28944-38636
1965	38637-46606
1966	46607-46608
1967	46609-46637
1968	46638-46656
1969	46657-46695
1970	46696-50978
1971	50979-61463
1972	61464-75602
1973	75603-95496
1974	95497-112803
1975	112804-130304
1976	130305-149625
1977	149626-169867
1978	169868-195067
1979	195068-211877

The following selected models were given their own number sequence. All models begin with number 101.

Artist Award Model

1965	AA 101
1966	AA 102-AA 113
1967	AA 114-AA 139
1968	AA 140-AA 157
1969	AA 158-AA 167

CE-100

1965	EF 101-EF 211
1966	EF 212-EF 396
1967	EF 397-EF 649
1968	EF 650-EF 719
1969	EF 720-EF 760

D-50

1965	AL 101-AL 192
1966	AL 193-AL 301
1967	AL 302-AL 513
1968	AL 514-AL 584
1969	AL 585-AL 698

DE-400

1965	EH 101-EH 126
1966	EH 127-EH 233
1967	EH 234-EH 276
1968	EH 277-EH 301

DE-500

1965	EI 101-107
1966	EI 108-116
1967	EI 117-136
1968	EI 137-141

F-50

1965	AD 101-119
1966	AD 120-190
1967	AD 191-291
1968	AD 292-355
1969	AD 356-418

S-200

1965	SC 101
1966	SC 102-153
1967	SC 154-166
1968	SC 167-191

Starfire II & III & III Spec

1965	EK 101-387
1966	EK 388-2098
1967	EK 2099-2819
1968	EK 2820-3028
1969	EK 3029-3098

Starfire IV

1965	EL 101-276
1966	EL 277-1167
1967	EL 1168-1840
1968	EL 1841-2223
1969	EL 2224-2272

Starfire V

1965	EN 101-194
1966	EN 195-927
1967	EN 928-1807
1968	EN 1808-2141
1969	EN 2142-2278

Starfire VI

1965	DB 101
1966	DB 102-174
1967	DB 175-274
1968	DB 275-329
1969	DB 330-339

Starfire XII

1966	DC 101-586
1967	DC 587-896
1968	DC 897
1969	DC 898-910

X-175

1965	EG 101-107
1966	EG 108-160
1967	EG 161-239
1968	EG 240-322
1969	EG 323-346

X-500

1965	DA 101-106
1966	DA 107-138
1967	DA 139-180
1968	DA 181-235
1969	DA 236-244

1964 Guild Polara. SN: 37766. $600. *Courtesy of Jay Pilzer, New Hope Guitar Traders.*

1973 Guild S100. SN: 8113. $650. *Courtesy of Jay Pilzer, New Hope Guitar Traders.*

1974 Guild S-100 Acorn. SN: 106301. $600 *Courtesy of Rumble Seat Music.*

1972 Guild Bluesburg Bass. Changed Bridge. SN: 89402. $800. *Courtesy of Bruce Diamond/Diamond Strings.*

1978 Guild S-300D. SN: 187391. $425 *Courtesy of Jay Pilzer, New Hope Guitar Traders.*

Hagstrom

Hagstrom guitars were produced in Sweden starting in 1957. Several brand names were used on their guitars during their production. Selmer U.K. imported guitars to England, that were marketed under the Futurama trademark name, and Hershman Musical Instrument Company imported them to the U.S. under the Goya and Hagstrom names.

Hagstrom's first models, the P46 solid body (Les Paul single cut-away shape), and the P24 hollow body featured solid pearloid fingerboards, sparkle finishes, and push button and roller controls (much like the Italian made guitars).

Hagstrom models from the 1960s included the pointed Strat-shaped guitars models I, II, and III. These featured a Strat-shaped headstock too, and were available in bass versions. The Viking model had a body with the shape of a Gibson ES 335 and a Strat-style neck, and the Coronado IV bass which featured an offset double cut-away body.

In 1973 Hagstrom redesigned its line of guitars. The Viking now had an asymmetrical 3+3 headstock. The newly introduced Swede was a fancy variant on a Gibson Les Paul. The Scandia was a hollow double cut-away model and the D'Aquisto archtop was a guitar that was designed by the late, great James D'Aquisto. He supplied the plans for the guitar, but had nothing to do with its construction. He also did not have anything to do with the Swede line of guitars and basses, as some people may have suspected.

Hagstrom guitar production ended in the early 1980s with little fanfare. The instruments they produced are of pretty decent quality and the enthusiast can add one to their guitar palate for as little as $200.

1970s Hagstrom Viking. SN: 866074. $450. *Courtesy of Gary L. Jacobs.*

c. 1973 Hagstrom Swede. SN: 53 021087. $550. *Courtesy of Jorgen Pettersson.*

1965 Hagstrom Bass II. SN: 756094. $300. *Courtesy of Flashback Guitars.*

1960s Hagstrom Model II. SN: 601164. $300.
Courtesy of Jay Pilzer, New Hope Guitar Traders.

1965 Hagstrom Coronado IV. SN: 658122. $450.
Courtesy of Bruce Diamond/Diamond Strings.

Hamer

Hamer originated in 1974 out of a small guitar shop called Northern Prairie Music, in Wilmette, Illinois. Concentrating on the restoration and repair of vintage electrics, the shop was able to gain a knowledge of the methods of construction that were used on these highly regarded instruments. Prairie Music's reputation grew and they became Gibson's first authorized service center. Jol Dantzig and Paul Hamer, two of the shop's key figures, were invited to tour the Gibson factory to gain better knowledge of Gibsons guitars. Not impressed with the guitars that were being produced at the time, Hamer and Dantzig decided to build their own instruments. A Flying "V" bass was the first such instrument. Jol used this bass in public performances and it started to attract interest. One of the interested people was Rick Nielson of Cheap Trick and a regular customer of Prairie Music.

Rick Nielson was the springboard that would put the "Hamer" guitar in the public eye. Jol and Paul decided on the name "Hamer" because it had a ring to it like Fender. Soon other professional players wanted Hamers and not long after that dealers wanted them too.

The Hamer U.S.A. Company incorporated and by 1975 the newly located Palantine, Illinois company debuted its first guitar. It embodied old-world craftsmanship with Gibson's Explorer design. Originally called "The Hamer Guitar" it would soon be known as the Standard. The guitar featured a two piece figured maple top, bound body, and a bound fingerboard with trapezoid inlays. Production was low, and quality was high. By 1977, when Hamer would introduce its second model, approximately only 50 Standards were built. The new guitar would also be based on a 1950s Gibson design, the double cut-away Les Paul Special and would be called the Sunburst.

1980 Hamer Special with factory custom graphics. $600.

In 1980 Hamer moved to a larger facility in Arlington Heights, Illinois, to supply the increased demand for their guitars. Many new models would be introduced in the next two decades, but it would be the two original models that proved the most enduring. Paul Hamer left the company in 1987 and in 1988 Hamer USA was acquired by Kaman Music Corporation. In 1997 Hamer's production was moved to Kaman's Ovation facilities in New Hartford, Connecticut. The original pre-1980 Standards are the most collectible models from Hamer's line.

Hamer Serial Numbers

Hamer has had two different sets of serial numbers. The information was provided courtesy of Frank Ridone, Hamer Product Manager.

The first set was used on Hamer standard models, multi-string basses and custom made instruments from 1974 to 1985. Stamped into the wood of the back of the headstock they were sequentially numbered from 0000 to 0745.

The second set was first used on the sunburst series in 1977. The first digit represents the year, followed by the production sequence. Early guitars were stamped and later models impressed on the back of the headstock. Eventually this system would be used on all domestic guitars and basses.

First series example:	1978 Standard: 0037
Second series:	1977: 7000
	1980: 01451
	1990: 024193

1978 Hamer Standard. SN: 0137. Changed bridge. $1400

1993 Hamer Archtop Studio. SN: 335778. $700. *Courtesy of Vince Perri.*

Hang Don

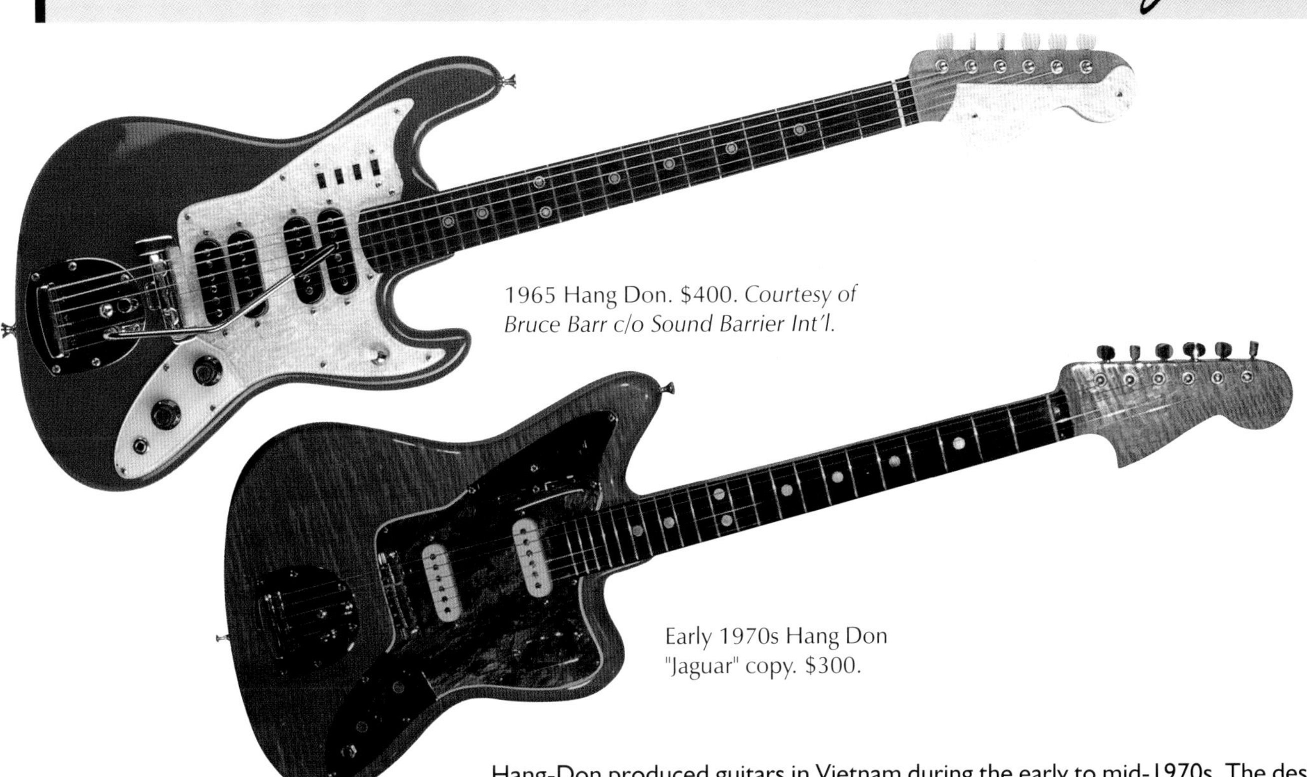

1965 Hang Don. $400. *Courtesy of Bruce Barr c/o Sound Barrier Int'l.*

Early 1970s Hang Don "Jaguar" copy. $300.

Hang-Don produced guitars in Vietnam during the early to mid-1970s. The designs are all loosely based on Fender models and some are downright copies. Construction features include maple necks (some are made from extremely flamed maple) with a highly radiused fingerboard, a non-adjustable solid steel neck rod, Strat-style headstock, up to 4 pickups, colored pearloid pick-guards, and a JazzMaster/Jaguar style vibrato. These guitars, even though they look pretty cool, are very crudely made and the Jaguar model that the author owned (for less than a month) was almost unplayable due to the extremely microphone pickups.

Harmony

During the late nineteenth century Wilhelm J.F. Schultz, a mechanic from Hamburg, Germany, immigrated to America and went to work for the Knapp Drum Company of Chicago.

Lyon and Healy, one of America's oldest and, at one time, largest musical instrument manufacturers, acquired Knapp, and Schultz was promoted to the foreman of the drum division.

In 1892 Schultz left Lyon and Healy and founded the Harmony Company. Buying a two room loft on the top floor of Chicago's Edison Building, Schultz and his four employee workforce started producing guitars. By 1894 the company's workforce had increased tenfold and several production locations in Chicago had been added. In 1904 the company consolidated to one location on 1748 North Lawndale Avenue in Chicago. In 1906 the original 30,000 square foot building was expanded, and by 1915 the Harmony Company employed 125 people.

In 1916 the Sears and Roebuck Company purchased Harmony in order to acquire their ukulele production which supplied America with a substantial amount of the then immensely popular instrument. By 1923 Harmony's annual production capacity was a quarter of a million instruments.

In 1925 Jay Kraus was appointed to Vice President of Harmony and in January of the following year he succeeded Wilhelm Schultz as president.

In 1928 Harmony introduced its Roy Smeck endorsed line of instruments. This endorsement, which lasted for at least three decades, would result in many electric models with his name on them.

By 1930 Harmony's annual sales were reported to be at a half-million units with nearly 40% of these being sold through Sears.

In 1940 Kraus acquired a controlling stock interest in Harmony, which continued to grow and prosper. At this time in Harmony's history it is reported that they were producing more than a half of America's total guitar production. In 1941 Harmony found a new larger home at 3633 South Racine Avenue in Chicago.

In 1947 Kraus and five other men founded the American Music Conference, of which he served as President, as he did for the National Association of Music Merchants (NAMM). By 1961 Kraus's Harmony company had outgrown their current facility and moved to a new 80,000 square foot factory on Kolin Avenue in Chicago. Even with the expanded production capabilities, Harmony couldn't keep up with the guitar boom that they were heading so they opened a second plant in 1964 on 44th Street, and a third location was acquired for warehouse purposes only.

1963 Harmony Rocket. $275. *Courtesy of Jeff Blakeman.*

1967 Harmony H-27 Bass, SN: 7579. $500. *Courtesy of Flashback Guitars.*

1960s Harmony Meteor. $375. *Courtesy of Pittsburgh Guitars.*

1967 Harmony H-75. $375.

Harmony Roy Smeck model. $300.

In 1968 Kraus died of a heart attack and was succeeded by longtime Harmony employee Charles RuBovits as president. Kraus had left the controlling stock of the company in a trust with which RuBovits had some business disagreements. This led to RuBovits's resignation as president in 1970. From 1971 until Harmony's demise in 1974, a trust-appointed president headed the company.

The Harmony trust tried to expand the business into a conglomerate by acquiring the Chicago-based distributor Targ and Dinner, and a couple of other companies, but in doing so found themselves in terrible debt. To satisfy creditors Harmony's factory equipment and other assets were sold at auction. Harmony guitars produced after 1974 were imported from Korea.

Harmony produced countless models of electric guitars during its history, all of which were sold through wholesalers. Most carry the Sears Silvertone name or the Harmony name but there are many other "house" brands that were built by Harmony.

Harmony's U.S. built electrics can have some pretty cool features and actually can play and sound fairly good. As a rule the fancier and more plentiful the pickups, the more it is worth, and general asking prices for Harmony made electrics are from $100 to $500.

Höfner

1958 Höfner Club 50. *Courtesy of Rumble Seat Music.*

Höfner was founded in 1887 by Karl Höfner. Originally located in what is now Czechoslovakia, Höfner built instruments in the violin family. By 1925 the company relocated to eastern Germany where they started production of their first guitars. In 1948 the company relocated again to Bubenreuth, in what was then West Germany.

Höfner debuted their first electrics in the very early 1950s based on archtop designs. They were only available to the domestic Germany market. In the mid 1950s what is referred to as the "Beatle Bass" made its debut. Designed by Walter Höfner, Karl's son, the violin bass is by far Höfner's most successful electric instrument.

Paul McCartney's own Beatle Bass, which he used with the band in its heyday. This was repaired at Mandolin Bros. Ltd. which was able to solve intonation problems which had plagued him since he obtained it. *Photo: Stan Jay/ Mandolin Bros.*

In 1958 Selmer of U.K. took over Höfner's distribution and the models that were destined for the British market differed from those made for the domestic German market.

In the 1960s Höfner's line of electrics expanded to include solid body models, some of which were finished in colorful vinyl. Höfner's instruments were distributed in the U.S. by Sorkin Music Company Inc. located in Hauppage, New York.

Currently Höfner continues to build instruments and at present is offering various re-issue models of their famous violin bass along with contemporary models. Distribution of Höfner instruments in the U.S. is now handled by Entertainment Music Marketing Corporation, Deer Park, New York.

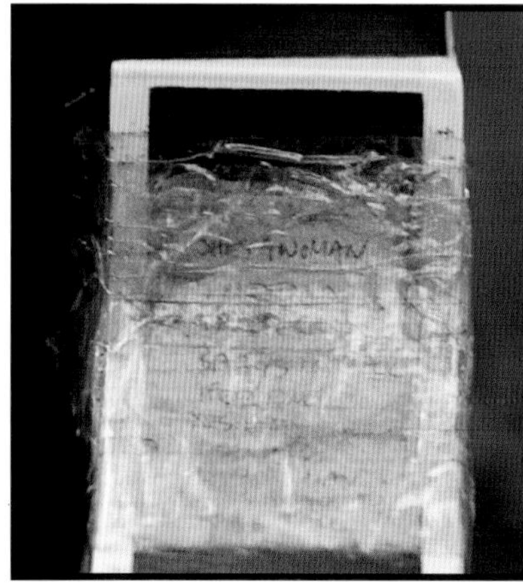

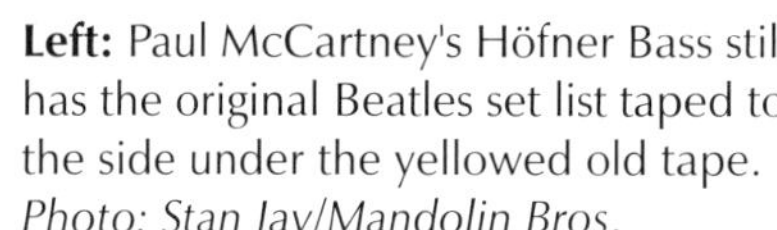

Left: Paul McCartney's Höfner Bass still has the original Beatles set list taped to the side under the yellowed old tape. *Photo: Stan Jay/Mandolin Bros.*

Right: John Hamel, Paul's assistant, guarded the instrument the three days it was in the Mandolin Bros. shop. The repairperson who performed the work was Flip Van Domburg Scipio. *Photo: Stan Jay/Mandolin Bros.*

1966 Höfner 500/1 "Beatle" Bass. $1500. *Courtesy of Gary's Classic Guitars.*

Höfner Serial Numbers

Höfner Serial Numbers are of no help in dating instruments. It is possible on electric models to date the era in which the instrument was made by the type of pickup that was installed. Also, instruments made prior to 1960 do not have an adjustable truss rod, and therefore also have no truss rod cover. Acoustic models often have the date of manufacture handwritten on the label inside of the instrument.

1953-1959: Fuma made, six star slot pole pieces
1957-1960: Bass guitar - Single coil sized plain top, plastic in black, white, or brown
1960-196: Bass/plain - Rectangular metal case with diamond logo only, rectangular metal case with 4 perforated slots and dia mond logo in the middle
1961-1962: Bass - Rectangle metal case with 4 screw head pole pieces and diamond logo
1962-1964: Bass - Rectangle metal case with 4 rectangle pole pieces and 4 slotted screw head pole pieces with a narrow surround
1961-1963: Guitar - Rectangle metal case with 6 pole pieces either slotted screw or rectangular and the Höfner diamond logo
1965-1966: Bass - Same pickup as the '61-64 style but with a wide pickup surround
1963-1967: Rectangle metal case with 6 slotted screw pole pieces and 6 rectangular pole pieces
1967 and later: Guitar/Bass - Rectangular metal case with 1 blade magnet plus a small slotted screw pole piece for each string

Recently Höfner has re-issued some of its classic instruments and these will have pickup styles true to their origin.

1967 Höfner 500/1 "Beatle" Bass. $1300. *Courtesy of Zapf's Music.*

Early 1960s Höfner bass. *Courtesy of Bruce Diamond/Diamond Strings.*

Ibanez

1977 Ibanez Rocket Roll Sr. SN: J775156. $800. *Courtesy of Marty's Music.*

1976 Ibanez Destroyer. Pickup covers removed. SN: J765616. $800. *Courtesy of Guitar Shelter.*

Ibanez is the trade mark name used since 1932 by the Japanese company Hoshino Gakki Ten Incorporated. The Ibanez line of instruments has been in continuous production since then except for a period in the 1940s when the factory was destroyed during World War II. After being rebuilt in 1950, Hoshino has come to produce some of the most respected instruments in the industry under the Ibanez name.

Ibanez guitars were first imported into the U.S. under the Elger brand name by Medley Music, a retail store in the Philadelphia suburb of Bryn Mawr. The first electrics appeared by 1965 with either an Elger or Ibanez logo. These were fairly crude entry level instruments of Ibanez's own design. By the early 1970s their guitars showed a much higher level of quality but also a much lower level of originality, copying, as they did, classic American designs. By the mid 1970s Ibanez got so good at the game that some of their copies were closer to the originals than Gibson's own re-issues.

They also made quality original models that were referred to as Artist models. The Artist name was also used to describe Ibanez's glued neck joint, which they utilized on any of their electric models.

By 1977 Gibson was so fed up with the blatant copies that they sued Ibanez. The case of Gibson vs. Elger would be resolved in a Philadelphia Federal District court in early 1978 when Ibanez agreed to stop making the copy guitars. With this, Ibanez incorporated their quality construction methods into original design instruments, spearheaded by the Iceman series of 1977. The GB10 George Benson signature model soon followed along with the neck through body Musician series and sort of Les Paul-looking Performer series.

In 1978 the Paul Stanley Signature Iceman, the PS10, made its debut in what would be a major marketing trend for Ibanez. During the next two decades they continued signing high profile guitarists to endorse their products. Players such as Steve Lukather, Steve Val, Joe Satriani, Reb Beach, John Petrucci, Frank Gambale, Phil Collen of Def Leppard, and Pat Metheny all had Signature guitars or complete series of guitars to their credits. With such a large pool of talented guitarists to draw ideas from, it is no wonder that Ibanez has been among the top group of guitar manufacturers in the world.

Even though it was the Super Strat-inspired guitars of the 1980s and 1990s that propelled Ibanez to a top contender spot in the electric guitar field, it is the glued-in set neck models of the 1970s that are of most interest to collectors.

1977 Ibanez Destroyer Bass. SN: H775157. $900

1981 Ibanez Destroyer 2. SN: L815135. $550. *Courtesy of Tone Zone.*

1982 Ibanez Rocket Roll 2. SN: E825777. $550.

1981 Ibanez PS-10. "Paul Stanley" Model. SN: 1816576. $1595. *Courtesy of Toys From the Attic.*

1976 Ibanez Bob Weir Professional. SN: 1766280. $1150.

1982 Ibanez Artist. SN: E825185. $600. *Courtesy of Toys From the Attic.*

1976 Ibanez Custom. $700.

Ibanez Serial Numbers

Starting in 1975 Ibanez started using a numbering system that indicated the date of manufacture. Many instruments produced just prior to 1975 don't have any numbers at all, and the models produced before this that have numbers can't be accurately dated by them. Serial numbers are found on the back of the headstock on glued in neck models, and on the neckplate on bolt on neck models.

From 1975 to 1988 a letter prefix was followed by a six digit number. The letter (A to L) indicated the month (Jan. to Dec.) and the following two digits indicate the year of manufacture. From 1988 to 1990 the letter prefix was deleted.

Examples

H775157 - 1977 Destroyer Bass produced in August

E825185 - 1982 Artist produced in the month of May

1991 Ibanez Universe Green Swirl. Very few made, probably fewer than 50. *Courtesy of Ed Roman Guitars.*

1979 Ibanez Artwood Twin, 2670. SN: D796222. $2500-3000. *Courtesy of Joe's Guitars.*

1977 Ibanez Double Neck Copy. SN: F770680. $800. *Courtesy of John Dolan*

Kay

Kay's history dates back to the Groeschel Company of Chicago, Illinois. Founded in 1890, Groeschel or Groehsl's primary production was of bowl back mandolins. In 1918 the company's name was changed to Stromber-Voisenet and in 1921 the company was incorporated with $50,000 of capital stock. Under the direction of the company's vice president, C.G. Stromberg (not to be confused with the Boston luthier family of Charles and Elmer Stromberg) the company began producing guitars under the Mayflower trademark. In 1928 Stromberg-Voisenet was purchased by Henry Kay Kuhrmeyer, who had previously held the several positions in the company, including those of secretary and treasurer. During this time Stromber-Voisenet marketed one of the first electric guitars. It was a hollow Spanish style instrument, offered with an amplifier. Being unsuccessful, very few were produced and today they seem to be nonexistent.

In 1931 Kuhrmeyer became president and changed the name of the company to Kay Musical Instrument Co. Kay produced mid-priced instruments, marketing them under the names of Kay or Kay-Kraft , holdovers from the Stromberg-Voisenet days. The business expanded rapidly and in 1934 Kay relocated from their 18,000 square foot, three story factory at 316 Union Park Court, to an even larger facility at 1640 West Walnut Street, both in Chicago. By the mid 1930s Kay introduced a new line of electrically amplified guitars that utilized a modern type of magnetic pickup. By 1938 Kay introduced its upright basses and cellos and also started to market some of its products through wholesalers.

Throughout the 1940s Kay's production steadily grew to a high of about three hundred instruments per day. Kay's electric guitars of the period featured one or two pickups that used a single bar design, mounted to a wood or plastic plate, or directly to the pickguard. The controls on many of these instruments were mounted on the upper bouts of the guitar's body to either side of the fingerboard.

In 1952 Kay was the first company to follow in Fender's footsteps of introducing an electric bass that was fretted and meant to be played in the same position as a guitar. The K-162 bass featured a hollow single cut-away body and one pickup.

In 1955 Kay Musical Instrument Company was purchased by a group of investors headed by Sidney Katz. Katz, formerly employed by Harmony as a service department manager, came from a wealthy family background. Investments in Kay by these well-to-do relatives enabled the company to increase its production substantially. Kay went head to head with Harmony in the lower priced brackets, selling much of their production through Sears under the Silvertone brand name. During this period Kay's guitars ranged from a $24.50 entry level instrument to the professional quality, $400 Barney Kessel-endorsed Jazz Special.

In 1964 Kay relocated to a 100,000 square foot facility near Chicago's O'Hare Airport. Production during this period peaked at about 1500 guitars per day, built by approximately 500 employees. Most of this production was in lower priced models and many of these were electrics.

In 1965 Kay, which was still financially sound despite the falling out of the guitar boom of the early 1960s, was sold by Sidney Katz. The new owners, the giant Chicago-based Seeburg jukebox company, owned Kay for two years. They sold Kay to Robert Engelhardt, Valco's owner of five years, in 1967, Engelhardt then moved Valco into the Kay facility where both Kay and Valco instruments were produced for two more years. By the end of the 1960s the under-financed company was shut down by creditors and both Kay and Valco were out of business.

The Kay trademark was acquired by WMI, a distributor for imported instruments, in 1973. Throughout that decade the Kay name was used on cheaply made imported guitars.

In 1980 the Kay trademark was sold to A.R. Enterprises and the name was again applied to a line of lower quality imported instruments.

During Kay's U.S. production the instruments ranged from fairly low quality entry level models to quite fancy and well made professional models. With this in mind, prices for these instruments can range from under $100 for the lowliest models to over $1000 for one of the Kessel models in really clean condition. The bulk of Kay-built guitars, though, will fall in the $100 to $400 range.

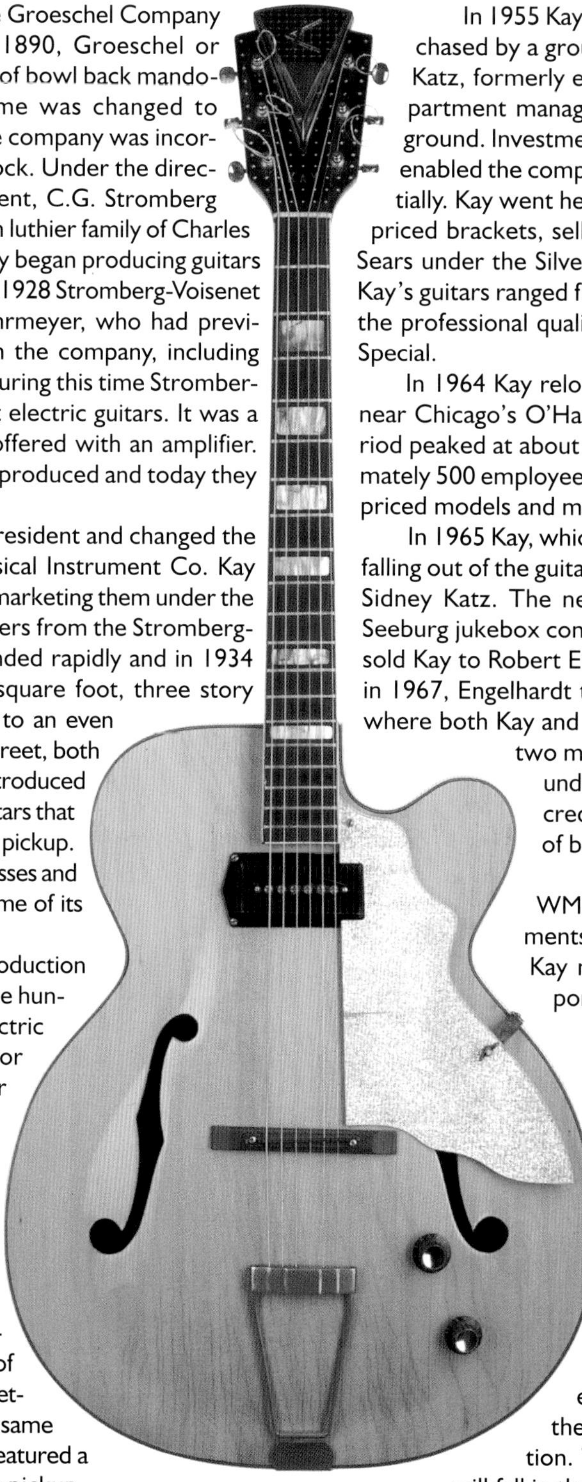

1957 Kay Upbeat. $700. *Courtesy of M.K. Music, David Comtois.*

Kramer

1985 Kramer Enterprise. 1 of 12. *Courtesy of Terry Boling, Kramer Krazy.*

Gary Kramer was a former partner of Travis Bean, the pioneer of the American-made aluminum necked guitar. In October, 1975, Kramer and Dennis Berardi joined forces to produce electric guitars in Neptune, New Jersey. In April, 1976, Peter J. LaPlaca joined the partnership, and the BKL Company was founded, taking its name from the first initial of each partner's last name. They opened their factory on July 1, 1976, producing Kramer guitars co-designed by luthier Phil Petillo and BKL. The first production run of aluminum necked instruments was completed during November, 1976. A month later Gary Kramer left the company. Ironically the guitars that bore his name would eventually become world contenders. Ultimately fourteen different aluminum neck models would be marketed up to the early 1980s. All of them featured a bolt-on aluminum neck which had two wood insert strips running down the back of the neck and a headstock shaped in the form a tuning fork. These early Kramers were usually very heavy and the necks had an unnatural feel. Additionally, they displayed tuning problems with temperature changes. These characteristics have kept the prices of these guitars down in the $300 to $600 range.

By 1982 the aluminum neck models were phased out of production and more conventional wood neck models, based on the "Super Strat" style guitar, began to appear. These guitars, with their exclusive Floyd Rose locking vibrato system and an endorsement by the groundbreaking guitarist Edward Van Halen, would propel Kramer guitars to new heights through the 1980s.

In 1985 BKL purchased the Spector Guitar Company and relocated the Spector production from New York to BKL's Neptune facility.

Kramer Guitars produced some acoustic/electric guitars in 1986 that were designed by luthier Danny Ferrington. These instruments, which resembled hollow body "Super Strats," were produced until 1991.

Kramer's product line during the 1980s was favored by the hard rock/metal "hair" bands that were popular at the time, and, as their popularity waned by the end of the decade, so did Kramer's guitars. In 1989 BKL went into bankruptcy and after several failed attempts at refinancing the Kramer Company was sold at auction to a group of investors who incorporated the company under the name of Kramer Musical Instruments (KMI) in 1995.

KMI also acquired the Spector operation, relocating both Kramer and Spector production to a new facility in Eatontown, New Jersey. KMI revived some of Kramer's early aluminum neck models, but, with a fairly low production, they never really put a dent in the market. After only two years in business KMI sold the Kramer trademark to the Gibson Corporation in 1997 and during the same negotiations Stuart Spector reacquired his namesake trademark, Spector.

Kustom

Kustom guitars and basses were produced from 1967 until late 1969 by the Kustom Amplifier Company in Chanute, Kansas. The company, whose Tuck and Roll amplifier lines were their claim to fame, produced three electric guitar models and an electric bass.

Kustom was founded in 1965 by Bud Ross, a musician who had a strong knowledge of electronics. Ross and his associate,Fred Berry, debuted their first amps at the 1965 NAMM show. These led to a massive line of Tuck and Roll models that ranged from small practice models to huge, complete public address systems.

In 1967 Ross collaborated with Doyle Reeding, Wesley Valorie, and Roy Clark (who later also endorsed Kustom amps) to design and market a line of electric guitars. All four models shared the same semi-hollow bodies that were produced by laminating a hollowed out two-piece top and back together. Models differed in hardware, decoration, and neck designs. The three guitar models were headed by the K200A with multi-dot fingerboard and Bigsby vibrato, the K200B with double dot inlays and trapeze tail piece, and the K200C with single dot inlays, a narrower headstock, and plainer hardware than the K200B. All models shared the same DeArmond pickups and available colors, which included black, black ash, white ash, natural, red, blue, sunburst, wineburst, and zebra finishes. The lone bass model, the K200D, utilized the guitar's body with a 21 fret bass neck that featured single dot inlays and a 2 + 2 headstock. Pickups were DeArmonds and it was available in the same glorious colors as the guitars.

By the end of production, in 1969, it is estimated that nearly 3000 instruments in total had been built.

1968 Kustom K200D Prototype Bass. *Courtesy of Bruce Diamond/Diamond Strings.*

Martin

Johann Georg Martin was a cabinet maker and carpenter in the village of Markneukirchen, Germany. The region was home to a guild of violin makers, for which Martin would sometimes build shipping crates.

Johann's son Christian Frederick Martin was born in 1796. He worked in the family business before going to work for Georg Stauffer in Vienna, where he learned the art of guitar and violin construction. Before long he became the shop foreman. In 1825 Christian left Stauffer to return to his family, where he and his father began to build instruments. This father and son team created serious competition to the local violin makers, which threatened to bring political pressure against them. Rather than fight against this resistance, the Martins emigrated to America. In 1833 they set up a music store at 196 Hudson St. in New York City. The business sold a complete line of instruments and music, as well as their own Stauffer-inspired Martin guitars. Not accustomed to city life, in 1939 Christian and his family decided to relocate to the rolling hills of Cherry Hill, a suburb of Nazareth, Pennsylvania.

1964 Martin F55. SN: 194983. $1000.

Christian Frederick Martin, Jr., was born in 1825. He gradually took over the management of the business, which was growing in its Pennsylvania location. By 1850 Martin's guitars started leaving their Stauffer roots behind, incorporating their own innovations, including the "X" braced soundboard. In 1857 Christian, Jr., purchased a block of land on North Main Street between North and High Streets in Nazareth. He first built a residence on the site, and then, by 1859, moved the entire business from Cherry Hill to the new location. In 1873 Christian, Sr., died at the age of 77. In 1887 the first of several additions was made to the factory. In November, 1888 Christian, Jr., experienced failing health and he passed away at the age of 63. The Martin business was then headed by Frank Henry Martin (1866-1948), who oversaw many factory expansions, increased production, and many landmark developments in the design of the acoustic guitar.

It wasn't until 1958, under the leadership of C.F. Martin III and Frank Henry Martin, Jr. that Martin would decide to market an electric guitar model. The prototype instrument was completed in 1958 and marketed in 1959. The D-18E was basically a D-18 model acoustic with two DeArmond pickups and their respective volume and tone controls mounted into the heavier braced top of the guitar. This model was joined by two other versions during its inaugural year, the 00-18E and the D-28E. The D-18E would only last one year, but the other two would carry on until 1964. During this time it was also possible to custom order any current production model with the DeArmond pickups installed. This feature would add the suffix "E" to the model's name and was available until 1971.

In 1961 Martin would introduce its first specially designed electric guitar models in its "F" series. These were all based on a single or double cut-away thin hollow body that was fitted with a traditional Martin neck. The F-50 was a single cut-away with one DeArmond pickup, the F-55 was a double pickup version, and the F-65 was the double cut-away, two pickup version. All of these models were available with an optional Martin stylized Bigsby Vibrato.

In 1965 the "F" series was discontinued and replaced with the single cut-away GT-70 and the double cut-away GT-75 models. Both models featured two DeArmond pickups, a wider headstock with pointed corners and binding, neck binding, and a Martin Bigsby Vibrato as an option. A twelve string version, the GT-75-12, was available, featuring the GT-75's body with a more traditional Martin twelve string neck. Production for the GT series would last until 1968, Martin did not market another electric guitar model until 1979. Production totals for the F and GT series are: F-50–519; F-55–665; F-65–566, GT-70–453; and GT-75–751.

Martin came back into the electric market with a solid body bass and two guitars in 1979. They all featured a double round cut-away body made of walnut-maple laminate, glued-in neck with a Stauffer inspired headstock shape with a 2+2 (bass) or 3+3 (guitar) tuner arrangement. Hardware was supplied by Leo Quan, Sperzel, and Grover, and all models used DiMarzio pickups.

Production of the E models ran from 1979 to 1982. 5,307 E-18 models were produced featuring covered pickups and two volume, two tone, selector, and phase controls. 5,629 EM-18 models were produced featuring exposed coil humbuckers and an added coil tap switch. 5,226 EB-18 model basses were produced featuring a singe exposed coil humbucker. From 1981 until 1982 Martin built an upmarket E-28, all-mahogany, neck-thru-body guitar and an EB-28 bass, with approximately 4,854 of each being produced.

In 1986 C.F. Martin IV assumed control of his family's company from Frank Henry Martin, Jr. During this period Martin imported a line of Korean-built solid bodies marketed under the Stinger trademark.

As Martin prepares to enter a new millennium under the control of C.F. Martin IV, the factory, which is unique in that it has remained under one family's control since it founding, continues to be at the top of its field. It is the standard by which all other acoustic guitars are judged.

Left: 1966 Martin GT70. SN: 208581. $1100. *Courtesy of Steve Senerchia, The Music Man.*

Below: 1979 Martin EM-18. $650. *Courtesy of Vintage Instruments.*

Martin Serial Numbers

Guitars have been chronologically numbered since 1898. The number shows the last instrument produced that year.

YEAR	LAST #
1898	8348
1899	8716
1900	9128
1901	9310
1902	9528
1903	9810
1904	9988
1905	10120
1906	10329
1907	10727
1908	10883
1909	11018
1910	11203
1911	11413
1912	11565
1913	11821
1914	12047
1915	12209
1916	12390
1917	12988
1918	13450
1919	14512
1920	15848
1921	16758
1922	17839
1923	19891
1924	22008
1925	24116
1926	28689
1927	34435
1928	37568
1929	40843
1930	45317
1931	49589
1932	52590
1933	55084
1934	58679
1935	61947
1936	65176
1937	68865
1938	71866
1939	74061
1940	76734
1941	80013
1942	83107
1943	86724
1944	90149
1945	93623
1946	98158
1947	103468
1948	108269
1949	112961
1950	117961
1951	122799
1952	128436
1953	134501
1954	141345
1955	147328
1956	152775
1957	159061
1958	165576
1959	171047
1960	175689
1961	181297
1962	187384
1963	193327
1964	199626
1965	207030
1966	217215
1967	230095
1968	241925
1969	256003
1970	271633
1971	294270
1972	313302
1973	333873
1974	353387
1975	371828
1976	388800
1977	399625
1978	407800
1979	419900
1980	430300
1981	436474
1982	439627
1983	446101
1984	453300
1985	460575
1986	468175
1987	476216
1988	483952
1989	493279
1990	503309
1991	512487
1992	522655
1993	535223
1994	551696
1995	570434
1996	592930
1997	624799
1998	668796

Micro-Frets

Micro-Frets was a small company located in Frederick, Maryland from late 1966 until 1974. Ralph Jones, the company's founder, implemented many innovative ideas to the basic guitar. These included: solid, hollowed out halves sandwiched together to form the body; the intonateable micro-nut; the cammed Calibrato vibrato tailpiece, which was supposed to keep all of the notes of a chord in relation to each other as the bar was depressed; and the Teleguitar of 1968, which was equipped with a built-in wireless transmitter.

In 1973 Jones passed away and was succeeded as president by form vice-president F.M. Muggins. In 1974 or early 1975 Micro-Frets closed and the entire operation was sold to Grammer Guitar president David Sturgill. Through 1976, Sturgill's two sons, John and Danny, assembled left over parts and sold the Micro-Frets guitars under the brand name of Diamond-S.

The various models of Micro-Frets guitars included the Orbiter, the Signature, the Spacetone, the Stage II, the Plainsman, the Golden Melody, the Husky Bass, and the Telecaster, which was later renamed the Teleguitar. All models shared the single coil pickups supplied by DeArmond and the Fender-inspired headstock design.

Micro-Frets Serial Numbers

It's not possible to pinpoint the date of manufacture of Micro-Frets guitars with the serial number, but they will indicate the production within a few years.

Serial Number	Years Made
1000-1300	1966-1969
1301-1322	1969
1323-3000	1969-1971
3001-3670	1971-1974

Late 1960s. Micro-Frets Plainsman. SN: 1202. $800. *Courtesy of Blue Note.*

Mosrite

1987 Mosrite, The Ventures Model. Signed by Semie Moseley on back of headstock. *Courtesy of Outlaw Guitars.*

In 1935 Semie Moseley was born in Durant, Oklahoma. When he was nine years old, he and his family moved to Bakersfield, California. While in the seventh grade, Moseley dropped out of school to play guitar with a traveling evangelistic group.

In 1953, at the age of 18, Moseley was hired to work at Rickenbacker by Paul Barth. While at Rickenbacker, Moseley worked with Roger Rossmeisl, whose German curve body contour was featured on many of his designs. Moseley would adopt this feature and use it later on some of his most famous Mosrite designs.

In 1955, Moseley lost his job at Rickenbacker for using their facilities to build his own guitar. During Moseley's stint as a traveling musician with the evangelistic group he had made an acquaintance with Reverend Ray Boatright, and it was Boatright who suggested to Moseley go into business for himself. Boatright co-signed for all of Moseley's wood working tools at Sears, and provided his garage in Norwalk, California for Moseley to use as a workshop. During this period Moseley, who named his company Mosrite by combining his name with Ray Boatright's, was doing custom guitar building for local musicians, most notably Joe Maphis and Larry Collins, building necks and doing inlay work for Paul Bigsby, and helping design Paul Barth's new line of Barth Guitars.

Moseley again hit the road to play guitar for another gospel group, and upon his return seven months later he relocated to Bakersfield, California.

While working out of a friend's barn, Moseley was approached by Bob Crooks of the Standel Company to design and build some guitars for him. Crooks asked for Moseley to design a guitar that would be similar to Fender's Stratocaster, and Moseley complied by just flipping a Strat over and tracing the body outline. Moseley would eventually build about twenty of these guitars and it is one of these guitars that the Ventures guitarist Nokie Edwards checked out while visiting the barn where Moseley set up shop. Nokie Edwards borrowed the guitar for a recording session and when he was finished and came back he told Moseley that the band loved it and he purchased it for $200.00 dollars. A few months later Moseley got a call from

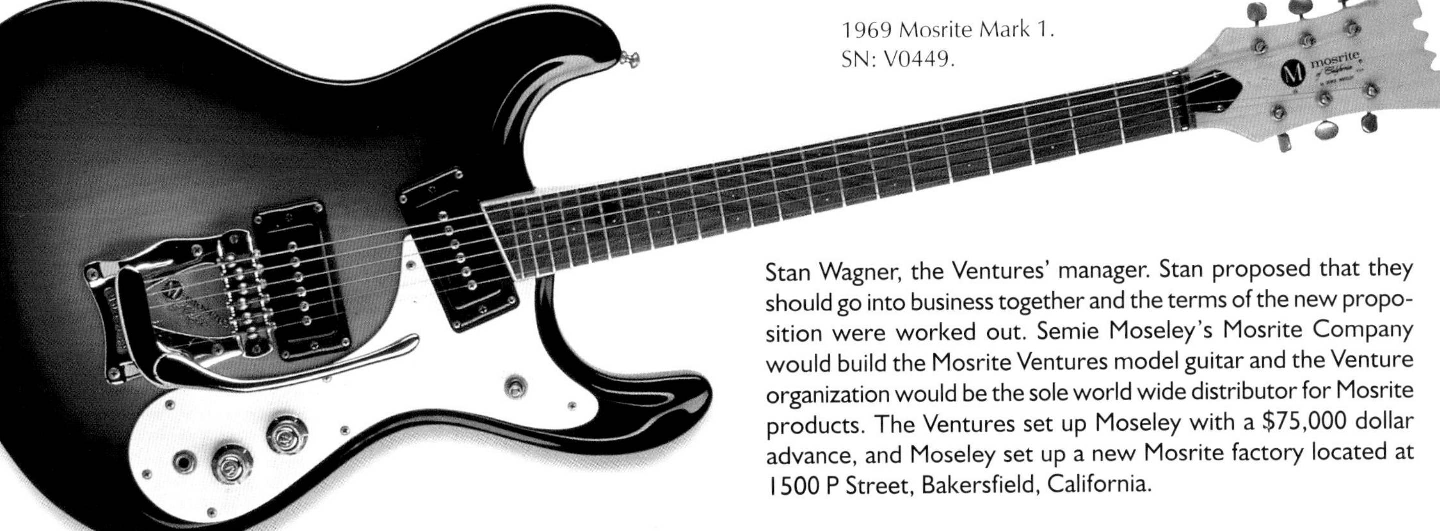

1969 Mosrite Mark 1. SN: V0449.

Stan Wagner, the Ventures' manager. Stan proposed that they should go into business together and the terms of the new proposition were worked out. Semie Moseley's Mosrite Company would build the Mosrite Ventures model guitar and the Venture organization would be the sole world wide distributor for Mosrite products. The Ventures set up Moseley with a $75,000 dollar advance, and Moseley set up a new Mosrite factory located at 1500 P Street, Bakersfield, California.

Mosrite was a success right from the start and before long they had leased another building down the street at 1424 P Street. Mosrite was building about 300 Venture model guitars a month and employed around 100 people.

In 1963, Mosrite acquired the Dobro Company and started assembling Dobro's out of the acquired stock of parts left over at the Dobro factory in Gardena, California. There were enough parts to make 150 or so complete instruments before Mosrite started to manufacture the Dobro parts. The later-built Bakersfield Dobros can be easily identified by their serial number location that is stamped into the end of the fingerboard like the rest of Mosrite's guitars.

Throughout the 1960s Mosrite's instrument line came to include many new models including the Ventures 12 string, the hollow body Celebrity series guitars and basses, the Ventures bass, available with one or two pickups, the Combo models which had a body that was made by hollowing out the back of a solid piece of walnut and then attaching a back (similar to some Rickenbacker bodies), the Joe Maphis model, which was similar to the Combo, but without a "F" hole, and was available in 12 string and bass versions, the Joe Maphis double neck which looked like a Ventures model with 6 and 12 string necks. The D-100 which was kind of across between a Celebrity guitar and a Dobro, and the Ventures II model, with the neck set further into the body giving the illusion of a shorter scale.

During the second half of the 1960s the Ventures had an independent company design a line of amplifiers and fuzz pedals for which they paid Moseley $5,000 dollars to use the Mosrite name. These amps proved to be the beginning of the end of the association of Mosrite and the Ventures organization. While the fuzz pedals and some of the larger models of amps worked fine, an entry level model featured an alarmingly high rate of failure and in covering for the defective amps the Ventures organization used up their line of credit and the bank shut down the organization. In doing so, Mosrite distribution was also shut down. Mosrite used Vox for a distributor for less than a year until Vox shut down.

During the 1970s and 1980s Moseley built Mosrite guitars sporadically and between building guitars he would return to the gospel music circuit. Final production was located in a converted Wal-Mart building located in Booneville, Arkansas, where Semie Moseley produced Mosrite model guitars under the company called the Unified Sound Association.

Semie Moseley passed away in 1992 and in 1994 Unified Sound Association, which remained open under the direction of Loretta Moseley, closed its doors.

Late 1960s Mosrite Celebrity. SN: KO353. $600. *Courtesy of Johnny's Guitars.*

1960s Mosrite Ventures Mark V. SN: B1025. $900. *Courtesy of Chris' Guitars.*

Mid-1960s Mosrite D-100. SN: D00081. $700. *Courtesy of Blue Note Guitars.*

1976 Mosrite Brass Rail. *Courtesy of Ken Kurosawa.*

Mosrite Joe Maphis Model. SN: 2J338. $1700. *Courtesy of Mimosa Music, Nashville, Tennessee.*

Mosrite Celebrity. 12-string. SN: W 0019. $500. *Courtesy of Palmetto Music.*

1967 Mosrite Strawberry Alarm Clock. *Courtesy of The Chinery Collection.*

1980 Mosrite Custom. *Courtesy of The Chinery Collection.*

1967 Mosrite, The Ventures Bass. SN: B0276. $1600.

1970 Mosrite Mark I Bass.
SN: B0180. $1200

1966 Mosrite Joe Maphis Bass.
$850. *Courtesy of Mimosa Music.*

Music Man

Ernie Ball Music Man. EVH. SN: 87767. $2000. *Courtesy of Cranford Guitar & Music Center.*

In 1972 ex-Fender executives Tom Walker and Forrest White founded Music Man in Orange County, California. White, once Fender's Vice-President, and Walker, a chief salesman for Fender, recruited many ex-Fender employees to come and work at Music Man.

Music Man's initial product offering was a line of successful hybrid tube and solid-state amplifiers that were rugged, well built, good sounding units. It wouldn't be until 1976 that Music Man would offer a guitar for sale.

In 1974 Leo Fender and George Fullerton, Leo's right hand man throughout their days at Fender, started to construct the facility that would house their next business venture, CLF Research. Due to a ten year (1965-1975) non-competition clause arising from the sale of Fender to CBS in late 1964, it was not possible to produce and sell guitars until 1975. In 1976 George Fullerton was made Vice President of CLF Research. That same year CLF concluded an exclusive agreement with Forrest White and Tom Walker to produce guitars for Music Man.

1991 Ernie Ball Music Man. EVH. SN: 80230. 30th one made. $2500. *Courtesy of Frank Palmisano.*

1996 Music Man 20th Anniversary Stingray Bass. *Courtesy of John J. Slog/ www.guitar-villa.com.*

The first model produced was called the Stingray I and it featured "Strat" styling with two humbucking pick-ups and an internal preamp. A bass version, also called the Stingray, was debuted at the same time; this popular instrument is still in production. Early versions of this bass featured a string-thru-the-body bridge, while current models do not. Other early CLF-made Music Man guitars included the Sabre guitar and bass models.

In 1978 the Music Man Company repeatedly made efforts to buy the CLF Research factory, but Leo and George repeatedly turned them down. Frustrated over the situation, Music Man started to decrease their orders for the CLF-built instruments. Late in 1979 CLF stopped producing the Music Man instruments altogether, and concentrated on new designs for Fender's final company, G&L (George and Leo).

In 1984 Ernie Ball, who was most noted for his guitar strings and the Earthwood acoustic bass, purchased the design rights and trademarks of Music Man and set up a production facility in the old Earthwood factory. Production for current model Ernie Ball/Music Man instruments remain at this location. The first Music Man instruments that Ernie Ball produced were the ever-popular Stingray basses. Throughout Ernie Ball's Music Man production many new, quality models of guitars and basses have been added to their catalog. All of the models share the unique asymmetrical tuner arrangements (4 + 2 for guitars and 3 + 1 for basses) on their headstocks.

There have been artist-endorsed models starting with a Eddie Van Halen model. Others included the Steve Morse, Albert Lee, and the Luke (designed for Steve Lukather) models. Other guitar models are the Axis, which replaced the Eddie Van Halen model after the end of his endorsement contract in 1995, and the Silhouette.

Other bass models that joined the Stingray are the Stingray 5, a five-string version, the Sterling, the Silhouette bass, and a rehashed Sabre model that was produced from 1988 until 1991. Celebrating Music Man's 20th Anniversary, Ernie Ball produced a special edition Stingray bass in 1996. The 20th Anniversary Stingray featured a highly figured maple top and the production run was limited to 2000 examples.

CLF Research- or pre-Ernie Ball-made instruments have production dates on the butt of the neck, where it bolts to the body. Neck removal is necessary to view this number. The serial numbers which are assigned to these instruments show no indication of the date of manufacture.

Ernie Ball-made instruments use a serial numbering system in that the first two digits of the number indicate the year of manufacture. Models that do not conform to this format are the 20th Anniversary editions of the Stingray bass (produced only in 1996) and the Eddie Van Halen model guitars (produced from 1991 to 1995).

National

1967 National Belaire. SN: X77883. *Courtesy of Darryl Agler.*

National Resoglass. Single pickup. SN: G25382. $450. *Courtesy of Blue Note.*

National was founded in late 1925 by brothers John, Rudolph, Robert, Emil Dopyera, and a few associates, including George Beauchamp, Paul Barth, and Ted Keinmeyer. Prior to National, John and Rudolph had been building banjos and repairing instruments in a small shop in Orange County, California. John met Beauchamp when he came into the shop in search of someone to build him a guitar with an amplifying system. It took him about six weeks to come up with an Amplifonic resonator guitar. Paul Barth spun the resonator cones. Financial backing came from Ted Keinmeyer, a wealthy distant cousin to Beauchamp. They located in Los Angeles where they hired tool and die maker Adolph Rickenbacker to make the dies for the metal guitar. Full production, with 30 employees, soon saw them producing about 50 resonator guitars a day.

In 1928 John Dopyera left National to form the Dobro Company. These instruments used a single resonator that resembled an aluminum speaker cone instead of National's three cone layout. National also came out with a single resonator style instrument with a resonator that looked like a reversed Dobro with a biscuit bridge at the peak of the cone. The Style O and the Triolian were offered in this style. National relocated to a new factory near Rickenbacker's shop and purchased new manufacturing equipment for him. In return Rickenbacker purchased 13 shares of stock in National and became the company engineer.

By the end of the 1920s George Beauchamp had successfully designed an electromagnetic pickup for stringed instrument amplification. His experiments led him to design a unit that utilized two horseshoe shaped magnets that surrounded the strings and the wire coil form which also housed magnet poles for each individual string. When National's other board members balked at the idea, Beauchamp, Rickenbacker, and others formed the Ro-Pat-In Corporation. This new company, founded October 15, 1931, set up a factory next to the Rickenbacker facility and exclusively manufactured electric guitars.

In 1932 the Dobro Company merged with National and National-Dobro marketed their first electric model. It was based on a 12 fret Dobro Model 37G, and, except for its volume knobs and output jack, looked identical to its acoustic brother. This guitar had an amplifier with a speaker cover matching the guitar's resonator cover. Commercially unsuccessful, only a few were built. National-Dobro revamped the electric model in 1933, calling it the Dobro All-Electric. The guitar featured a 14 fret neck joint and solid metal cover plate with lightning bolts etched into it. This model also proved unpopular.

In 1935, they reentered the electric market. Following Rickenbacker's success with the aluminum Hawaiian models, National-Dobro marketed electric models of aluminum lap steels, mandolins, and Spanish-style guitars under the National, Dobro, and Supro brands. In 1936 National-Dobro opened a Chicago office to better serve their association with Regal who had marketed the Resophonic guitars with Dobro parts since 1932. Regal had supplied bodies and necks for National-Dobro electric Spanish-style guitars since 1935, and acquired exclusive rights to manufacture and market Dobro model resonator guitars in 1937. Early National archtop electric models included the Electric Spanish and New Yorker models. These featured bodies and necks supplied by Regal and the dual blade pickup that was used on all of National-Dobro's 1930s and early 1940s electric instruments.

CMI (Chicago Musical Instruments Co.) became National's exclusive distributor in 1941, and National-Dobro moved its entire operation to Chicago. In 1943 Victor Smith, Al Frost, and Louis Dopyera bought out National-Dobro and reorganized it under the Valco name. They continued the production of the National, Dobro, and Supro models, and also built guitars for Sears, Montgomery Ward, Spiegel, and other mail order houses. In 1944 CMI became the exclusive distributor for the Dobro brand. Through the 1950s Valco made many models of archtop electric guitars most with bodies coming from outside sources including Kay, Harmony, Regal, and even Gibson. Some models include the Supro El Capitan, the National New Yorker, the National Sonora , the National Model 1155 electric flat-top, the National Club Combo, the National Debonaire Custom, and the National Bel-Aire. In 1948 Victor Smith retired, resonator production was nearly at a halt, and Valco's production centered mostly around electrically amplified instruments.

In 1952 Valco produced its first solid body models. National models included the Glenwood with diamond-in-block neck inlays, "Les Paul" shaped body, two pickups, and Bigsby vibrato. They also produced the Town and Country with parallelogram inlays and two pickups, the Avalon with two pickups, the Bolero with a single pickup, and the Model 1102 Stylist with a single cut-away body equipped with two pickups and block neck inlays.

In 1962 Valco introduced fiberglass as a new body material for some lines. Called Res-O-Glas, the bodies were constructed in two halves and laminated together with plastic edge binding. National's Res-O-Glas models included two map-shaped styles, each available in three different trims. Models included the Glenwood 98 with diamond-in-block inlays, two standard pickups, and a bridge mounted pickup, the Glenwood 95 without the bridge mounted pickup, the Newport 88 with quarter circle neck inlays, two standard and a bridge mounted pickups, the Newport 84 with a standard and a bridge pickkup, the Newport 82 with a standard pickup, and the Newport 85 bass. A single cut-away budget Res-O-Glas model called the Studio 66 was made in the early 1960s. A wood map-shaped model called the Westwood series, included the 77 with block neck inlays, two standard pickups, and a bridge mounted pickup, the 75 with one less standard pickup, and 72 with only one standard pickup. By 1965 the Westwood series was out of production, and production ceased on the Res-O-Glas models. By 1970 Valco was out of business. Its trademark was acquired by the Chicago-based Strum 'n Drum company and applied to a line of imported instruments.

Aside from National's original resonator model guitars, it is the fancier Res-O-Glas models that attract the most attention from collectors.

Ovation

Born in 1919 in Washington, D.C., Charles Huron Kaman was the son of a construction supervisor. Charles took up guitar playing at a young age, being taught by his father. By the time he was in high school he was playing with a local radio station group, WJSV's Originality Boys. In 1937 he turned down a spot in Tommy Dorsey's band, which offered a salary of $90 per week, and, instead, attended Catholic University in Washington. He graduated in 1940 with a degree in aeronautics. His first job was with United Aircraft designing helicopter rotor blades. In 1945 Kaman struck out on his own, founding the Kaman Corporation, which has since grown to a conglomerate of nearly 30 different companies.

Being a guitarist, Kaman wanted to get into the music industry and, after being turned down in his attempt to purchase Harmony and Martin, he decided to start from scratch. Development on Ovation's now classic bowl back design began in 1964. Kaman employee Jim Rickard's prewar Martin D-45 was used as a guide for tone tests. Along with John Ringso and Kaman the synthetic parabolic body shell was developed using technology that had been acquired from the company's helicopter rotor blade work.

The first guitar prototypes and initial production took place in the rotor blade plant in Bloomfield, Connecticut.

Still needing a name for these early guitars, Kaman turned to a local folksinging group call The Balladeers, which had purchased some of the earliest production. The group earned a standing ovation at the Eastern States Exposition, a large state fair, where they had performed using the guitars. About two weeks later Kaman decided to call the company Ovation and their initial offering the Balladeer.

In February, 1967, Kaman moved Ovation to an old textile mill located in New Hartford, Connecticut. Early on Glen Campbell endorsed Ovation's bowl back guitars and did much to give the company a legitimate image in the acoustic field. Other early endorsements came from Charlie Byrd and Josh White.

In 1968 Ovation introduced its first electric guitar and bass models. Based loosely on Gibson's semisolid ES-335 style guitars, the series of instruments, which were called the Electric Storm models, included the Thunderhead (1968-1972), the twelve string Hurricane (1968-1969), the Tornado (1968-1973), the Eclipse (1970-1973), and the Typhoon bass models (1968-1972).

In 1971 Ovation would enter into the solid body segment of the market with the radically shaped Breadwinner (1971-1979). This model featured active electronics with an onboard FET preamp, making it one of the first commercially available production guitars to be so equipped.

In 1972 Ovation would debut a fancier version called the Deacon (1972-1980). Other solid body electrics marketed by Ovation in the 1970s were the Viper (1975-1983), the Preacher (1975-1978), the Deacon twelve string (1976-1980), and the Magnum series of basses (1974-1983).

In 1980 Ovation experimented with an alternative body material on the UK II (1980-1983). The UK II (UK stood for Ultra Kaman) featured a body core of aluminum covered with Urelite, a type of urethane.

In 1984 they marketed an imported line guitars called the Hardbody series. It featured domestically made pickups, German hardware, and Korean bodies and necks. In 1988 Kaman acquired the Hamer Company, moving Kaman into successful solid body guitar production.

Ovation's domestically made electric guitar models, like Martins, were never considered a huge commercial success and both companies now focus on acoustic models only.

1976 Ovation Deacon 12 string. SN: 5939. $700.

Ovation Serial Numbers

Ovations Electric Guitars and Basses have serial numbers starting with a letter. Models made from 1970 to 1973 begin with an H, I, J, or L. Guitars from 1973 to 1981 begin with an E, and basses from 1974 to 1979 begin with a B.
The following list which contains Ovations entire production, acoustic and electric, is courtesy of The Kaman Music Corporation and was researched and compiled by Paul Bechtoldt.

1966: Red 3 digit number	006-319
1967 (Feb-Nov): Red 3 digit number	320-999
1967 (Nov)- 1968 (July): Black 4 digit number	1000-
1968 (July-Nov): Letter A prefix plus 3 digit number	
1968 (Nov)-1969 (Feb): Letter B prefix plus 3 digit number	
1968 (July)-1970 (Feb): Serial number with a For G prefix	
1969 (Feb-Sept): Letter C prefix plus 3 digit number	
1969 (Sept)-1970 (Feb): Letter D prefix plus 3 digit number	
1970 (Feb)-1972 (May): 5 digit serial number	
1970-1973 Electric Storm model	
Number with a H, I, or L prefix	
1972 (May-Dec)	000001-007000
1973	007001-020000
1973 (Jan)-1975 (Feb): Solid electrics	E prefix plus 4 digit number
1974	020001-039000
1974-1979: Magnum Electric Bass Letter B prefix plus 5 digit number	
1975	039001-067000
1975 (Feb)-1980: Solid Electrics	Letter E prefix plus 5 digit number
1976	067001-086000
1977 (Jan-Sept)	086001-103000
1977 (Sept)-1978 (April)	103001-126000
1978 (April-Dec)	126001-157000
1979	157001-203000
1980	211011-214933
Late 1980-1981: (UK II Electrics) Letter E prefix plus 6 digit number	
1981	214934-263633
1982	263634-291456
1983	291457-302669
1984 (Elite Models Only)	302670-303319
1984 (May-Dec): (Balladeer Models Only)	315001-339187
1985-1986	303320-356000
1987	357000-367999
1988	368000-382106
1989	382107-392900
1990	403760-420400
1990	421000-430680
1991	400001-403676
1991	430681-446000
1992	402700-406000
1992	446001-457810
1993	457811-470769
1994	470770-484400
1995	484401-501470

The following serialization is for Ovation's Adamas model only.

1977	0077-0099	1987	4284-4427
1978	0100-0608	1988	4428-4696
1979	0609-1058	1989	4697-4974
1980	1059-1670	1990	4975-5541
1981	1671-2668	1991	5542-6278
1982	2669-3242	1992	6279-7088
1983	3243-3859	1993	7089-8159
1984	3860-4109	1994	8160-9778
1985	4110-4251	1995	9779-11213
1986	4252-4283		

1980 Ovation Preacher. SN: E17768. $350. *Courtesy of Johnny's Guitars.*

1972 Ovation Typhoon. SN: H341. $400. *Courtesy of Jim Heflybower.*

Paul Reed Smith

In the mid 1970s Paul Reed Smith constructed his first guitar for a music class while attending college. By combining his prowess around the wood shop with a musical background he earned an "A" for the project. After school Smith began building and repairing guitars out of his home and, later, out of a small shop. Throughout this period his instruments were constantly evolving to what would eventually be the classic Paul Reed Smith guitar. By 1982 the guitar design that would bring him recognition in the electric guitar world was completed and by 1985 the original factory in Annapolis, Maryland was opened.

The Paul Reed Smith guitar embodied old world craftsmanship with the highest quality materials to create a modern guitar design that took the world by storm. Early users of the Paul Reed Smith guitars were Carlos Santana, who would eventually get his own signature model, and Ted Nugent. By the late 1980s Paul Reed Smith's guitars had become second to none by bringing a new level of excellence to the world of guitar manufacture. They consistently used an outrageously figured maple on the tops of the instruments. They produced many limited runs of certain models featuring exquisite neck inlays. Every model featured perfectly applied finishes. These factors combine with the terrific playability and ergonomics of the guitar's basic design to make these stunning instruments some of the most sought after modern guitars today.

In 1996 Paul Reed Smith completed the move to a new, much larger factory located in Stevensville, Maryland. Here Paul Reed Smith guitars continue to evolve with the addition of new designs, like the McCarty models and hollow body models, while retaining all of the qualities that have brought this company to the forefront of modern guitar manufactorers.

1994 PRS Dragon III. SN: 4 19555.
Courtesy of Ed Roman Guitars.

1993 Paul Reed Smith Custom 24 in whale blue finish.SN: 315918. $1,600.

1994 PRS Dragon III. SN: 4019812. $20,000. *Courtesy of Garrett Park Guitars.*

1993 PRS Dragon II. SN: 3 17170. $20,000. *Courtesy of Ed Roman Guitars.*

1997 PRS McCarty SN: 7 34505. $1800. *Courtesy of John SanGiacomo.*

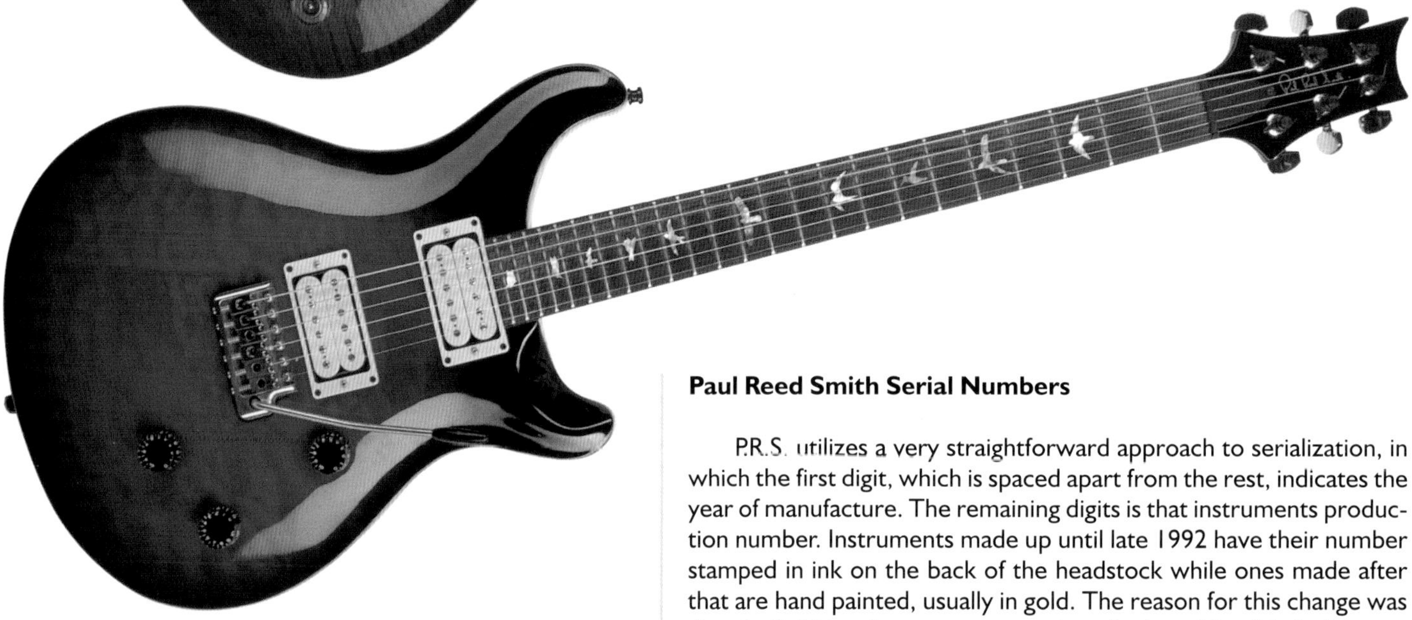

1990 PRS Custom 24. SN: 0 7997. $1595. *Courtesy of John SanGiacomo.*

Paul Reed Smith Serial Numbers

P.R.S. utilizes a very straightforward approach to serialization, in which the first digit, which is spaced apart from the rest, indicates the year of manufacture. The remaining digits is that instruments production number. Instruments made up until late 1992 have their number stamped in ink on the back of the headstock while ones made after that are hand painted, usually in gold. The reason for this change was that the finishing department sometimes had trouble with the ink running or bleeding!

Examples
6 1635 Inkstamped - 1986 Custom, 1635 instrument made
3 15918 - 1993 Custom 24, 15918 instrument made
6 29052 - 1996 Rosewood Ltd. 29,052 instrument made

1997 Paul Reed Smith McCarty Gold Top model. SN: 7 29939. $1,400.

1998 PRS Private Stock Custom Order. 24K gold inlays SN: 8 36358. $20,000. *Courtesy of Garrett Park Guitars.*

1996 PRS Rosewood Limited. SN: 6 29052. $8500 *Courtesy of Garrett Park Guitars.*

1977 PRS Bass. The first bass made by Paul for Peter Frampton's bass player.

Peavey

Hartley Peavey was raised in Meridian, Mississippi where, as a youth, he repaired record players for his father's music store. By high school he was building guitar amps for his peers. His reputation and the demand for his amplifiers grew to the point where Hartley decided to put off college and start his own business. Peavey Electronics was born in 1965 in the basement of Hartley's parent's house. Peavey saw a greater need for sound reinforcement equipment than for guitar and bass amps and concentrated his production on that.

In 1968 Peavey built a small factory and hired his first employee to satisfy the demand for his products. Throughout the 1970s Peavey established a reputation for offering high quality, reasonably priced equipment and his Meridian, Mississippi company grew exceptionally throughout the decade. As the company grew, so did the models of guitar and bass amps, as well as P.A. equipment.

In 1977 Peavey decided to expand its business into the instrument market. A bass, the T40, and a guitar, the T60, were built under the leadership of Chip Todd (the "T" in the instruments name from Todd's last name) and were debuted at the 1978 NAMM show. The guitars featured unique wiring so that as the tone control was rolled off the pickups would change from single coil to double coil mode. The guitars also featured the industry's first automated construction techniques. This allowed Peavey to market a high quality instrument at an exceptional price.

Throughout the 1980s Peavey's guitar line expanded and took on many new shapes. Peavey soon sought the endorsements of some guitar playing heavy hitters and this resulted in guitars such as the Adrian Vandenberg model. Peavey's latest foray into the endorsement field is with the legendary Edward Van Halen with whom Peavey was already making the 5150 line of guitar amps. The Peavey Wolfgang, named after Eddie's son, is Peavey's latest guitar. Designed by Van Halen, this instrument should carry on Peavey's proud tradition of offering high quality, USA built products with exceptional value.

1979 Peavey T-60. SN: 00656016. $400.

Late 1980s Peavey Vandberg. SN: 0005274. $750. *Courtesy of Guitars Rescue Society.*

1998 Peavy Wolfgang. SN: 91004841. $1200. *Courtesy of Guitar Haven.*

Premier

Premier was the brand name of guitars marketed from the 1950s to the mid 1970s by the Sorkin Music Company of Hauppage, New York. Early models were made by The Multivox Company of New York and the solid body models featured a scrolled upper horn and a bolt-on neck. By the mid 1960s Premier guitars started featuring imported parts and by the 1970s the guitars were completely imported.

c. 1950s Premier Archtop. SN: 2983. $450. *Courtesy of Rumble Seat Music.*

When Sorkin went out of business in the mid 1970s, The Multivox Company took over the Premier guitar line as well as the distributorship of Höfner Instruments from them. Currently, both Premier and Höfner are distributed by Entertainment Music Marketing Corporation of Deer Park, New York. Premier guitars are currently entry level instruments made in Korea.

Rickenbacker

1957 Rickenbacker 365. Prototype.

1960 Rickenbacker 375F. One of three made.

Adolph Rickenbacker was born in Switzerland in 1892 and immigrated to the United States as a young child in 1918. He moved to Los Angeles, California where in 1925 he founded the Rickenbacker Manufacturing Company, a tool and die business. Adolph Rickenbacker changed the spelling of his name replacing the "H" with a "K" to take advantage of the association of World War I Flying Ace, Eddie Rickenbacker.

It is Rickenbacker's company that was hired by the National's founders, and during the late 1920s he was completing experiments on the idea of an electrically amplified guitar. He had successfully designed an electromagnetic pickup, which incorporated two horseshoe magnets that surrounded a coil that housed six individual pole pieces, one for each string. This pickup is the granddaddy of all modern pickup designs. Unfortunately, the rest of National's principles were not as enthusiastic about the idea of an electrically amplified guitar as Beauchamp was, and he was finally ousted from the Company in November, 1931, due to conflicts of interest after Adolph Rickenbacker and he formed the Ro-Pat-In Company, a month earlier to produce electric guitars exclusively.

1979 Rickenbacker Model 4080. SN: SC1399. *Courtesy of Dean from Plasma.*

The first product was an aluminum electric Hawaiian model that had a small round body that earned it the nick name "Frying Pan". About a dozen of these Frying Pans were built that were based on a wood bodied prototype.

A Spanish hollow body was also available. Built with a harmony supplied archtop body and neck. It also utilized the horseshoe magnetic pickup that would become a company Hallmark. Very few of these guitars were built.

In 1934, the Company changed their name to the Electro String Instrument Corporation and the instruments were marketed as Rickenbacker Electro models, compared to the previous name of only Electro. A curious note is that on all early Rickenbacker labeled instruments the name for an unknown reason is spelled with a "H" instead of a "K".

In the mid 1930s Rickenbacker marketed a Spanish version of their model, Bakelite lap steel called the Electro Spanish. This model was available with an optional vibrato system designed by Doc Kauffman, who would later be teamed up with Leo Fender with their K& F Company of the mid 1940s.

In 1937, a motorized Vibrato version was offered that was called the Rickenbacker Vibrota Spanish. Both of these guitars could be considered one of the world's first solid body electric Spanish guitars.

Through out the rest of the 1930s and up until the U.S. involvement in World War II most of Rickenbackers production was in the Hawaiian or lap steel segment of the market, while the Spanish models offered were based on archtop designs, with bodies supplied by other manufacturers.

In December of 1953 Francis C. Hall, the founder of the Radio-Tel-Electronics Company and one of Fenders early distributors purchased the company from Rickenbacker. Under his leadership the Company produced the sleek electric guitars and basses that it became famous for. Throughout the rest of the 1950s and 1960s Rickenbacker introduced many influential models and many of these utilized the horseshoe style pickup.

1990 Rickenbacker 325 3/4 scale. SN: TF2442. $900. *Courtesy of Brockton Music Works, Inc.*

Rickenbacker popularized the neck through body construction technique that would be featured on almost all of their models and in 1957 a new under the string pickup brought the company up to modern standards.

In the 1960s Rickenbacker's popularity mushroomed with their association with the Beatles and throughout the decade they garnered a strong loyal following.

In 1965 Hall reorganized the company keeping the Electro name for the manufacturing part of the business and naming the sales and distribution part Rickenbacker, Inc.

By 1970 Rickenbacker stopped making the lap steel style guitars that their company had been founded on, and concentrated on their booming electric Spanish model production.

In 1984 Francis C. Hall's son, John, purchased both Rickenbacker Incorporated and electro string instrument corporation from his father and formed Rickenbacker International Corporation by combining both interests.

Rickenbacker continues to produce guitars in southern California where they have been made since the inception of the Company, and current production includes both reissues of classic models as well as fresh new designs.

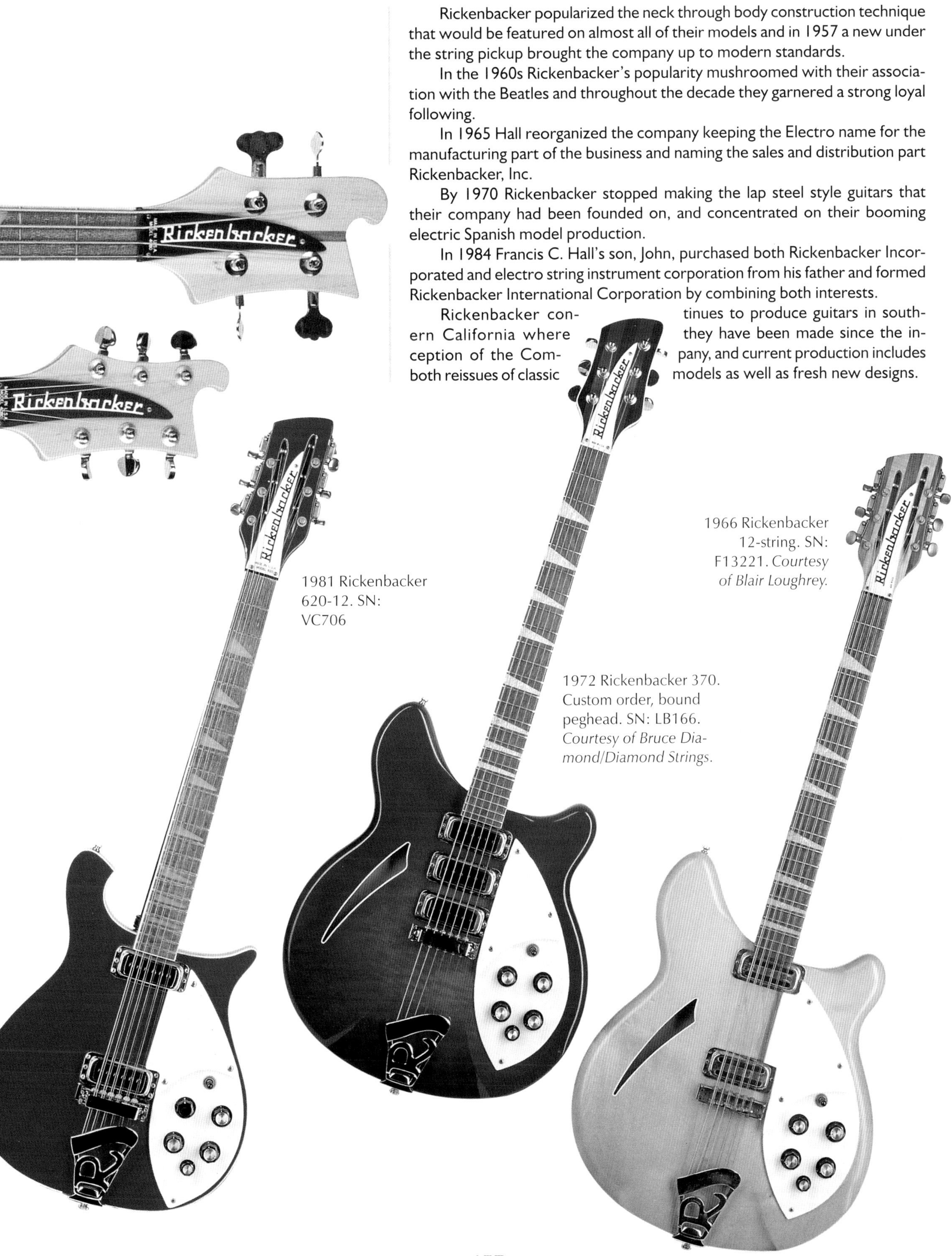

1981 Rickenbacker 620-12. SN: VC706

1966 Rickenbacker 12-string. SN: F13221. *Courtesy of Blair Loughrey.*

1972 Rickenbacker 370. Custom order, bound peghead. SN: LB166. *Courtesy of Bruce Diamond/Diamond Strings.*

1978 Rickenbacker 320. SN: SF 2800. $700. *Courtesy of Neil's Guitars.*

1965 Rickenbacker 360-120S. SN: EH 539. $8000. *Courtesy of Mark Hoover, Guitars Plus.*

1967 Rickenbacker Model 370. $1800. *Courtesy of Palmetto Music.*

Rickenbacker Serial Numbers

Numbers on instruments produced from 1931 to 1953 give no indication of production. Instruments produced from 1954 to 1961 utilize four to seven digit numbers. The number that immediately follows the letter in the serial number indicates the year of manufacture. From 1961 to 1986 serial numbers used a two letter prefix. The first letter (A to Z) indicates the year and the second letter (A to L) indicates the month (Jan-Dec).

1961	A	1974	N
1962	B	1975	O
1963	C	1976	P
1964	D	1977	Q
1965	E	1978	R
1966	F	1979	S
1967	G	1980	T
1968	H	1981	U
1969	I	1982	V
1970	J	1983	W
1971	K	1984	X
1972	L	1985	Y
1973	M	1986	Z

Examples:
R9143 1959 4000 Bass
OD19121975 480 model produced in April

From 1987 to 1996 the numbering sequence was changed so that there was only one letter prefix in the number. This letter (A-L) indicated the month, while the following digit indicated the year.

1987	0	1992	5
1988	1	1993	6
1989	2	1994	7
1990	3	1995	8
1991	4	1996	9

Example:
BG9189 1993 Tom Petty Signature Edition manufactured in February

1965 Rickenbacker. SN: EB202. $1500. *Courtesy of Pittsburgh Guitars.*

1975 Rickenbacker 480. SN: OD1912. $550. *Courtesy of Pittsburgh Guitars.*

1993 Rickenbacker Tom Petty Signature Guitar, Jetglo. S/N B69189. $1400. *Courtesy of Mark Hoover, Guitars Plus.*

1980s Rickenbacker 4003S Bass. S/N 126680. $800. *Courtesy of Blue Note Guitars.*

1996 Rickenbacker V-64 12 String. S/N H95903. $1300. *Courtesy of Mark Hoover, Guitars Plus.*

1960 Rickenbacker Model 4000 Bass. $4000 *Courtesy of John J. Slog/www.guitar-villa.com.*

Robin

Robin guitars have been built in Houston, Texas since 1982 by company founder David Wintz. In 1972 Wintz and an associate opened a guitar shop in Houston that specialized in the repair and restoration of vintage guitars. This led to the building of complete instruments that often used certain qualities of vintage models in a modern interpretation. Parallels can be seen between Robin's Machete model and Gibson's Fire Bird, Robin's Savoy and Avalon models and Gibson's Les Pauls, and Robin's Flying Wedge to Gibson's original Korina-styled instruments. Robin's guitars are of very high quality and just about anything or any option can be ordered from them.

1996 Robin Flying Wedge. S/N 960053. $1600. *Courtesy of Coleman Music.*

Schon

In the mid 1980s Neal Schon, the guitarist for the rock band Journey, designed and financed the production of his own signature guitar. Built by the Charvel/Jackson Company of California, these guitars embodied Schon's unique single cut-away design with Jackson's high end neck-through body construction. Every Schon guitar that I have seen was built in 1986, again proving that even though it was a very solidly built instrument, its controversial styling caused it to be commercially unsuccessful.

1986 Schon NS1, Neil Schon. #NS60081. $600. *Courtesy of Nationwide Guitars.*

S.D. Curlee

Randy Curlee was the owner of a Chicago area music store during the early to mid 1970s. During this time he saw the need for a high quality, no-frills instrument that was reasonably priced. From 1975 until 1982 he produced guitar and bass models which featured rock maple necks that extended into the mahogany body all the way back to the bridge. The hardware used was made out of brass, including the nut, to supposedly increase the sustain. The pickups were by DiMarzio, and the tuners by Schaller. These well made oil finished instruments sold new for less than half the price of their contemporaries, and in today's market they still can be had at very reasonable prices.

Randy Curlee also imported versions of his instruments in order to fend off unlicensed copying, which was so prevalent in the late 1970s. These instruments will usually be labeled as S.D. Curlee Design Series, Aspen, or S.D. Curlee International models. These instruments are worth considerably less than their American made counterparts.

S.D. Curlee 1977 Guitar. *$450. Courtesy of Joeís Guitars, Langhorn, Pennsylvania*

Silvertone

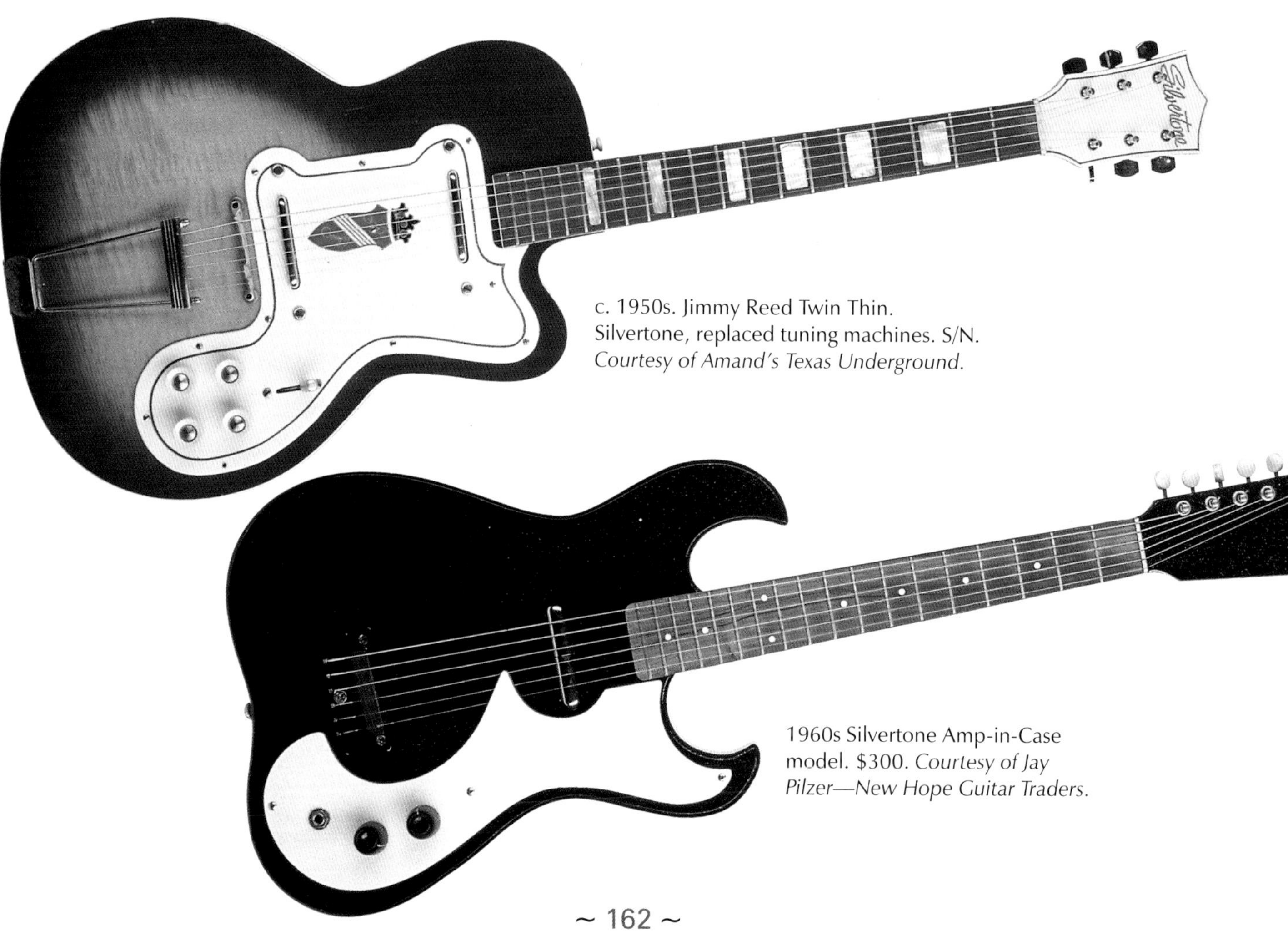

c. 1950s. Jimmy Reed Twin Thin. Silvertone, replaced tuning machines. S/N. *Courtesy of Amand's Texas Underground.*

1960s Silvertone Amp-in-Case model. $300. *Courtesy of Jay Pilzer—New Hope Guitar Traders.*

Late 1950s Silvertone U-1. $400.

1959 Silvertone U-1. $400. *Courtesy of Rumble Seat Music.*

1960s Silvertone. Amp in case model. $500 with case. *Courtesy of Garret Park Guitars.*

Silvertone is the trademark name owned and used by Sears since the late 1930s. The name was used on guitars as well as amplifiers and radios marketed by Sears. Silvertone instruments were built by Kay, Harmony, Valco, Danelectro, and Teisco. None were built by Sears although they did own Harmony from 1916 to 1940.

Today the Danelectro-made models, easy to distinguish with the "Lipstick" tube pickups, are usually the ones that collectors prefer, and a clean two pickup amp-in-case model can bring as much as $600. Values on the models made by the other manufacturers depend on how fancy and unique the instrument is, as well as how well it plays and sounds, and prices usually range from under $100. to about $500.

Guitars built from the early 1970s and later were of cheap Asian construction and have no value to collectors.

Steiberger

1990 Steinberger Custom Koa. $3000. *Courtesy of Ed Roman.*

1991 Steinberger Guitar. Custom Maple Top by Ed Roman. S/N 2920. $2000. *Courtesy of Ed Roman Guitars.*

1980s Steinberger XP-2 bass. $700.

During the early 1970s Ned Steinberger was a sculpture major at the Maryland College of Art. After graduating, he moved to New York, where he began work as a cabinet maker and furniture designer. By 1975 Steinberger moved to a woodworker's co-op in Brooklyn, New York, where he met guitar and bass luthier Stuart Spector. During 1976 Steinberger collaborated with Spector on the design of Spector's NS-1 bass and the follow-up NS-2 model (NS stood for Ned Steinberger, and the number refers to pickup quantity). In the early part of 1978 Steinberger had built his first prototype headless bass guitar, constructed entirely of wood. Steinberger was not completely satisfied with the finished product. The instrument showed promise, but displayed dead spots on the fingerboard due to sympathetic vibrations in the neck. He solved the problem by coating the entire instrument in a layer of fiberglass, which also increased the sustain and improved the tone of the instrument. Throughout 1978 he continued his experiments with resins and reinforcing fibers of glass and carbon.

In 1979 Steinberger built another bass, this one almost entirely of carbon graphite. He displayed it at some music trade shows, where he had hoped to sell the design to an existing manufacturer. No buyer was found, so, in 1980, Steiberger took on partners Robert Young, a plastics engineer, Hap Kuffner, and Stan Jay of Mandolin Brothers, a large New York based vintage and new musical instrument dealer, and founded the Steinberger Sound Corporation.

The Steinberger Bass was debuted at the 1980 NAMM show and at the Musicmesse in Frankfurt, Germany. Throughout the 1980s Steinberger's headless guitar and bass designs became huge successes, defining the look of many of the pop bands of the era.

In 1986 Ned Steinberger agreed to sell his company to Gibson and by 1990 the takeover was complete. Steinberger has been run as an independent company owned by Gibson and Ned Steinberger has stayed on with the company as a design consultant.

Supro

The Supro line of guitars was manufactured and marketed by the Valco Company of Chicago from 1935 until 1967 as their budget model line.

The first electric models were lap steels and hollow bodies followed in 1952 by solid wood bodied electrics. In 1962 Valco introduced fiberglass bodied Supros, which were produced until 1967 when Kay acquired Valco. Supros were then produced by Kay up until their bankruptcy in 1968.

The Supro trademark was then acquired by the Strum and Drum Company of Chicago, but nothing was ever done with it.

In the early 1980s, Archer's Music of Fresno, California acquired the Supro trademark and some of the original stock with which they produced a limited number of new instruments.

Even though Supros were originally marketed as entry level guitars they are pretty cool, and many of them play and sound really good. Values can range from $200 for the simplest models, up to $700 for some of the more extravagant models in mint condition.

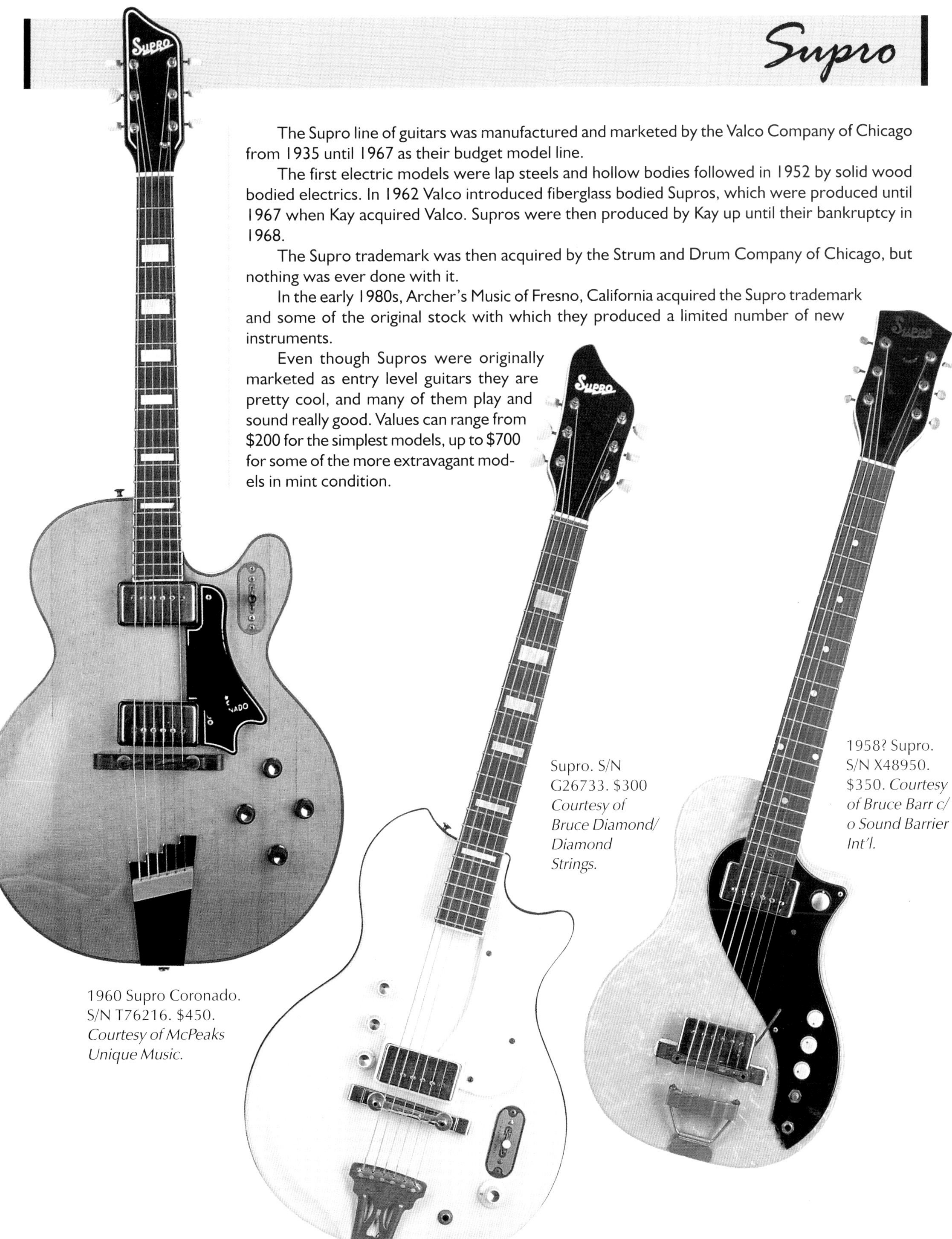

1960 Supro Coronado. S/N T76216. $450. *Courtesy of McPeaks Unique Music.*

Supro. S/N G26733. $300 *Courtesy of Bruce Diamond/ Diamond Strings.*

1958? Supro. S/N X48950. $350. *Courtesy of Bruce Barr c/o Sound Barrier Int'l.*

Teisco

Teisco electric guitars were built in Japan from 1956 until 1967 by the Nippon Onpa Kogyo Co., Ltd. They were imported to the U.S. by Westheimer Musical Instruments under various trademark names, including Teisco, Teisco Del Ray, Kingston, and Swinger.

In 1967 the Kawai Corporation bought the Teisco Company and continued the production of Teisco guitars, which now were sometimes labeled a Kawai.

Teisco guitars have been built in countless styles and designs, and all were entry level quality guitars. Values on these instruments usually range from $50 to $300 depending on the coolness and strangeness factors, but some models like the Spectrum 5, which Kawai has recently re-issued for their domestic Japanese market, can bring upward of up to $1000.

1960s Teisco three pickup model. $250.

1960s Teisco two pickup model in blue metallic with a striped anodized aluminum pickguard. $300.

Tokai

Tokai, the Hamamtsu based company started building electric guitars in the 1960s. These early models used American themes in their original designs, but by the late 1970s the guitars were downright copies, almost to the point of forgeries of American designs. The quality of these instruments was high, higher in fact than the American made models that were being built at that time (this could be argued). But this all came to an end with legal threats and Tokai now makes high quality original and American influenced guitar models.

Tokai Strat copy. $500.
Courtesy of Monkton Guitars.

Universal

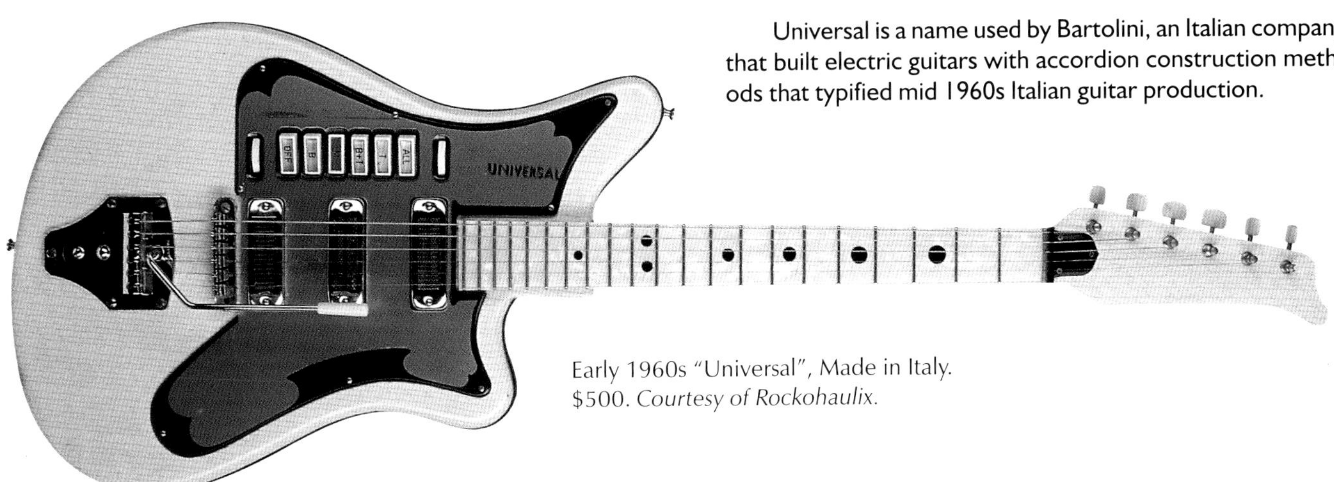

Universal is a name used by Bartolini, an Italian company that built electric guitars with accordion construction methods that typified mid 1960s Italian guitar production.

Early 1960s "Universal", Made in Italy. $500. *Courtesy of Rockohaulix.*

Veillette-Citron

In 1966 two former students of noted flat-top guitar luthier Michael Gurian, Joe Veillette and Harvey Citron, met in college. During the early 1970s they started doing instrument repairs and building experimental guitars. In 1974 they founded Veillette-Citron, and at the 1976 NAMM show, they displayed their prototype models. From that point until the company's demise in 1983, Veillette-Citron handbuilt their exquisite and expensive neck-through body design basses and guitars.

1979 Veillette Citron bass. #73. $1500. *Courtesy of The Bass Place.*

Vox

Tom Jennings was the owner of a music store in Dartford, England during the 1940s. In 1951 Jenning's along with Derek Underdown, produced and marketed the Univox Organ. Jennings Organ Company was formed and the business became a success.

In 1957 Tom Jennings, with longtime friend and electrical engineer Dick Denny, would design a guitar amplifier. This amp, model AC 15, would be marketed under the Vox brand name.

In 1958 Jennings would reincorporate Jennings Organ Company which would now be called Jennings Musical Instruments Ltd. (JMI).

In 1959 JMI followed the 15 watt AC 15 with the AC 30, the company's most famous and desirable model.

In 1961 Vox introduced its first line of electric guitars and a bass model. These models started out as entry level quality instruments, but that soon improved. Models introduced in 1961 included the Ace (1961-1966), Super Ace (1961-1966), Stroller (1961-1966), Consort (1961-1965), Shadow (1961-1965), and Bass Master Electric Bass (1961-1964).

By 1962 Vox instruments were fitted with necks built by the Italian Eko Company and this change made for a much better instrument. Jennings didn't stop there. In his quest to improve on quality, a group of three engineers was assembled that included Bob Pearson (Quality Control), Ken Wilson (Styling), and Mike Bennett (Design Prototypes). This team would be responsible for the design of Vox's original and classic "Tear Drop" shaped Mark series and "coffin" shaped Phantom series guitars. Instruments debuting in 1962 were the Phantom I (1962-1963), Phantom II (1962-1963), Phantom VI (1962-1967), and the Sound Caster (1962-1966).

In 1963 Vox added the Mark VI (1963-1967), and Phantom XII to their guitar line and the Phantom IV Bass (1963-1967) to their bass line.

In 1964 Vox moved the entire guitar production to Italy where most of the models were built by Eko, but a few were produced by the Crucianelli Company. New models for 1964 included the Lynx (1964-1967), Super Lynx Deluxe (1964-1967), Mandoguitar (1964-1966), Mark VI Special (1964-1967), Mark IX (1964-1967), Mark XII I 1964-1967), Lynx Bass (1964-1967), and the Mark IV Bass (1964-1968). During this year Jennings sold a large amount of the stock in his company to the Royston Group in order to gain capital, and later in the year they acquired the remaining shares, and JMI was renamed Vox Sound Ltd.

In 1965 Vox introduced new models which included the Bobcat (1965-1967), Harlem (1965-1966), Mark VI Acoustic (1965-1967), Phantom Guitar Organ (1965-1967), Spitfire VI (1965-1967), Spitfire XII (1965-1967), Hurricane (1965-1967), Tempest XII (1965-1967), Tornado (1965-1967), and the Typhoon (1965-1967).

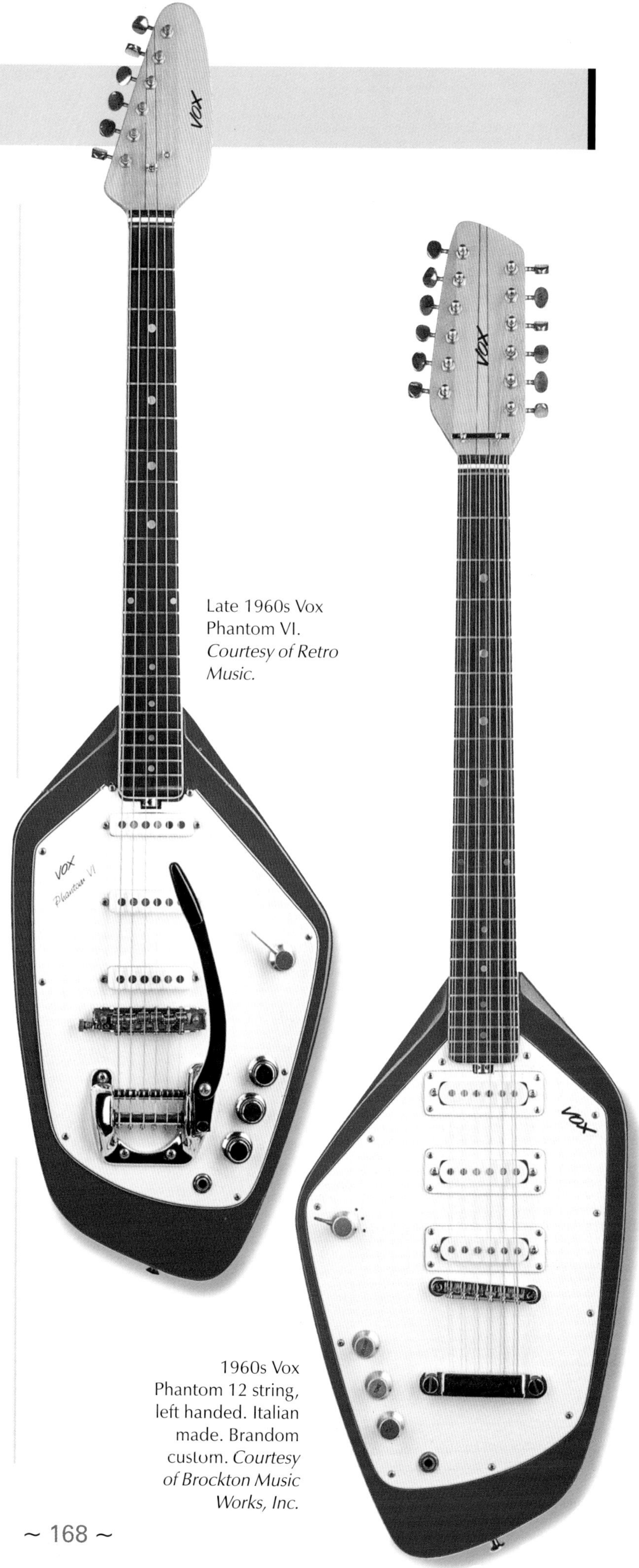

Late 1960s Vox Phantom VI. *Courtesy of Retro Music.*

1960s Vox Phantom 12 string, left handed. Italian made. Brandom custom. *Courtesy of Brockton Music Works, Inc.*

In 1966 Vox introduced the rare Bulldog (made in 1966 only), the Phantom XII Stereo (1966-1968), and the Wyman Bass (1966-1967) which was endorsed by Bill Wyman of the Rolling Stones.

Instruments introduced in 1967 were the Invader (1967-1969), Grand Prix (1967-1969), Delta (1967-1969), Cheetah (1967-1969), Bossman (1967-1969), Apollo (1967-1969), Ultrasonic (1967-1969), Thunder Jet (1967-1969), Starstream (1967-1969), Starstream XII (1967-1969), Apollo IV Bass (1967-1969), and the Astro IV Bass (1967-1969).

In 1968 Vox introduced the Viper (1968-1969), the Stinger IV Bass (1968-1969), and the Constellation IV (1968-1969).

By the end of the 1960s the production of the unique Italian Vox guitars had ceased. During the 1970s and 1980s there have been guitars of Asian origin sporting the Vox name on their headstocks.

The most recent owners of Vox is the Japanese company Korg, who acquired them from the then defunct Rose-Morris Company in 1992. Korg has set out to revive the Vox name by offering high quality Vox AC 30 re-issues that are currently made in England at the Marshall factory.

1966 Vox Bulldog. SN: 240757. This model was only produced during the one year. $700.

Vox Meteor. S/N 289580. $450. *Courtesy of Select Guitars, Inc./Bob Gasster.*

Vox Constellation Bass 1966, #360410. $600. *Courtesy of Flashback Guitars.*

1966 Vox Saturn IV. S/N 401408. $700. *Courtesy of Select Guitars, Inc./ Bob Gasster.*

c. 1967 Vox Phantom Bass. #363160 *Courtesy of Chicago Music Exchange.*

Wandré

Wandré Pelotti (1916-1981) was an Italian artist who liked motorcycles and guitars. During the mid 1950s he started designing the electric guitars that can't be confused with any other brand of instrument. Produced by various Italian manufacturers including himself, Wandré guitars are a sight to behold.

The first production period from 1956 until 1960 were Pelotti made. The 1960 to 1963 guitars were built by Framez of Milan and Sport Framez Pickups. Davoli built the guitars from 1963 until 1965, and Pelotti oversaw the final production run up to 1969 at his own facility. The guitars built from 1963 until 1969 use Davoli Pickups.

The actual construction of these guitars was quite unique for the time, with a neck and headstock made of an aluminum assembly which Wandré referred to as the Duraluminum neck. The hardware's styling was inspired by motorcycle parts, and the finishes on these oddly shaped guitars ranged from wild multi color paint jobs to sparkled colors. Values for these unique guitars is in the $1000 range, due mostly to their eye catching aesthetics.

Right: 1960s Wandré Avalon. *Courtesy Craig Brody, The Guitar Broker.*

Far right: 1960s Wandré Jazz model. *Courtesy Craig Brody, The Guitar Broker.*

Washburn

1994 Washburn N4. S/N 9402090. $800. *Courtesy of Guitar Haven.*

Washburn was the brand name applied to the Lyon and Healy Company's line of fretted instruments. Lyon and Healy's history dates back to 1835 when the company's founder Oliver Ditson founded the Oliver Ditson Company Inc., an east coast based music publishing company. In 1864 Ditson founded Lyon and Healy, named after business associates George Washburn Lyon and Patrick Joseph Healy, as his Chicago based distribution company. In 1887 the Washburn trademark name was filed for by the Lyon and Healy Co. and Ditson was now in the instrument manufacturing business. Throughout the rest of the nineteenth century and early twentieth century, Washburn mass-produced high quality and often superbly decorated instruments.

In the early part of the century, Lyon and Healy's Washburn plant suffered a disastrous fire and production was shifted to outside suppliers such as Regal and Vega.

In the late 1920s Tonk Bros., a large distributor took over the Washburn trademark name. The same outside manufacturers continued to produce the Washburn instruments until Tonk Bros. discarded the trademark name.

In 1964 the Washburn name was revived on a line of imported Japanese made acoustic guitars. In the late 1970s electric models became available.

Currently Washburn guitars are made in the U.S. (High End), Japan (Mid priced), and Korea (entry level), and are distributed by Washburn International of Vernon Hills, Illinois.

1970s Yamaha. S/N 28818. $1000

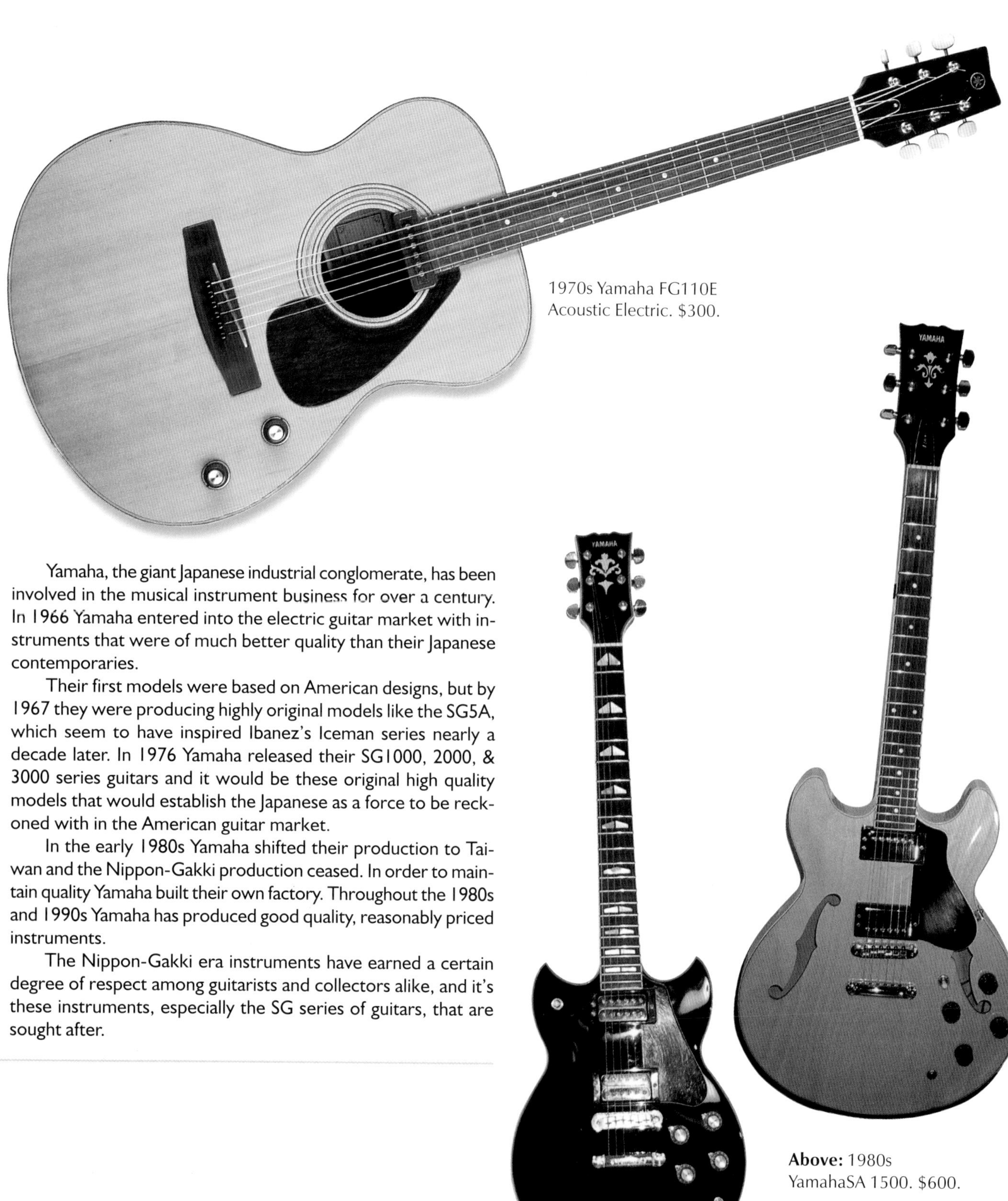

1970s Yamaha FG110E Acoustic Electric. $300.

Yamaha, the giant Japanese industrial conglomerate, has been involved in the musical instrument business for over a century. In 1966 Yamaha entered into the electric guitar market with instruments that were of much better quality than their Japanese contemporaries.

Their first models were based on American designs, but by 1967 they were producing highly original models like the SG5A, which seem to have inspired Ibanez's Iceman series nearly a decade later. In 1976 Yamaha released their SG1000, 2000, & 3000 series guitars and it would be these original high quality models that would establish the Japanese as a force to be reckoned with in the American guitar market.

In the early 1980s Yamaha shifted their production to Taiwan and the Nippon-Gakki production ceased. In order to maintain quality Yamaha built their own factory. Throughout the 1980s and 1990s Yamaha has produced good quality, reasonably priced instruments.

The Nippon-Gakki era instruments have earned a certain degree of respect among guitarists and collectors alike, and it's these instruments, especially the SG series of guitars, that are sought after.

Above: 1980s YamahaSA 1500. $600.

Left: 1982 YamahaSBG 2000. $800.

For two decades John R. Zeidler has been building world class archtop and flat-top guitars in Philadelphia, Pennsylvania. His impeccable attention to detail stems from backgrounds in various craft trades and current instruments show his highest degree of quality yet. Although he is not known for solid body electrics, he built at least the one pictured in this book during the mid 1980s.

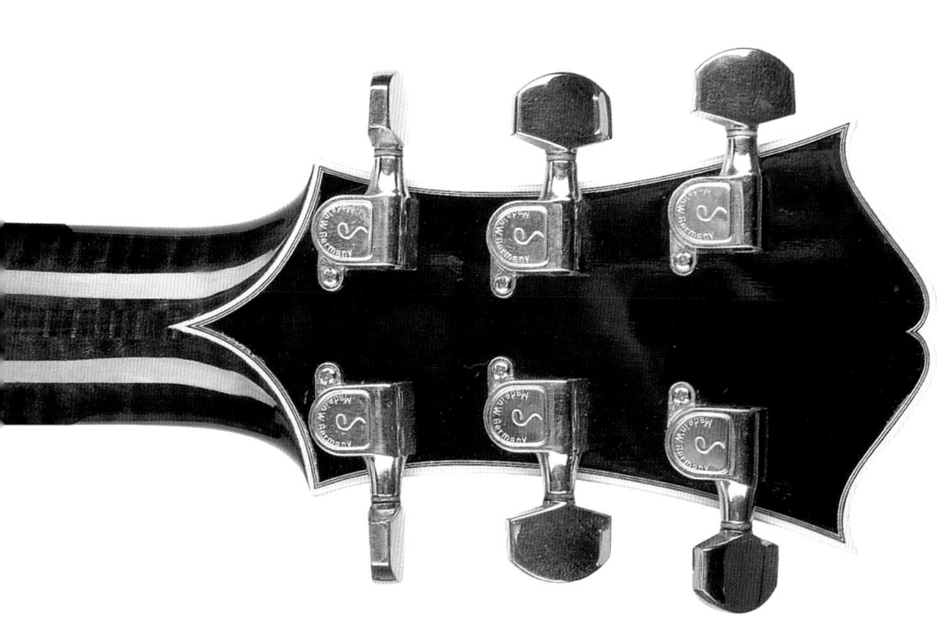

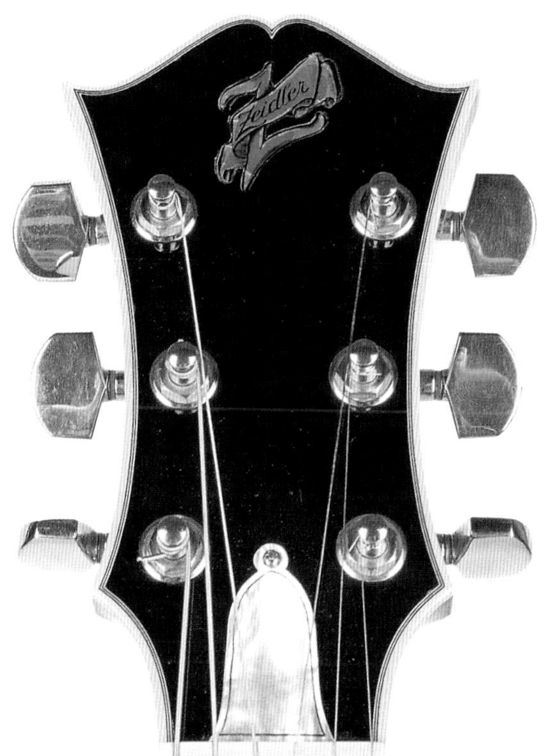

Zeidler 1980 (mid) Les Paul style. 67. *Courtesy of Martynís Guitars, Lansdale, Pennsylvania*

Zemaitis

Antanus Casimer Zemaitis was born in England in 1935 of Lithuanian descent. Going by the English translation of his name, Anthony Charles Zemaitis left school and became an apprentice in a cabinet making shop when he was 16. Zemaitis' first foray into guitar making involved the rebuilding of an old acoustic guitar that he had found in his parent's attic. In 1955 Zemaitis completed his first guitar of decent quality, a classic model. During the next couple of years he served in Britain's National Service, and when he became a civilian again he continued his hobby of guitar building. As his reputation grew in the early 1960s, Zemaitis' guitars found a small market, some of which ended up in the hands of some famous musicians, including Jimi Hendrix.

By 1965 Zemaitis' guitar making had outgrown its hobby status and the building of acoustic and electric guitars became his profession. By the end of the decade he had built guitars for Ron Wood of the Rolling Stones and other top guitarists of the time.

Tony Zemaitis continues to build electric and acoustic guitars and basses at an average of about ten instruments a year. His solid body electrics with engraved metal or pearl tops have gained a fairly strong following, strong enough, in fact, that there have been many forgeries built. Zemaitis instruments are quite valuable and appraisals from a knowledgeable authority should be had to determine value and authenticity of a particular instrument prior to any kind of transaction.

Zemaitis 1984 Metal Front. *Courtesy of Peter Garofalo.*

Zorko

The Zorko trademark name was used by the Dopyera Brothers of National Valco and Dobro Fame, to market a down-sized, upright electric bass. The instrument which was about the size of a cello featured a hollow plastic body. In 1962 Ampeg purchased the design rights to the instrument, and after some design and pickup refinements, marketed it as the Baby Bass.

Zorko Electric Bass. Predecessor to the Ampeg Baby Bass. 161. $2000. *Courtesy of Chicago Music Exchange.*

GLOSSARY

Abalone. A rock clinging mollusk, the lining of which is used for decorative inlay. More colorful than mother of pearl.
Acoustic. Describes unamplified instruments
Action. Refers to the distance of the strings from the fingerboard and the ease of playing the guitar
Active electronics. Instrument equipped with battery powered preamp and/or tonal circuitry
Alnico. Iron, aluminum, nickel, and cobalt battery used in pickups and speakers
Anodized. Electrolized finish on metal, used to refer to late 1950s Fender pickguards
Archtop. Guitar with a curved or arched top, formed by carving solid wood or press-forming a laminate
Bakelite. Early trademarked plastic used for many parts on guitars from the 1930s to 1950s.
Banjo tuners. A tuning mechanism mounted perpendicular to the face of the peghead with a rear facing tuner button
Baritone. A G-string guitar with a 30 inch scale length, tuned between the standard and the bass guitar
Bass. A 4 to 6 string instrument with a 30 to 34 inch scale, tuned one octave below a standard guitar
B-bender. A device meant to change the pitch of the "B" string to give a pedal steel guitar effect
Bezel. Ring of metal, plastic, or wood that molds the pickup to the guitar body
Bigsby. A simple single spring vibrato designed by Paul Bigsby
Binding. Plastic, wood, abalone, or metal strips or pieces used for protective and decorative edging
Bird's eye. Describes highly figured maple.
Blonde. Natural or semitransparent finish usually used on maple or ash guitars
Bobbin. The form on which a pickup coil is wound.
Bolt-on neck. Form in which the neck is bolted or screwed to the body
Bookmatched. Wood grain patterns that are symmetrical.
Bound. Refers to part of an instrument with binding
Bout. The widest parts of a guitar's body, above or below the narrowest point or waist.
Bracing. Strips of wood used to support the tops and backs of hollow bodied guitars
Bridge. Unit on the body that supports and spaces the strings.
Capacitor. Electronic filter used in most tone circuits
Capo. Movable clamp to change tuned pitch
Center block. Solid wood block used in middle of semisolid guitar or bass
Coil tap. A switch that grounds out one coil in a Humbucking pickup, making it sound like a single coil pickup.
Coils. Coil of wire in a pick. Strat pickups have one, Humbuckers have two.
Controls. Volume, tone, and pickup selector switches.
Cut-away. The area on the body at the neck joint where wood is removed for easier access to the neck. A single cut-a-way has wood removed only on the treble side and a double has both sides removed.\
Dog ear. Gibson P-90 pickup mounted on the surface of the guitar
Dot neck. Gibson's ES 335 guitar with dot fingerboard inlays
Dreadnought. Large bodied acoustic guitar pioneered by Martin
Droopy headstock. Gibson 1958 Explorer design, later used by nearly every manufacturer of a super-Strat model
Ebonized. Wood stained black to resemble ebony
Ebonol. Synthetic material emulating ebony
Ebony. Extremely dense hard wood, usually black or very dark. Used as fingerboard material on premium models
F-hole. Decorative and functional sound holes on archtop hollow body guitars
Fingerboard. Part of the neck where the strings are pressed to change notes, usually of maple, ebony, or mahogany
Flame. Grain figure in curly maple that resembles flames
Flat-top. A guitar with a flat top, usually acoustic
Floating bridge. A bridge held in place only by string tension
Floating pickup. A pickup mounted in such a way as to not touch the guitar's top
Fret. Raised metal pieces on the fingerboard properly spaced to facilitate playing notes of the musical scale
Fretless. An instrument without frets on the fingerboard, usually found on basses
Glued neck or set neck. Guitars with neck glued into a routed pocket in the body, creating a permanent joint
Hard tail. Describes bridge on non-vibrato equipped Fender Stratocaster models
Headless. Instrument without a peg head or headstock, and with body mounted tuners.
Headstock. Portion of the neck which provides a place for mounting tuners
Heel. The part of the neck that attaches to the guitar's body
Horn. Portion of the body's cut-away that ends in a sharp or rounded point
Humbucker or Humbucking. Any two coil pickup that is hum cancelling
Impedance. Measurement of electrical resistance used to measure output of pickups
Inlay. Decorative or functional marquetry.
Input jack. Place where guitar cord plugs into the guitar
Jack plate. Metal or plastic plate that secures the input jack to the guitar's body
Kerfing. Method of slotting the guitar linings. Used for attaching the pieces of a hollow guitar body.
Laminate. Two or more pieces of wood or plastic glued together to form a thicker piece. Can also refer to layered pickguard material.
Lining. Strips of wood, usually slotted or kerfed used to join the pieces of a hollow back instrument.
Locking nut. A type of nut usually used with a vibrato that clamps down on the string for more stable tuning
Locking tremolo. A type of vibrato that clamps down on the ball end of the string for more stable tuning
Locking tuner. A type of tuner that locks the string to the string post for more stable tuning
Machine head. Any geared tuning system.
Mint. A condition of an instrument that is factory new.
Mini-switch. Small switch usually used to split pickup coils or phase pickups together
Mother-of-pearl. Lustrous internal portion of the shell of some mollusks used for decorative inlay work. Usually less colorful than abalone.
NAMM. National Assembly of Musical Merchants
Neckplate. Metal plate used to secure the bolt-on neck to the body
Neck tilt. Mechanism used to change the angle of the bolt-on neck to the body.
Nut. Piece of wood, plastic, metal, bone, graphite or a combination of materials placed opposite the body end of the fingerboard to properly space and elevate the strings.
PAF. Early Gibson humbucking pickups with a Patent Applied For sticker. Appeared from 1957 to as late as 1964
Passive. Standard electronic wiring on an electric guitar or bass
Pearloid. Fake mother-of-pearl, usually of plastic and pearl dust
Pickguard. Plastic or metal plate to protect the surface of the guitar from wear
P-90. Gibson's first adjustable pole single coil pickup. Originally coded PU90 it has been in production in some form since 1945

Polepiece. Magnetized metal cylinder or screw in a pickup used to transfer the vibration of the string into an electrical current. Usually there is one polepiece per string per coil
Position markers. Markings on the fingerboard to aid in proper fingering
Potentiometer. A variable resistor used for the volume and tone controls, called "pot" for short
Preamp. Part of the active electronics that boosts the signal.
Pre-CBS. Fender guitars produced before January, 1965, when Columbia Broadcasting Systems acquired the company
Post-CBS. Fender guitars produced after March 1985 when CBS sold the company to William Shulz et al
Purfling. Binding
Quilt. Grain figure in maple that resembles the reflections of water in a pool.
Radius. The amount of curvature on the surface of the fingerboard
Ribs. Sides of a hollow body instrument
Saddle. Part of the bridge that makes contact with the strings. Number can range from one, as on most acoustics to one for each string as on Fender's Stratocaster. Many saddles are adjustable for string length or height.
Scale. Length of the string from the nut to the twelfth fret multiplied by two
Scalloped fingerboard. A fingerboard with wood removed or scooped out between the frets. Can aid playing in some styles
Scratchplate. Another term for pickguard
Selector switch. Toggle or blade switch used to change from one pickup to another
Semi-acoustic or semisolid. A hollow body with a built-in solid wood block running down its center.
Shielding. Protective metal or metallic paint used in the control cavities of solid body instruments to keep out electronic interference
Single coil. A pickup with only one coil
Slab board. Used to describe Fender's use of a thick rosewood fingerboard from 1959 to late 1962
Soap bar. A nickname give to Gibson's P-90 style pickup, which does not sport the mounting "ears"
Soundboard. Top of a hollow body guitar
Sound hole. Any hole placed in the soundboard
Spaghetti logo. Describes Fender's earliest style logo font
Stop tail/Bridge. Describes solid mounted bridge and tailpiece combination, like those on 1950s Les Paul Junior models.
Stop tail or stud tail piece. The same as the stop tail/bridge, but used only as a string anchor in conjunction with a separate bridge.
Strap button. A small button used to attach a guitar strap
String tree or string guide. Small metal guide on the headstock used to add downward string force on the nut
String length. Length of string between the nut and the bridge
Sunburst. A multicolored finish, usually with the brightest color in the middle and the darkest at the edge of the guitar's body
Superstrat. Describes the "hot rodded" Strat style guitars popularized in the early 1980s by Charvel/Jackson
Table. Soundboard
Tailpiece. General term for the string anchor
Thinline. A shallow depth hollow body guitar
Through-neck. A solid body guitar construction that uses the neck as the centerpiece of the body
Tigerstripe. Describes the grain figure in maple resembling the fur of a tiger
Trapeze. Tailpiece that attaches to the end of the guitar or butt of the guitar and hinges forward to a bar that holds the ball end of the strings. Used on most hollow body archtop instruments
Tremolo. Misused term describing the vibrato mechanism
Truss rod. An adjustable rod or mechanism inside the neck used to counter the tension of the strings
Truss rod cover. Plastic or metal plate covering the truss rod
Tune-O-Matic. The separate adjustable bridge designed by Gibson around 1952. Now used generically
Tuning peg. A machine head
Vibrato. Mechanism used to alter the pitch of the strings
Waist. Narrowest portion of the guitar's body
Whammy bar. Nickname for vibrato
Zero fret. Fret place right at the nut to guide the strings height

BIBLIOGRAPHY

Bacon, Tony. *The Ultimate Guitar Book.* London, England: Alfred A. Knopf, Inc., 1991.

Cherne, Steve, and S.P. Fjestad. *Blue Book of Guitars, Fourth Edition.* Minneapolis: Blue Book Publications, Inc., 1997.

Duchossoir, A.R. *Gibson Electrics: The Classic Years.* Milwaukee: Hal Leonard Publishing Corp., 1994.

___________. *The Fender Telecaster.* Milwaukee: Hal Leonard Publishing Corp., 1991.

___________. *The Fender Stratocaster.* Milwaukee: Hal Leonard Publishing Corp. 1988.

Evans, Tom and Mary Ann. *Guitars: From the Renaissance to Rock.* New York: Facts on File, 1977.

Fliegler, Ritchie. *Amps: The Other Half of Rock 'n Roll.* Milwaukee: Hal Leonard Publishing Corp., 1993

Gruhn, George, and Walter Carter. *Electric Guitars and Basses: A Photographic History.* San Francisco: An Imprint of Miller Freeman Books, 1994.

Moseley, Willie G. *Classic Guitars U.S.A.* Fullerton, CA: Centerstream Publishing, 1992.

___________. *Stellas and Stratocasters.* Bismarck, ND: Vintage Guitar Books, 1994.

Greenwood, Alan and Cleo, Editors. *Vintage Guitar Magazine.* Bismarck, ND: Vintage Guitar, Inc.

Wheeler, Tom. *The Guitar Book: A Handbook for Electric and Acoustic Guitarists.* New York: Harper & Row Publishers, 1974, 1978.

___________. *American Guitars: An Illustrated History.* New York: Harper & Row Publisher, 1982.

Wright, Michael. *Guitar Stories, Volume One.* Bismarck, ND: Vintage Guitar Books, 1995.